STATUTE MILES

TEXAS

TO KANSAS CITY 600 MILES NEARER THAN TO WEST COAST OF U.S.

Fuerte

Agiobampo Lagoon

San Blas

La Logia

Los Justes

Los Mochis

Topolobampo

Topolobampo Bay

San Ignacio Bay

FARALLON I.

ICO

GULF OF

MEXICO

Mexico City

A Southwestern Utopia

A
SOUTHWESTERN
UTOPIA

by Thomas A. Robertson

Drawings by Cas Duchow

The Ward Ritchie Press: Los Angeles
1964

COPYRIGHT 1947
BY THOMAS A. ROBERTSON

REVISED AND ENLARGED, COPYRIGHT 1964
BY THOMAS A. ROBERTSON

Library of Congress Catalog Card Number 64-16139

Printed in the United States of America

*Dedicated to the
memory of those hundreds
of colonists who gave up
their lives to the pursuit
of a noble idea.*

Foreword

*Better a day of strife than a century of sleep.**

EXCEPTING only the urge to provide food, shelter, and safety—the necessities of life—for himself and his loved ones, there is no instinct stronger in man than the desire for adventure.

Some of us express that desire in travel; others in hunting, fishing, or sports; and others in business speculation or in experiments in science, foods, forms of government, or ways of living. Children read books on adventure, play Indian, cowboy, soldier, sailor, with a vigor that only an inherent adventurous instinct could supply.

This instinct for adventure, combined with the urge for preservation and advancement of self or of family, has drawn across the seas to the Americas people of many nations. Along the coasts, up the rivers, over the mountains, across the plains they have come—to build our country—pioneers, adventurers, challenging and conquering nature—adjusting themselves to the ways of living and working required to survive and to succeed.

Today travelers east and west across the continent find everywhere trails of those adventurers of the past: Indians, trappers, traders, covered wagon trains, cattlemen of the old west, prospectors, and farmers who combined raising crops with fighting Indians.

More than any other area, the southwestern United States bordering on Mexico has retained the influence of that past.

This is a story of the country still beyond that old southwest, and of a group of adventurous souls, now forgotten, who over a half century ago dreamed of a new life, a new order, to be built by themselves in the undeveloped land of Sinaloa, lying along the eastern shore of the Gulf of California.

*Father Ryan.

[vii]

Travelers by the southwestern route across the continent now move eastward and westward through Tucson, Arizona —by train, by bus, by car, by plane—thousands of persons daily.

Some stop over to steep in the warm dry sunshine, the scenery and traditions of the old southwest.

Of these some few take the trip seventy miles or so by train or by car to the border town of Nogales, the gateway to the west coast of Mexico. A part continue southward, down the Magdalena River valley, onto the plains and so through a brush-covered country to Hermosillo, capital of the State of Sonora, or on to Guaymas, famous fishing resort, or perhaps continue by the Southern Pacific of Mexico Railway through the States of Sonora, Sinaloa, and Nayarit, turning south of the quaint old city of Tepic to climb the mountain ranges to the plateau of the State of Jalisco—on to its capital of Guadalajara with nearby Lake Chapala, and finally onward to the tourist haven of Mexico City.

Adventurous car drivers may continue through from Guaymas south to the Yaqui and Mayo Rivers, onward to the great Fuerte River valley and the sugar-cane fields, factory, and city of Los Mochis—may continue yet farther, subject to condition of roads and weather, even beyond the tropical port of Mazatlan, Sinaloa. Through this country the westcoast branch of the International Highway is now under construction. Over it fly daily great passenger airplanes with many visitors to our neighboring Mexico.

Few of these visitors would know that here not long ago roamed tribes of Indians fierce and primitive—and that off the roads and beaten trails many Yaquis and Mayos still live much secluded, their men and boys scantily and comfortably clad in loin cloth, spending much time hunting small game, or the larger game animals, deer, and peccary, not only with rifle, but with bow and arrow, or snaring them, for their food.

Along these woods traveled Juan Bautista de Anza on the pilgrimage that eventually led his band through many Indian tribes, across the blazing desert to California, and northward to the vicinity of San Francisco Bay.

Up this wilderness slowly, precariously, moved the Spanish priests, even though the fierce Mayos and Yaquis had whipped the Spanish soldiers; these priests winning with their good works and their religion what the soldiers lost through barbarism greater than that of the Indians.

Slowly, dangerously, this northwest coast was partially occupied by the Spaniards. This process of penetration was continued by the Republic of Mexico after its overthrow of Spanish rule, yet today there are areas in the Yaqui country not safe to any but the Yaquis.

It has been my good fortune, or so it has seemed to me, to have spent all my boyhood, and some of the years beyond, in the west-coast country below the Mexican border.

That country, its woods and mountains, its many miles of seashore, islands, and inland ocean water, its fishing and its wild game, the Indians, the Mexican people, the adventure of life in an American colony there, all have been a source of interest and pleasure.

These many years later, on a pleasant *hacienda* in the foothills of southern California, gathered around the family fireplace evenings I have sometimes told incidents of the life in Mexico, and finally have thought to preserve some of the record of those Americans, of their lives and adventures in those early days of pioneering in Sinaloa. There are two stories to be told, one of a cooperative colony, begun in 1886, where perhaps two thousand Americans attempted to work out a new social, economic, and political destiny for themselves—a new "Utopia in Sinaloa."

The second story is of the country, the Mayo Indians, the poorer Mexicans, the wealthier *hacendados* and merchants, the story of life for Americans on a Mexican frontier from the turn of the twentieth century, through the days of the Mexican revolution to the present day. Those are the "Memories of Sinaloa."

1947

With the completion of the long contemplated railroad from Texas to the port of Topolobampo there was a renewed interest in this book and the story it told of the region and the people who settled it. To this reissue of the original edition has been added an epilogue which brings the story up to date.

1963

Table of Contents

PART I

Utopia in Sinaloa

[xi]

PART II

Memories of Sinaloa

List of Illustrations

PART I

Utopia in Sinaloa

Ranch scene, Sinaloa. Corral is of hardwood upright posts, house of local hardwood, brush-walled, with dirt roof. Corn fodder is stacked on roof. Upright poles in foreground support wooden arm for hoisting leather water bucket from well in dry season.

CHAPTER I

Mexico of Yesterday

Doth any man consider what we waste
Here in God's garden? While the sea is full,
The sunlight smiles, and all the blessed earth
*Offers her wealth to our intelligence?**

THE NORTHWEST coast of Mexico is a territory of potential wealth in minerals, agriculture, fishing, and sporting which surpasses anything known or dreamed of except by a very few Americans. There is mineral wealth in this northwest area to be counted in billions, enough for the government, education, and sanitation of the whole nation for generations to come. There is land and there is water, in the rivers and underground, to irrigate the land, millions of acres, enough to supply winter fruits and vegetables in abundance to Mexico, the United States, and Canada. Yet its agriculture in years past has been carried on to a great extent on small one-man farms along river banks or in mountainous places too inaccessible for modern farming. Much of the land is still worked with plows drawn by oxen and weeded with hand tools such as *machetes, coas,* or *tlaxpanas.* The Sea of Cortez—Gulf of California—is generally believed to be the greatest sportsman's fishing place in the world, yet its resources in commercial and sporting fishing have scarcely been touched.

This great undeveloped wealth lies in a country of generally rather poor people who could benefit immeasurably in health, in education, and in comfort of living through development of these resources. It lies next to a country outstanding in the world for pioneering, for production, and for making natural resources into sources of better living.

There are some fundamental reasons for that area's being still largely undeveloped. The United States was pioneered

*From "Waste" by Charlotte Perkins Stetson.

[3]

by men and women who worked to build homes, farms, cattle ranches, mills, stores, something on which to establish themselves individually and in independence of domination by a ruling group or class. The land to which our ancestors came was sparsely peopled by Indians who lived largely by hunting, who shifted with the seasons, who had little interest in permanent settlements, and who resented to their death the intrusion of Europeans on their domain. They could not be absorbed in any appreciable numbers into the new order, were therefore inevitably destroyed, and the building of the new country was accomplished by the invaders who are the blood race of our present day.

In contrast to the Indians of the north, the Indians of central and southern Mexico at the time of their conquest by Spain were a settled people who had lived for generations in one village or locality, who built houses, raised corn, beans, tobacco, cotton, and other crops, made cotton garments, were advanced in pottery making, basket weaving, and other primitive arts, and in most cases had a communal government within their various tribes.

Tribes usually were governed by a ruler and council, apt to be absolute in matters of property, of life or death. The common class of Indians therefore was submissive and easily fell under the domination of the Spanish invaders. Although often enslaved and killed in great numbers during the conquest, Indians still remained in numbers sufficient so that today they are the predominant blood strain of the Mexican people, still retaining to a marked degree the characteristics, the native crafts, and the habits of living of their ancestors of over 400 years ago.

The Spaniards established themselves as the ruling class. They did not work individually or in families in the tilling of the soil, in mining, or in fishing. Instead, they were overlords, directing and making use of the toil of the Indians to gain a greater degree of wealth and comfort for themselves. The Church and Government of Spain worked parallel to each other, and diligently, although not always in harmony, in the establishment of spiritual and physical rule in the New Spain. Unfortunately, in this effort the true spiritual and physical well-being of the natives was often of secondary importance to the interest of the ruling classes.

[4]

It would be unfair to say that Mexico has not progressed. Within the limitations suggested above, through the years Spaniards, Indians, and Mestizos have arisen to become leaders in progress, in culture, in better government. In the future there will continue to be others, and from this mingling of fewer Spaniards and more Indians one of the strong nations of the world should eventually emerge to enjoy its rich material wealth in minerals, farm lands, timber, fishing, and other resources yet untouched.

Four hundred years of lowland heat and mountain chill have passed over the northwest of Mexico since the Spaniards first established the new "Province of Sinaloa," later

divided into the three Mexican west coast states (from Arizona south) of Sonora, Sinaloa, and Nayarit.

To sense the feeling of time elapsed, consider that the west coast of Mexico had formed a part of the colonies of Spain in the New World for 250 years before the American Colonies declared themselves a republic 170 years ago.

There have been many changes in government in Mexico during its known history. There were centuries upon centuries of Indian tribal rule. Then came the domination of the Indians by Spain, which brought about the slow building through three centuries of the mixed Spanish and Indian middle class, the Mestizos, and their emergence under the leadership of the patriot priest, Miguel Hidalgo, and many others, as the dominant factor in securing independence from Spain, in a struggle beginning September 16, 1810, and continuing for eleven years thereafter. Later the great Oaxaca Indian Benito Juarez gave Mexico her republican constitution, separating church from state and paralleling the Constitution of the United States in establishing the rights of the people.

Then followed the latter part of the 19th century, when Mexico entered into the period of greatest development of its natural resources, its greatest period of prosperity. This was an era of large expansion in Europe, in the Western Hemisphere, and more particularly in the mining, industrial, and agricultural development of North America. Mexico as a storehouse of mineral wealth, oil, hardwoods, and potential farming lands became a source of interest to, and a place of investment for, thousands of Americans. Some were individual seekers of fortune; some were groups of pioneers in farming, railroading, water transportation, mining, and other enterprises. The new republic grew in wealth. Food, clothing, and the various necessities (and some of the luxuries) of life were enjoyed by an increasing number of people.

The ruling aristocracy created at the time of the Spanish conquest was not confined in later years to the Spanish families, as it once had been. It often developed within one family generation through the accumulation of wealth in lands, mines, and industry. This aristocracy generally was well educated and diligent in the education of its children. It possessed a degree of business, scientific, legal, and other training comparable to that of similar people of any other country. There existed the happiest relationship of any period of our national life between our government and that of Mexico, between our people and Mexican people of all classes, including the poorer classes often employed by Americans in business in Mexico.

There were inevitable clashes between the rich and the poor. The native aristocracy generally regarded the lower classes, especially the Indians, as their inferiors—the Indians were simply *Indios*, whereas the Mexicans were *Gente de*

Razon, people who reason. The Indians in their turn clung tenaciously to the knowledge that the lands now occupied by the Mexicans had once been theirs; compelled as they were to become servants or sharecroppers, they retained through the centuries the tradition of their ownership of the land. However, holdings of lands were increasingly concentrated. Ownership was largely by the fewer families of the aristocracy of wealth, and admittedly the aristocracy of knowledge, material progress, and achievement.

In the country were all the elements with which to make a nation great: a well-planned constitutional government, good relationships with other countries, much developed wealth and far more potential wealth, an educated, intelligent, sometimes brilliant leadership in the aristocracy, a great mass of people ripe for education in farming, commerce, industry, and self-government. Many adult people of Mexico were being educated by practical means as railroad workers, longshoremen, sailors, factory workers, agricultural workers, miners, all those occupations leading to a greater Mexico with more wealth and higher standards of living.

The time was right for the establishment of a national school system free and available to all classes of children. Many other countries were going through this forward movement in education, but in Mexico there was the great difference between the ruling aristocracy and the lower classes, the lack of interest in many persons of the lower classes in their own and the national welfare, and, most important, the unsettled conflict of right to land, which the education of the Indian and the lower classes would have forced as an issue, a grievance against those in power. To put into effect an adequate national school system would have taken a strong leader, determined in the right, ready to risk a life-and-death struggle against powerful elements in the governing aristocracy, and determined to force education even against the inclination of many of the lower classes.

Porfirio Diaz, another Oaxacan, of Mestizo blood, rising from poverty to fame as a General and becoming a man of wealth, ruled Mexico as President for thirty years, from 1876 (except for one term, 1880-1884) until 1910. In many ways he was progressive, forward looking, a great figure in the world. However, he feared to or did not wish to bring about

[7]

national education. He ruled through appointed *Jefes Politicos* in the various states and in the subdivisions of states, giving these *Jefes* local dictatorial power, yet retaining absolute and ruthless control over all by means of a strong army. The forms of elections were carried out for all those years, but the candidates elected were chosen by the government before election. The *Jefes Politicos* usually were of the aristocracy.

Generals of the Army were apt to become large landowners or property owners through the years, as also were large landowners or property owners apt to become Generals.

There was order in the land. There was respect for property rights by the common people. There was more food and clothing at a cheaper price, if the price of personal liberty were not considered. There was a certain paternalism, a protection, given to employees at the will of employers; through the plenty of production and competition for labor that paternalism was often an important contribution to the well-being of the working classes. But there was not popular representation, in government, there was not general free education, there were too many poor people witnessing the pleasures of too few rich people, too many people subjected to the rule, tyrannical or benevolent as it may sometimes have been, of too few other people.

Such was the Mexico of the latter part of the nineteenth century—a country rich in its resources, proud in its ruling aristocracy, submissive in its lower classes, generally in harmony with the economic and social practices of the world of that day, its top leadership receptive to development of its resources by investors from countries with industrial facilities or technical or practical knowledge more advanced than their own.

CHAPTER II

The Fuerte River Valley of Colony Days

TO THE FUERTE RIVER

An Ode *by Wm. Ross*

Thou ever winding stream, if we only could but dream
Of the millions yet to teem, in thy vale—
Or foretell the future rank, of the cities 'long thy bank
Where no tyrant fetters clank; What a tale!

Though no more in modern days thou may'st meet the red man's gaze
Still upon thy winding ways thou shalt roll.
Though the red man sink to rest, his canoe forsake thy breast;
Of this beautiful Southwest still the soul.

And though many a stately arch, some day hence may proudly perch
O'er thy current on its march to the sea;
Still the rainbow in the shower, in the joyous summer hour
From yon clouds will form a bower over thee.

And while Phoebus glads each morn, thy bright valley to adorn
Future kindred yet unborn, will thee bless.
And the snows that softly lay, massed on mountains far away,
Shall leap down the canons gray, to thy kiss.

And though years may roll along, and the gay and joyous song
Shall resound great halls among, it was toil
That at first thy valley sought, and most wondrous changes wrought
And abundant treasures brought, from its soil.

When our great commercial marts, shall resound with trade and arts
Bringing wealth the people's hearts to regale;
Then may those who foremost trod, thy own fair and virgin sod
Sleep forgotten 'neath the clod of thy vale.

But some stranger brown with toil, from the far Atlantic soil
Like a Pilgrim of the Nile yet may come
To search among the heaps, that moulder by thy deeps
Where desolation sleeps, ever dumb.

But though institutions grand, shall occupy this land
Or crumbling ruins stand, all sublime;
Still wilt thou meander on, till eternity has gone—
Until breaks the dial stone of old time.

FROM THE Sierra Madre Mountains the Fuerte River flows westward to the coastal plain at San Blas, forty miles on a direct line from the Gulf, sixty miles following the winding course of the stream. This fertile plain, extending northward and southward, apparently without end, evidently was formed partly by the recession of the sea, as marine fossils can be found in the woods even up to the foothills. It was also formed by erosion from the mountains and by decomposition from its dense woods.

The deeper river bed of the Fuerte varies from a quarter of a mile to a mile wide. Sometimes in flood the waters run twenty-five feet deep, spreading several miles into the higher lands; however, during the dry season of May and June before summer rains fall in the Sierras eastward, the river may be almost dry.

On the Mexican west coast, summer (July through September) is the wet season. There may be a second rainy season about the end of the year and for a month or two after.

The alluvial soil deposited along the river course is particularly fertile and is mellow for cultivation. Here is the heaviest growth of trees (cottonwood, willow, *guamuchil*, mesquite, and many others) and of vines and thorny undergrowth.

Here too has always been the greatest concentration of animal and human life; the river vegetation is always green, and there is water for animals and for people. Away from the river the woods grow thick but not so profusely. Shortly after the beginning of the wet summer season all the woods become green and are beautiful with bloom; during the spring months the woods away from the river bottoms become dry, water holes are depleted, and wild life must move or do without water. Wells are dug for cattle and for domestic use, but on this higher plain farming is not very successful without irrigation.

The Spaniards found the Mayo Indians populating the margins of the Fuerte River. Their little villages and farms extended along the river course from the mountains to the sea. The villages were organized with a headman for each, and groups of villages were joined into a tribe. The Spaniards, partly by force and partly by the persuasion of the priests, took possession of sites along the river for *pueblos* and

churches. Upon the east bank of the Fuerte from San Blas to
the sea, about twelve miles apart, are old missions (such as
Charay, Mochicahui, San Miguel, and Ahome). The grants
of Spain for colonization (on lands belonging to the Indians)
called for the location of a central plaza and a church, for
homes extending from this plaza, for common pasture
ground, and for the right of individuals to cultivate a portion each, the community eventually ceding to each the portion taken, to be held in perpetuity by the heirs.

The Spaniards and their descendants encroached increasingly on the hunting grounds, the farms, and homes of the
Indians. By 1870 almost all the river area from above the
city of Fuerte to the sea a hundred miles below was owned
by old established families, no longer by Indians. Extending
from Fuerte (the district seat) down river, some principal
owners were Ibarra, Orrantia, Vega, Borboa, Renteria, Qui-
ñonez, Quintero, Lugo, Valenzuela, Ochoa, Zakany, Cruz,
Padilla, Luque, Lopez, and Castro. Most of these families
were extensive in their relationships and intermarriages.
Their names loom large in the history of the Fuerte River
valley and in some instances in the history of far more distant places.

Often they were at once landowners and town merchants.
They farmed principally through *partidarios* or *medieros*
(sharecroppers), the usual arrangement being for the landowner to furnish the land, the oxen or mules, the plow, the
seed, and sometimes the *medieros'* home. The landowner advanced corn, beans, and other limited necessities to the *mediero*; these advances were deducted from the renter's share
of crop returns. The crop usually was divided half and half
in the field. At times the sharecropper got away with a large
half through diligent stealing before the time of division. At
other times the landowner charged exorbitantly for advances
made to the *mediero*. Usually, however, there was a strict
accounting and an honest liquidation. Crops were cheapest at
harvest time and largely passed from the renter's hands into
possession of the merchants for resale later at higher prices.

The homes of the *hacendados* and of the principal merchants were apt to be extensive: brick houses built on an L or
a square, with large rooms, high ceilings, and an inner court
surrounded by servants' quarters and storehouses, or with

part of the rear court enclosed by high brick walls. All articles of value were kept in the house or enclosed court. This was barred at night at front and rear gates, these gates being large enough to accommodate passage of wagons, carriages, or coaches. The front gate, a huge folding hardwood door, was the entrance to the home. It opened into a cobblestone corridor, thence into the porch and patio and on back to the stables. Rooms and porches had either cement or brick floors. Walls, of brick or plastered adobe, were sometimes three feet through. Roofs were a double layer of thin brick laid in lime mortar on heavy hewn hardwood rafters and were only slightly sloping, giving the general effect of a flat Moorish top. Thick walls and high ceilings made the houses cool in summer, especially when servants sprinkled the floors of the rooms.

High brick walls surrounded rear parts of the courtyard. Often there was a layer of broken glass bottles cemented into the top of the wall, in lieu of more modern insurance. Windows were iron barred to keep out petty thieves and to keep the *señoritas* in of evenings, or the young men out, while the *señoritas* were being serenaded.

Freighting of merchandise was a usual business, by ox-cart or in cumbersome homemade heavy wagons drawn by eight or more little mules, the Indian driver riding the right-wheel mule while handling reins, whip, and brake rope with the admirable skill of experience.

There was one main *Camino Real* from *pueblo* to *pueblo*. In that fine alluvial soil, soon after each rain it was ground to powder, and the dust was suffocating. Men rode with bandanas over their noses, *señoras* and *señoritas* with *rebozos* covering their heads and faces except for the eyes. Upon alighting at their destination they were vigorously slapped by their friends with cloths or feather dusters as a first courtesy to the guest.

Stagecoaches were the railroads and bus lines of that day. These coaches were high-seated, with covered roofs and with leather or canvas dust curtains. The coach bodies often were slung on great leather straps for springs. Coaches were drawn by mules, the all-weather, all-duty animal of Mexico, heat resistant, long enduring, and easily supported. Coaches rolled along from one picturesque village to another, mules at a gallop for hours, changing teams every twelve miles or so.

Just a few months ago in the northeast corner of Sinaloa we drove with a station wagon over a portion of the old stage-coach road (Fuerte, Sinaloa, to Alamos, Sonora) scarcely traveled now, but cut in some places three or four feet deep into the hard mountainsides.

Those were the days before pumping plants for irrigation. The river banks stood some twenty to twenty-five feet above the river bottom. The larger *hacendados* built high-water canals from the river, sometimes several miles long, to cover their land when the river came into flood; the canals were dug at a sharp angle downstream to take the best advantage of the slight fall available. Some canals were twenty feet deep and fifteen feet wide at the bottom, with correspondingly more width at the top. They were dug by the Mayo Indians, first with shovels, then by carrying out the earth in turtle shells or baskets.

Labor was extremely cheap, six pesos a month perhaps, plus rations of corn and beans, altogether probably fifteen American cents per day. Still the cost for construction was tremendous, sometimes a lifetime project to build and pay for. Considering these costs, the charge of one-half the crop made by the landlord does not seem severe. Crops on irrigated lands were planted according to the luck in getting rises of river water into the canal. Some years there was no high water. Some crops were planted on high lands without irrigation as soon as the summer rains began. Crops on the low lands were planted at the end of the rainy season; then sometimes late floods drowned or washed the crops away.

Low or high water, when planting season came the Indian must plant. He moved down to the low land, built a small temporary brush shelter for himself and family, and put his yoke of oxen to his wooden plow. When floods came, news was sent down river from *pueblo* to *pueblo* by couriers on horseback. *Hacendados* then gave attention to the flooding of their lands by means of their great high-water canals.

The Indians had (and still have) their own means of communicating up and down the Fuerte River. Living at intervals, one family or a group of families, along the river banks, they were joined into well-organized tribal groups corresponding to the area influenced by each of the old mission *pueblos.* From up river a hundred miles the rawhide-covered tom-toms began beating out the message of the coming of the flood waters. The sound carried well, across and down the wide river bottom, and the message was relayed from one post to another—the primitive forerunner of modern telegraphic communication.

Sometimes, especially when floods came at night, isolated Indian families failed to hear the warning, or delayed too long in removing their families and their small possessions, or perhaps in gathering their oxen, burros, or other livestock from the wooded river bottom. Those who couldn't get out of the river bottom ahead of the rush of water climbed the nearest cottonwood trees or were drowned.

There were many dugout cottonwood canoes along the river for transporting travelers, livestock, or grain. These were pressed into service by other Indians and Mexicans during each flood, to pick the unfortunate Indians off the limbs of the cottonwoods, or off some floating tree.

The current of the stream during flood was so swift that before undertaking a crossing canoes were poled or paddled along the banks well above the destination on the opposite shore. Sometimes there were whirlpools of water, especially about sunken trees, that threatened to engulf the canoe. However, most native canoemen were bold and skillful; even during floods they ferried passengers, goods, and livestock. Cattle were made to swim, towed by a rope tied about their horns and pulled short into the stern of the canoe. Horses swam easily alongside with a longer rope to keep them under control; in fact, they sometimes helped tow the canoe. But mules were obstinate—and burros were impossible.

To illustrate, one day my brother and I were on a return trip from a week's stay with our friends, the Padilla family, at Higuera de Zaragosa, a *pueblo* down river, Don Victor Padilla and his son Carlos accompanying us, all riding mules. At the river bank we removed saddles and bridles, putting them in a big dugout canoe manned by a couple of stalwart Mayo Indians, persuaded our mules, two on either side, into the water, and took off for the opposite shore some three hundred yards away. The mules swam well and easily. About midstream there was a bank under those swirling, muddy waters. The mules felt bottom with their feet, and there they

[14]

stuck, water almost back high, noses out, refusing to move a step further. The big canoe swung below with us hanging onto our lead ropes. Time passed. Don Victor was a good-hearted but cantankerous old patriarch. That day he was furious. I have never heard such a selection of Spanish epithets as he bestowed upon those obstinate brutes. We pulled and paddled, we yelled, we swore. For all our efforts we seemed glued to the river to wait for dry season.

Finally the mules wearied and were edged off the bank.

One, then another, drifted down stream and swam furiously at the end of the lead ropes. The pull from them, with the pull of the canoe in the swift water, dislodged the others, and soon all four were swimming for the river bank. We saddled and rode the wet little animals, not much larger than donkeys, along the pleasing, green-bordered road, past La Logia, the old American colony site, to Ahome, Aguila, and Los Mochis.

Those river roads were interesting! They were worn deep like canals and were bordered by great trees: banyans, their cousins the *higueras*, giant mesquites, *guamuchils*, and many others, all enveloped at the base with green brambles and climbing vines such as blue and purple morning glories. Occasional glimpses through rough-hewn wood gates into small clearings showed clumps of bananas, papayas, mangos, guayabas (the larger Mexican guava), *ciruelas* (native plums), *zapotes*, and orange and lime trees.

Cottontails and big whitish jackrabbits were everywhere. Coyotes, wildcats, ocelots, even mountain lions and occasional jaguars, fed on all the smaller birds and animals. Now and then there would be the flash of a native deer, the "Arizona whitetail," or a group of wild pigs, peccaries, crossing from one feeding ground to another.

There were birds everywhere: quail in droves; white-winged doves in the fields and trees; turtledoves, lovely, dainty little creatures cooing plaintively on the fences and in the low bushes; always vermilion flycatchers and cardinals.

The *cuichi* (the native pheasant called *chachalaca* farther south) sat hidden in the brambles or upon the dense branches of the taller trees. It resembles an elongated brown leghorn hen in appearance, not unlike the smaller native gamecocks of the country.

Commonest of the many birds are the blackbirds: the smaller ones common in California; the redwings; the larger, yellow-breasted ones; the still larger *zanates*, brilliant, purple-black fellows with long tails; the yet larger *grajos* (grackles), almost half the size of crows; the crows and ravens; all appearing to be of the same family.

Mockingbirds were abundant. Flocks of *catalinos* (parakeets) moved like swift, compact little green clouds from one dense bush to another, effectually camouflaged as they sat among the green leaves.

The *pericos*, larger parrots, red- and yellow-headed fellows with green bodies and multicolored bright wings, flew noisily over in pairs or in flocks, or sat on the tops of the green cactus trees, blending perfectly in color with their perches.

Mockingbirds (*zenzontles*), doves (*palomas*), parakeets, and parrots were most commonly tamed by the natives, mockingbirds and doves being kept in neatly built cages of split bamboo, parakeets and parrots, wings clipped, on little perches hung from the roofs of the *adobe* or brush houses.

The smaller native houses along the river road were intriguing. Usually they stood back some twenty-five yards or more from the highway and were viewed through a foreground of vine-covered road on either side of an old gate of horizontal hardwood bars, looking into a yard with clumps of bananas and other native trees. Sometimes there was a little vegetable garden, always with green onions, garlic, and chili peppers. A wide path led to the house, which was essentially a large porch with a room or two or three at the rear. About the porch would be vines—morning glories, lantanas, trumpet flowers, and others—and in clay pots or tin cans, set on stands or suspended from the low roof to keep them out of reach of pigs and chickens, were geraniums, begonias, ferns, and other little plants.

Under the porch there would be a cool *olla* (pottery jug) of drinking water, set on a three-pronged base formed by branches of some small mesquite tree cut for the purpose and buried like a fence post into the dirt floor of the porch. Under this porch the family lived and visited. Here they set out for us visitors their native hardwood chairs, those of the rawhide or leather bottoms, or circular homemade stools with rawhide or fiber seats on them. Here too they would sit chatting with us, the man usually with his big straw hat hung on one knee. He would presently be rolling a long and thick cornhusk cigarette filled with powerful homegrown tobacco. The cigarette between draws was held artistically between the thumb and smaller fingers, sometimes cigarette hand on knee or farther away when the pungent *macucho* tobacco smoke became too offensive to the nostrils.

The *señora* and whatever *señoritas* had "become of age" would sit too, while the man, pulling at his long drooping mustache between puffs at the *cigarro*, did most of the visiting—that is, unless one knew the family well. Then the man usually had to take a back seat, so to speak, while the *señora* questioned at length as to the health and occupation of all the visitors' relatives and friends, and entered into long discussions of her own, particularly in regard to sicknesses, and about conversations held by the estimable lady with various people, demonstrating her wisdom, wittiness, and good will.

All the while she and the man of the house would be ordering the younger children, and after a courteous interval the younger *señoritas*, too, about the business of preparing some coffee. Small boys would scurry about for wood, small girls would build the fire and toast the coffee in half-round pottery bowls over the fire, a *señorita* would grind it in the little hand grinder on the wall, or on the stone *metate* used for grinding their corn for *tortillas*, which are used instead

[17]

of bread. The actual making of the coffee was the climactic operation, and at this point the *señora* likely would excuse herself with a good-natured complaint about not trusting those ingrate children (*ingratos niños*), and take over.

When the coffeee was served it was ink-black and strong as the kick of a mule. The *muy hombres* took it straight, except for about three spoonfuls of sugar. I would try to tactfully put over the idea that I knew this was the perfect way to drink coffee, but that disgracefully (*desgraciadamente*) it had been my misfortune to have a sensitive stomach and nervous system, and with profound regret (*Que lastima!*) I accepted a dilution of hot water or milk, being properly commiserated over by the hosts—this too giving our lady an opening for another amiable and breezy discussion of maladies of friends not heretofore recalled.

We would discuss the origin and merits of the lady's chickens, the characteristics of the household cat, its ability as a rat and bird catcher, details of its conquests, the sterling qualities of the fleabitten dogs—probably nothing of the pigs wandering about (they were just "razorback" pigs) until finally we would arise with the excuse of whistling to the mockingbird, dove, parakeet, or canary in the cage, or of engaging the parrot in conversation at his perch under the porch, about the kitchen, or on the branch of some tree in the yard; and so by degrees, after discussing the construction of the oxcart standing in the yard, looking over the calves in the little stake corral, and hearing of their lineage and that of their mothers—the fathers were not important—perhaps next admiring the gentleman's saddle horse just enough not to have him offered for sale (a delicate balance in courtesy), after extending thanks to everyone, greetings to all their relatives and to mutual acquaintances, then shaking hands first with the hosts, next all around, with little compliments to the children (careful, nothing but a handshake and our pleasure at seeing the *señoritas*), we put on our spurs, then, after another handshake with the gentleman of the house (and perhaps with the lady if she is quite a well-known acquaintance) we mount our mules or horses and proceed on our way, talking to each other in admiration of the yard, a mango tree, something that may please the pride of the owners, until we are out of hearing.

CHAPTER III

Albert Kimsey Owen—
Day Dreamer, Unlimited

Mourn not for vanished ages
With their great heroic men
Who dwell in history's pages
And live in the poet's pen
For the grandest times are before us
And the world is yet to see
The noblest worth of this old earth
*In the men that are to be.**

HISTORY is largely the story of the lives of leaders of men —and of women—and of their influence upon the lives of others.

The history of the American colonization of the Fuerte River valley of Sinaloa is curiously and intricately bound up with the life of an intriguing personality, a youthful civil engineer, Albert Kimsey Owen. Born at Chester, Pennsylvania, about 1848, he was the son of Dr. Joshua K. Owen, a Quaker physician who was Senior Surgeon of Volunteers in the Civil War, serving under General Ben Butler. The father was a personal friend of Abraham Lincoln, of General Ulysses S. Grant, and of many other notable characters of that period. The boy's mother, who died during his childhood, was Harriet Moffit, sister of Samuel Moffit, State Treasurer of Maryland.

The father, Dr. Joshua K. Owen, wrote some most interesting letters to Albert and to an older brother Alfred (who later became a physician, but who died at an early age, as a victim of yellow fever, while attending yellow-fever patients at the Naval Hospital, Pensacola, Florida). These letters tell the story of the young Owen whom we see reflected in the

*Ella Wheeler Wilcox.

unusual dreamer, pioneer, and promoter of later years. The letters were written while Dr. Owen, then a widower, was serving in the Union Army, and are divided between personal narrative and stories of the advance of Grant upon Richmond and his plan for capturing the Rebel army of General Robert E. Lee.

Taking bits from these many letters; the Quaker father says:

> Thy letters are beautiful and thoughtful . . . when you, my sons, shall retrospect your thoughts to the scenes of your childhood you will find many pleasant memories to lure your meditations . . . among your earliest traits were your fondness for the daring . . . yet with stability of character. [Later.] Another theater opened its panorama for you—mighty armies and their equipment, mighty battles and their results . . . the mighty materials of warfare that test the resources of a nation . . . the exposures and privations of a soldier— you left your beautiful home, its comforts and its privileges, and for two years followed the Army of the Potomac [the boys were orderlies on the General Staff] witnessing its battles . . . assisting the wounded, mingling your sympathies with the dying and the dead. . . .
>
> The novelty of boys of your years joining in the ruggedness of campaign life rendered you favorites with officers and men—you were not limited to particular command, you visited forts, pickets, trenches, rifle-pits, breastworks, fortifications with opportunities granted to few . . . these privileges you improved with an ardent desire for observation—the advantages you derived will be appreciated more, as time shall reveal to your maturer years . . . your impatience to trace on the map the localities of opposing forces . . . you acquired the first knowledge of your country without even the consciousness that you were studying its geography and its history . . . the knowledge of one country leads to the study of others. . . .

Here we see the development of interest that had so much to do with the years of our story.

Albert Owen's life was one of unusual experience. The

father describes an earlier journey with him and the brother
to where "Westward the Course of Empire makes its way,"
presumably with some Army command:

> to the land of the antelope and the buffalo, where hun-
> gry wolves follow you by day, and howl around your
> camp at night—the sterile desert of burning sand hills,
> where the wild sage and cactus grow, where rattle-
> snakes, lizards and horned toads in multitudes find con-
> genial burrows—scorpions and tarantulas luxuriate . . .
> the country of the desperate Navajoe . . . the war trail of
> the merciless Apache . . . over the far reaching plains;
> these same plains in the depth of winter; six consecu-
> tive weeks, through three terrific snow storms . . . such
> was your boyhood, filled with more stirring and prac-
> tical events than that period has furnished to any other
> person within my knowledge.

Continuing, the father writes,

> A most extensive combination of the Cheyennes, Ar-
> apahoes, Kiowas, Sioux, Comanches, Utes and others
> have since waged war upon the white man with savage
> ferocity in that section where you were, between the
> Platte and Arkansas rivers . . . how interesting these ac-
> counts must be to you who have been among these very
> Indians, visited the Chiefs in their own lodges, talked by
> signs with them, even traded with them. . . .
> They have murdered 3,000 white men, captured
> many trains, run off numerous herds, burned every-
> thing in their way. General Blunt is in command against
> them. You will remember him. . . .

In 1863, probably during this same western trip, the father
and the two boys went to New Mexico, stayed overnight with
Kit Carson at Los Pinos, and in El Paso were guests of Colonel Bowie.

Although the boys' young lives were taken up with so
much adventure, the father was diligent in their training.
He describes their home, built almost entirely by himself and
the boys,

> . . . by its associated harmonies of beauty, elegance and
> grace it was hoped to inspire your admiration and to im-

press your growing minds with the beautiful, the artistic, the graceful . . . to institute a silent though
effective influence upon your refinement and taste.

This unusually able and thoughtful parent refers to their
scientific collection, to an extensive library, to lessons in
piano, in drawing—of building with them a skiff which they
rowed and sailed on the Delaware River; tells of a private
park where the boys assisted in the care of flowers, and kept
bees, birds, animals, and fish in its aquarium.

The young Owen was sent to study mathematics under
James W. Dale at Media, Pennsylvania, and there learned
civil engineering. The able father counsels the sons on education:

Let your aim be to ballast your ship with mathematics
and language; you can dress it with sails—other studies
—at your pleasure, and rely upon a composed security
that no storms or adverse winds can deprive you of your
resources to weather against them.

In a letter from James River, Virginia, dated October 21,
1864, the father reviews the Civil War struggles from the
viewpoint of a close observer, telling of many historic incidents such as the battles of Malvern Hill, Harrison's Landing, Chickahominy Ridge, and many others, reciting in dra-
matic detail the Battle of Malvern Hill.

In a later letter he says,

I shall endeavor to be home soon. I must not fail to
give President Lincoln my assurance of his faithful
stewardship. I am inclined to believe the re-inaugura-
tion will return every sword to its scabbard.

In April, 1866, the father and sons, Albert and Alfred,
sailed for Europe, during the following fourteen months visiting England, France, Malta, Syria, Egypt, Palestine, Sicily,
Italy, Savoy, Switzerland, and Germany.

Three thousand miles of this pilgrimage was made on foot
in order to more closely observe the countries and their
people.

One must greatly respect and admire this Quaker father
for his "faithful stewardship" of his young sons, as well as

for his evident talent for planning and carrying through such a varied yet purposeful program for their education.

The father and Alfred returned to the United States. Young Albert, now a tall vigorous young man of nineteen years, remained for two months, walking eight hundred miles through England, Scotland, and Ireland, living that period mostly in the open country, asserting that he made the whole two months' excursion on only thirty dollars— fifty cents per day—for expenses.

Soon after his return Albert began his career as a civil engineer by serving as chainman of the survey for Chester Creek Railway, near his home. He next assisted in laying out parts of Chester City and of the Fourth Ward, Philadelphia, thus acquiring experience in city planning as well as in railroad construction.

After serving a term as City Surveyor of Chester, Pennsylvania, with a letter from a friend of the Civil War days, General E. F. Beale of Chester, who by then had become prominent in railroad development, he went to Colorado and found employment assisting in the location of Clear Creek Canyon Railroad.

Evidently his talents in this type of work were sufficient to determine General William J. Palmer, closely associated with the Denver and Rio Grande Railway, to invite Owen to join his expedition, as engineer, into Mexico.

Together with Governor H. C. Hunt of Colorado, Owen went from Colorado Springs via Santa Fe, El Paso, and Chihuahua to Queretaro, Mexico, presumably generally following on horseback or by stagecoach the rail route now used by the *Ferrocarriles Nacionales de Mexico*.

At Queretaro they met General Palmer and General William S. Rosecrans, another builder of the New West, whose grandson, William S. Rosecrans, has for many recent years been prominent in the development of the water, land, and manufacturing resources of southern California.

Owen remained to survey the possibilities for railroad development, from the viewpoint of construction and of economic benefits to be obtained. During eleven months this young American engineer traveled five thousand miles, about three thousand four hundred on horseback.

His travels presently led westward over the Sierras of Central Mexico to the Pacific Coast. He must have followed the wide cobblestone *Camino Real* (Royal Road) over the route first used by the Indians, later by the Spaniards, and by the time of Owen's explorations in 1871, a broad highway for freighting with oxen and mule teams, and for stage coaches, to the Barrancas of Jalisco, then by pack train over the mountain ranges to find again a broad cobblestone highway leading down to the City of Tepic and thence down another fifty miles to the sea at San Blas—now State of Nayarit. No doubt from the period of Owen's first trip into the southwest in 1863 he had begun to learn some Spanish, so that after the few years spent in Colorado and the months in Mexico, with his educational background he probably had done much to master the language, which he spoke quite fluently in later years.

From San Blas, Nayarit, Owen traveled by coastal sailing sloops or small steamers northward from one small port to another, determining possible harbor facilities, for the purpose of reporting to Generals Rosecrans and Palmer on the merit of a railway line projected to be built from Colorado Springs southward through the deserts of Sonora to various ports along the eastern shores of the Gulf of California—the northwest mainland of Mexico.

During his explorations of the west coast, destiny brought two important events into the story of Albert Kimsey Owen. First, he found as a traveling companion for a part of the trip a young General, Manuel Gonzales, then Military Commander of the West Coast and Lower (*Baja*) California. The two men became good friends, apparently with many interests in common. Ten years later, after the first term of General Porfirio Diaz, General Gonzales became President of Mexico.

Second, at the tropical seaport of Mazatlan, Sinaloa, then vying with Guaymas, Sonora, for first importance as a seaport of the west coast, Owen made the acquaintance of Dr. Benjamin R. Carman. This story is best told in an article from *El Gazetero*, a Spanish-English newspaper published at Topolobampo by John G. Dawkins, issue of March 1, 1903:

> Dr. Benjamin R. Carman was the U.S. Consul and leading physician at Mazatlan during about 30 years. It

Native home, Sinaloa. Only articles not of home manufacture are clothing and Singer sewing machine.

Potter at wheel, El Valle, Sinaloa. Potter's wheel is propelled by quick kicking motion of foot against lower solid-wood wheel.

One of many smaller coves of Tompolobampo Bay.

*Excursion of colonists from La Logia to Estuary of Toriguara
near mouth of Fuerte River.*

was he who first told Mr. Owen that there was a place known as Topolobampo. This was in August, 1871. . . . Dr. Carman had gotten his information from two American miners who had been working in the Sierra Madre eastward of Topolobampo and who, wishing to go on some vessel going down or up the coast, followed the mule path which led from the rich copper mines of Bohuerachic to the "Smugglers' Retreat" where these ores were shipped secretly to Swansea, Wales. There was a heavy duty on the exportation of ore in those days. Dr. Carman was of an old Philadelphia family, a man of distinguished presence, and the best known person on this coast, due to his generous hospitalities. The officers of the U.S. Navy always knew that at Mazatlan Dr. Carman would have entertainment for them, and in consequence he made many strong friendships with them, and when he asked Commodore Wm. I. Truxton to make a personal visit and examination of Topolobampo the Commodore went with the U.S.S. "Jamestown," took soundings, made a map of the harbor and gave a private report to Dr. Carman. This map and report have since become a part of the records at Washington. Topolobampo was never published on a map issued by Mexico or the United States until Mr. Owen published his "Map of the Republic of Mexico," Philadelphia, 1882.

Owen continued his explorations northward, up the Gulf to Guaymas, passing the scarcely known and uncharted *Bahia de Topolobampo* with its many inland bays without entering, but determined to return.

With his return really begins the story of the Topolobampo Colony, which was to touch on the lives of people in every principal city and many lesser towns in the United States, and to be a subject of comment in many countries. The opening of this story fortunately we have, expressed in his own words.

CHAPTER IV

The Dream

IN "TOPOLOBAMPO—A REMINISCENCE," printed in the
Credit Foncier of Sinaloa, issue of Feb. 15, 1889, Albert Kimsey Owen wrote:

> I recall the occasion as though it were yesterday; one
> evening in September [1872] myself and my compan-
> ion [Fred G. Fitch, engineer] came on horseback, at the
> close of a beautiful twilight, upon some Indian fishers
> encamped among the bushes on the west shore of Ohuira
> Bay.
> Some giant *pitahaya* [cactus] trees stood nearby. Un-
> der one of these we unsaddled. A fire of dried cactus was
> blazing. A dozen dogs, a goat or two, some sheep, two
> women, three men, an urchin and a few milch cows . . .
> fish were hanging from the mesquite trees. The flesh of
> the green sea turtle, cut in strips, was dangling from the
> arms of the *echos*. [Giant cactus; more branched than
> the Sahuaro of the Southwest.] Many shells of turtles
> were lying around. Some served for seats, others held
> salt and fish. One was used for a cradle.
> We were tired. Within a few minutes we were
> stretched on our blankets near the fire. I fell asleep. It
> may have been near midnight I awakened—fire smoul-
> dering—the moon had climbed above the mountains,
> and had thrown a soft light upon the camp.
> An Indian came through the bushes from the beach
> with a turtle on his shoulder—let it fall to the ground—
> it flopped violently. He turned it on its back—it was

*Ella Wheeler Wilcox.

[26]

quiet. He put a fish upon the live coals, seated himself upon a turtle shell, turned the fish once, and when it was brown and steaming, he took off skin and scales as one skins an eel, and thus prepared, he ate it.

After this, he placed a peccary skin over the breast plate of a turtle, threw himself on top of both, and with a turtle shell for a pillow and his feet upon a sleeping dog he was, in a few minutes afterward, breathing heavily.

I had traveled many days through the wilderness and over swollen rivers [500 miles from Mazatlan during the rainy season] in search for this out of the way and but little known bay. My curiosity was keen to see the water and to investigate my surroundings. I stole from my blankets, went through the bushes and looked. What a panorama—there was Ohuira—an inland sea!

Mountains rose directly from out the water to the east and south. Ripples played on the edge of the incoming tide, and a dugout canoe was lying far up on the shore ... to the north and east stretched a level plain of grass and chaparral.

Thought I, if the morning should discover a deep and safe channel from this inland sea to the Gulf of California, then here is the site for a great metropolitan city. On that water, now without a sail, will one day come the ships of every nation. On this plain will dwell happy families. The Australasian will crowd this shore to be welcomed by the European, who shall come by train from the Atlantic seaboard, over the plateaux and across the Sierras.

As I stood and afterwards strolled along the beach, these thoughts grew into fancies. I pictured the shipping lying at anchor, saw the flags of many nations, heard the striking of the city clocks, was attracted by the chimes as they played "Sweet Home" from the tower of the Normal Industrial School, looked at the stone quays shaded by tropical plants and flowers, listened to the birds singing within the courts of Spanish-Moorish houses—and only awakened from my trance after the dawn had tinged the eastern horizon.

Everything we examined combined to impress us with

the importance of these Straits and Bays for a safe, deep and extensive anchorage. I settled that from that time on I would never rest until "Topolobampo" became a "household" word among commercial people, until the Republics of North America had utilized its advantages and Topolobampo had become a favorite place for the exchange of trade between the peoples of the world.

Let us recall that in 1872 there was no Panama Canal. There were no railroads extending from the United States southward to the dense tropics of Mexico. There were no great paved highways, nor automobiles, nor truck transportation. The first great transcontinental railroad was recently built, others were still building. The heads of the great railroad companies were called the "Empire Builders" of that day.

The dream of Albert K. Owen was to shorten transcontinental railway transportation, measured from key points such as Kansas City, Missouri, and Galveston, Texas, by 400 to 600 miles over the distance from those same points to the harbors of the Pacific Coast of the United States.

On a total haul of 2,000 to 2,500 miles that reduction in distance would have made a most substantial saving.

Shipping to the Orient and up and down the West Coast of the Americas would have been the principal business. However, back from Topolobampo for forty miles or more, and far to the north and south lies that great fertile coastal plain, eastward lie mountains rich in precious metals and in timber, beyond is the cattle and farming country of Chihuahua to the American border. These were all potential sources for freight products and passenger transportation.

The harbor then newly explored by Owen deserves description. Marked by Farallon Island, a Gibraltar-like rock rising from deep out of the Gulf of California about sixteen miles offshore, the harbor entrance lies about three miles across between two long narrow drift sand peninsulas—Las Copas to the southeast, Santa Maria to the northwest. Shoreward of these peninsulas, particularly northward, is a series of great bays and estuaries, miles upon miles of them. The estuaries are really the continuation into the bays of dry washes from the coastal plain. Into them flow peacefully inland with the rise of tide great ocean streams, through miles of evergreen marshes, the mangroves called in Spanish *mangles*.

At low tide vast areas of sand bars and mud flats are uncovered, leaving only the smaller channels extending into the *esteros* (estuaries).

Southeastward of this series of brilliant green mangrove-bordered bays lies a chain of high rocky hills, forming the opposite shore.

Along the southerly shore of Ohuira Bay continues the chain of hills; along its northerly shore are more estuaries bordered with mangroves, then a sloping beach with woods above. In the bay are several small islands. The scenery of this area justifies an extended exploration.

No doubt filled with a young man's plans and fancies, Owen rode with Engineer Fitch northeastward across the fertile plains of Los Mochis to the river and on a hundred miles from the ocean to the picturesque little city of Fuerte, in the foothills and overlooking the Fuerte River.

Here they laid their project—their dream—before Don Blas Ibarra, one of a long line of wealthy *hacendados* and merchants, a line continuing through all adversities to the present day.

Evidently convincing Don Blas, it was agreed that Fitch should survey and map the lands on the plain between the mountains and the sea, including the harbor area, receiving 5% of the land for his labor; that the land, presently found to be 111,000 acres including the harbor area, should be "denounced" (filed upon)—for Don Blas Ibarra and Dr. Benjamin Carman jointly, each retaining a divided half interest, but operating together. For preparing all necessary papers and filing, an attorney, Carlos Retes, son-in-law of Ibarra, was given a 5% interest.

Owen was given a 20% interest, and a complete power of attorney from all interested parties, to sell, hypothecate, arrange for concessions from the government for railroad and harbor building, colonization, or for any purpose, on 75% of all the lands.

Fred Fitch remained at Fuerte to marry a lovely high-class Mexican *señorita*, Rosario Burgos.

Armed with his extensive authority, the young engineer

Owen, now perhaps twenty-four years of age, crossed the Sierras to learn more of the proposed rail route, and dedicated the succeeding years largely to the promotion of his dream.

There surely was something compelling about this tall, well-built, black-mustached young engineer. From various sources we know that in May, 1873, he was permitted to present to the Governors' Convention of the Southern States, meeting at Atlanta, Georgia, an extensive plan for a railroad to be built from Norfolk, Virginia, via Austin, Texas, to Topolobampo.

This Convention, meeting eight years after the close of the Civil War, was absorbed in the problems of rehabilitation for the south, and was particularly interested in the opening of new routes for commerce. The Convention approved Owen's plans, including colonization along the proposed route. However, the hard times of the seventies prevented this project from carrying through.

From boyhood association through his father, Owen was friendly with General Ulysses S. Grant, now President of the United States. Pressing his project before the General, Owen secured the assignment of young Commodore (later Admiral) George W. Dewey, U.S.N., to survey and map the entrance of Topolobampo Bay.

By 1873 he had arranged for the consent of Mexico, then had urged before committees of the United States Congress the ordering of a survey for a postal route from Austin, Texas, to Topolobampo. This survey would serve to determine the most feasible route for all purposes, the interest in a postal route serving as legal justification for action by Congress.

The postal survey was approved, to include timber and land resources enroute. A 68-page report was given by the War Department, which presumably was entrusted with the survey.

At the Governor's Convention at Atlanta in 1873 the young Owen formed a strong friendship with Duff Green, a character famous in history as one of the "Kitchen Cabinet" of President Andrew Jackson. Green, who later broke with Jackson in favor of his rival, John C. Calhoun, was a liberal journalist, a Missouri State Senator, and Editor of *The Republic*, which fought the "spoils system" of Jackson and advocated free trade with other countries.

Here we have the first intimation of Owen's later known political and social philosophy.

Green was also the eminent authority of the time on relations with Mexico. Appointed by John C. Calhoun, then Secretary of State, as Consul to Galveston, he acted as adviser on the annexation of Texas. After the close of the war with Mexico, Green was sent by President Tyler to negotiate payments by the United States for land taken during the war. This elderly statesman no doubt was very helpful in his advice to young Owen.

Owen soon interested Governor Kemper of Virginia in his project, and through his assistance secured the passage in the spring of 1874 by the Virginia Assembly of a Charter for the "Southern Settlement Society" still for the purpose of planting colonies from Norfolk to Topolobampo.

By December, 1874, he had persuaded Honorable William D. Kelley to present to the U.S. House of Representatives and Honorable (General) John B. Gordon to the Senate a "Memorial of A. K. Owen, Civil Engineer—The Great Southern Trans-Oceanic and International Air Line—Asia to Europe via Mexico and the United States."

This memorial urged the shorter route, and further urged that it be built with "Treasury Money"—Greenback Currency—which had been issued during the Civil War.

From that time until 1879 Owen continued to urge this project before Congress. We know that at one time President Grant had a special board of U.S. Army Engineers convened to examine Owen on the project, this board being Major Generals Wright, Abbott, and Warren.

Those must have been strenuous years, for we know that Owen meanwhile had earned his living from civil engineering, part of the time in the mountains of Colorado.

In the winter of 1873 Owen had become one of the organizing board for the first "Greenback Club" of Pennsylvania, advocating the use of paper currency without gold reserve, and discontinuance of the practice of Government borrowing and payment of interest. He began writing articles in favor of this monetary reform, in favor of free trade, and of equal suffrage for women.

[31]

In 1876 Peter Cooper, the wealthy manufacturer, designer of the first steam locomotive in America, and a noted philanthropist and reformer, ran for President on the "Greenback" ticket. Owen was one of the electors and active in his campaign.

He belonged to the Brotherhood of the Union, Knights of Labor, and was a Mason. He wrote a series of letters entitled "The West and the East" directed to President Grant and to his friend, General (later President) Gonzales of Mexico, discussing the desirability of trade with the Orient.

During all the years up to 1879, according to Owen, the transcontinental railroad lobbies had succeeded in blocking every effort made to secure Federal support for his project, despite his (and his influential friends') having at one time secured a unanimous approval for their plans by the Railroad Committees of both House and Senate.

No doubt in some degree discouraged if not embittered by the long opposition and delay, in 1879 Owen, now just past thirty years of age, went to Mexico City with a letter from the Mexican Minister in Washington, Señor Don Manuel Zamacona, for the purpose of laying before President Porfirio Diaz, then completing his first term, a plan for building a World's Exhibition. Here again the young engineer must have made an unusual impression, for we know that President Diaz and Señor Don Matias Romero, Secretary of the Treasury, asked Owen to prepare plans and form a company to undertake the drainage of the great valley about Mexico City.

In his proposal, entitled "Texcoco-Huehuetoca Canal," Owen suggested its financing through issuing of Mexican Treasury money—the "Greenback" plan again. He further submitted to President Diaz a plan for "The Military, Postal and Commercial Highways of Mexico and the United States, Their Construction and Management," together with suggestions on reconstruction of Government, City, and Public Buildings and means of payment for such public works.

Here surely was the "Day Dreamer, Unlimited." His plans must have fired the imagination of Diaz, then in the bloom of his youth and in the first term of a rule destined to last, with only one four-year interruption, for thirty years. The plan was translated into Spanish by the Diaz Cabinet and presented to the Mexican Congress. It was approved, and Owen immediately returned to the United States, apparently now on the highroad to success.

In the United States Owen soon formed a syndicate with Major General Alfred T. A. Torbert as President, for the purpose of building this great drainage system for the area of the Mexican national capital, and to continue with other construction outlined by him in the pamphlet translated to the Mexican Congress, including a national system of railways for Mexico.

On August 25, 1880, General Torbert, Owen, and fourteen other members of this syndicate sailed for Mexico on the ship *City of Vera Cruz.* On August 29th a hurricane caught this ship off the coast of Florida and dashed it to pieces. Seventy-four persons were drowned, all of the members of the Torbert party excepting Owen. Perhaps because of his youth and his evident determined will, Owen survived the ordeal of twenty-four hours of storm, finally washing ashore on the Florida coast, one of four survivors. In a night of driving wind and rain he made his exhausted way to a settler's cabin where he was given shelter and help.

So at thirty years of age this zealous young man faced another setback, in fact, a major disaster. However, with admirable perseverance Owen returned to New York to begin again. This time he must have again turned to his father's friend, President Grant, for a new syndicate was created with Ulysses S. Grant, Jr., as its president and Owen as chief engineer.

This delay was fatal to his purpose. Concessions were given elsewhere for the draining of the Valley of Mexico and for the building of the Mexican Central Railway from El Paso to Mexico City.

The great commercial rivalries of that day over interests in Mexico, as between individuals or companies, and as between the nations foreign to Mexico, make interesting reading, but are not a part of our story.

Accepting the inevitable, Owen once again turned his undivided attention to his dream of 1872, and by 1881 he had secured a concession from the Mexican Government, his friend General Gonzales now being President, for a railroad from Topolobampo across the Sierras, to be built by the

"Texas, Topolobampo and Pacific Railroad and Telegraph Company," with himself as chief engineer. The concession called for 2,000 miles of road and for a subsidy of sixteen million dollars.

The names of many of those directly interested by Owen in this project are historic: General U. S. Grant; Ulysses S. Grant, Jr.; Mayor Frederick O. Prince of Boston; General Ben Butler, once a candidate for President; Wendell Phillips, orator, statesman, and reformer; E. A. Buck, Editor of *The Spirit of the Times*, New York; Señor Don Matias Romero, by then Minister at Washington; United States Senators John B. Gordon of Missouri, Joseph E. Johnson and Ben Hill of Georgia; General Samuel B. Price of Missouri; Governor John U. Brown of Tennessee; Chief Engineer Sickles of the Union Pacific Railway.

At this time he likewise secured a concession for colonization, and for construction of a city surrounding the harbor of Topolobampo, more particularly along the west side of Ohuira Bay.

The first President of this Texas, Topolobampo, and Pacific Railroad and Telegraph Company was Mayor Prince of Boston. From 1883 to 1889 we find as President the Honorable William Windom, once Secretary of the Treasury of the United States.

With this organization accomplished, in 1883 Owen returned to Sinaloa to locate one hundred miles of the projected railroad from the ocean across the plain to the city of Fuerte. He returned to this work in 1884, and by February 1885 clearing of right-of-way and grading inland from the hills at Topolobampo had begun.

CHAPTER V

The Credit Foncier of Sinaloa

By hidden waters' lovely bay
Pacific's future mart shall rise
A greeting to the New Born Day
The growing light, the brightening skies!

In fair proportions she shall rise
Her commerce visit every strand
While eager waits the iron horse
To bear her traffic o'er the land.

Her palaces and homes shall rise
In graceful forms to greet the sun
While in them rest the sons of toil
When labor's lightened task is done.

With warm full hearts we welcome him
Who through long years, with patient plan
Hath wrought to found an empire here
Whose chiefest cornerstone is Man.

And who shall say that where we stand
What noble city shall arise
Upbuilt to freedom and to man
A true terrestrial paradise.

Perchance these plains of Mexico
These giant hills that round us rise
Shall feel the first warm thrill and glow
*Of Freedom's Sun, of Freedom's Skies.**

SO ONCE MORE by 1885, the young engineer—promoter—dreamer, backed by many men of wide influence in the United States, was at the point of launching a great enterprise—the construction of a shorter transcontinental rail route, the building of a great metropolitan seaport, the colonization of an area then and now a potential empire in its natural resources.

The governments of both countries were friendly to the project.

*From "Libertad" by colonist S. A. Merrill.

No doubt President Gonzales of Mexico, who granted the concessions, envisioned great benefits to his people through increased production and transportation, both by rail and by sea. Owen's support in high places in the United States has already been referred to.

Up to this time there had been no hint, no indication as to the method of establishment of the seaport, the colony, and the railroad. The determination of these matters lay with the thirty-seven-year-old engineer and promoter of the vast project, as events will show.

What were Owen's ideas? What were his plans? We find the answer by picking up the threads of his personal associations of the preceding years.

Of his associations with persons well known to history in political and financial circles we already know. Among them was Wendell Phillips, the great orator and reformer—champion of abolition of slavery, prohibition, women's suffrage, penal and legislative reforms. Another was the "single taxer," Henry George. A very close friend was John W. Lovell, who became a millionaire through publishing low-priced editions of popular books whose copyrights had expired, so making them available to the great masses of people. Lovell was a philanthropist, and in political conviction a Socialist and reformer.

Owen was a relatively poor man. During his travels in Europe, the West Indies, and Mexico he had no doubt been in close contact with persons in poverty. His early training and his Civil War experiences must have made him of sympathetic mind.

In 1875 he became acquainted with two unusual persons, Edward Howland and his wife Marie, both of whom afterwards figured strongly in the beginnings of the colony. A novel by Marie Howland, with the rather misleading title of *Papa's Own Girl*, was provoking much comment at the time for its frankness of statement, and after reading the book Owen visited the Howlands at their home near Hammonton, New Jersey.

Marie describes Albert Owen ". . . in the prime of early manhood, in exuberant health and spirits, graphically describing the nature and promise of this wonderful country; all were carried away by his magnetic eloquence. . . ."

Edward Howland was an unusual personality. He was born at Charleston, South Carolina, September 15, 1832, son of a cotton commission merchant who was widely known for his benevolences. The father was founder of the first public library in the city and of the New Boys' Lodging House in New York.

Edward was eighth in direct line of descent from John Howland, who came to America in the Mayflower. He was a classmate of Charles W. Eliot at Harvard (class of 1853).

Howland is described as of medium height, athletic in build, esthetic in appearance, with blue-gray eyes, high forehead, thick mustache, thin beard shaved part way back in the fashion of the day. He was a writer and a translator of rare old volumes from many languages, traveling to foreign countries with expenses and salary paid by publishing houses to search for these volumes for translation.

Among his associates and contemporaries were Thomas Bailey Aldrich, William Dean Howells, and Albert Brisbane, father of the late Arthur Brisbane, famed columnist of the Hearst newspapers.

During his residences in Europe Howland became a student of, then a disciple of, the great French Socialist leader Fournier, and later of the Socialist leader Godin.

Marie was a New England girl, educated in the United States and Paris, where she became interested in "Familistere," the Socialist colony at Guise, France, developed by Godin.

These two writers met in New York, were married in Scotland, and spent their honeymoon in Scott's "Lady of the Lake" country, afterwards lived in St. John's Wood, London, in Amsterdam, and in Belgium.

Returning to America, the Howlands purchased five acres near Hammonton, always an unprofitable enterprise. During this period as a part-time farmer Howland became interested in farm problems. When the Grange movement started in New Jersey he supported it with enthusiasm. The first Grange of New Jersey was said by the Howlands to have been organized at Casa Tonti, the Howland home. Howland was chosen first State Master and went as state representative to the Grange national meeting in St. Louis in December, 1873.

Marie writes, "Mr. Howland took the most active interest in Mr. Owen's plans for colonization. . . . I urged the starting of a little paper to print some of the letters [from people interested by Owen in the proposed colony]. Owen lacked money; finally we began the paper June 9, 1885. . . ."

What other influences Owen may have had to determine him we do not know—it matters not. In 1885 we find this statement of his intention: "During the past six months Mr. Owen has, in connection with the railroad, suggested a cooperative colony to be located in Sinaloa . . . it is a new departure in laying out, settling and managing a city . . . there are over 1,400 persons already enlisted, and over $300,000 in money associated for carrying out the enterprise. 'Integral Co-operation' is now being published in Spanish at the Mexican Capital. . . ."

"Integral Co-operation," written by Albert K. Owen, is an elaborate plan for reorganization of society by substitution of Integral Cooperation for our system of free enterprise. He states that there are two principal problems, production and distribution; that production deals with labor, machinery, inventions, chemistry, science; that distribution deals with wages, transportation, manners of payment. He maintains that the two problems must be treated together—that the production problem is well in hand, but distribution is very inefficient, unequal, and unfair. Quoting him, "The mission of Socialists is to force upon the consideration of our people of every class the vital issues underlying the second part of the problem [distribution] and to urge by organizing cooperative industries and exchanges the application of equity in the affairs of mankind . . . by incorporating earnest, industrious and responsible men and women into associations. . . . Mexico is the best locality for a cooperative colony . . . virgin soil, great resources, good climate, removed from evil influences of the trade and political centres of the world. . . ."

The application by Owen of the term "cooperative colony" to an essentially socialistic enterprise can easily be misleading.

Through the years since this young dreamer planned for a better world there has been a progressive development of cooperatives in many countries, notably the United States, England, Sweden, and Denmark.

[38]

Present-day cooperatives, although encouraged by government, are essentially products of the private enterprise system. In the United States they consist of groups, usually farmers, joined together for one or several purposes, as purchasing of supplies, transportation and sale of products, for financing the purchase of property, or financing of production.

Consumer cooperatives have grown to be important factors in the buying and selling markets of Great Britain.

In Sweden and Denmark, countries whose agricultural economies are largely dependent on the production of strictly standardized, highest quality products for sale abroad, such as ham and bacon, butter and cheese, cooperatives are sponsored by government and favored to a degree to almost exclude competition for individuals not members of cooperatives.

It has been my privilege to be member and director of farm cooperatives, first in Mexico, then California, then nationally in the United States. Such institutions have a place in a democratic world. They tend towards more efficient production and distribution of the world's goods, with consequent benefit to both producer and consumer. They tend to educate their members in the art of cooperation, of thinking and planning collectively for the common good—an education which makes better citizenship in any country.

There is a similarity in sharing among farmer members of cooperatives with the profit sharing by employees in certain private industries, which has been successfully accomplished by some forward-looking industrial concerns.

It is my growing conviction that the way to the most abundant life for both capital and labor lies in these fields of cooperation and profit sharing, rather than in either extreme capitalism or extreme socialism.

The plan of Owen for this cooperative colony called for eliminating private wealth and the use of money in the way we consider it, substituting a system of credits for the labor of each, and providing that homes be built by the colony for its citizens, with lifetime right for their use, further providing for building by the colony of all community improvements—roads, schools, hospitals, libraries, manufacturing plants—eventually everything needed and possible of production by the colony. This social-economic philosophy or plan of life began with the assumption that labor is the main

source of all wealth, and proposed distribution of all wealth
—the product of labor—through credits for labor.

Colonists were to build the harbor facilities, the "Pacific
City," the railroad; to clear the land and produce the food
needed; presently to create many small industries whose
products would be for the use of all the colonists and also for
sale in order to secure other necessities of life. Likewise the
operation of the railroad was to be by the colonists on a cooperative basis, returns to apply towards the upbuilding of
the colony commonwealth and the security and comfort of
its citizens.

Payment for the railroad was to be largely by subsidy from
the Mexican Government.

Colonists were required to sign an agreement to comply
with the principles laid down in "Integral Co-operation."

For their belongings such as plows, wagons, livestock, tools,
even books and artist supplies, they were given paper credits,
on the assumption that these items contributed to the collective good of the colony.

In order to finance this vast enterprise there was created
"The Credit Foncier of Sinaloa," with Owen as chairman of
its board of directors, which offered for sale to friends of the
plan throughout the world shares of stock which corresponded
in value to the script or credits given for labor, so that investors in stock might later make their home in the colony
with the benefits of community development and personal
residence being available to them.

The term "Credit Foncier" is said to indicate credit based
on the family, the home.

The board of directors for administration of the Credit
Foncier Company was elected by the stockholder members.
The chairman, elected by the directors, formed departments
to be under the charge of the various directors.

A newspaper, *The Credit Foncier of Sinaloa,* edited by the
Howlands at Hammonton, New Jersey, made known these
plans to the interested public. Owen and his fellow planners
held meetings. Credit Foncier Clubs were organized in one
large city after another, in many smaller towns, and in several other countries. Support sprang up like a flame, spread
like a prairie fire. Stock subscriptions poured in from thousands of persons, usually in small amounts, no doubt by rela-

tively poor contributors. Enthusiasm grew. Members of Credit Foncier Clubs began selling their homes, their farms, their businesses, to move to the new Utopia in Sinaloa.

In Sinaloa there was nothing prepared. The dream was still on paper. Only one small party making the railroad survey and cutting line for the right-of-way of the Mexican-American Construction Company, organized by Owen with private capital, was working near Topolobampo in November 1886.

In California the Credit Foncier movement was led by an interesting personality, Dr. Edwin J. Schellhous. His parents from Vermont, Edwin J. Schellhous was born in Huron County, Ohio. His father had been a brigadier general during the War of 1812 under General Harrison. He had also been a delegate to the constitutional convention to create the state of Michigan, and had served several terms in the Michigan State Legislature.

Young Shellhous attended Michigan State University in 1837, took a medical course in Cincinnati, Ohio, married in 1848, moved to California in 1852. He chose to teach for thirty years, rather than follow his medical profession, although he was a graduate of the Medical Department, University of California. Of his wife we know nothing; he mentioned a daughter of whom he seemed very proud.

From 1876 he began publishing articles on political and financial reforms, edited a paper, *Emancipation*, and was a delegate to the Greenback-Labor Convention in 1884, probably meeting Owen at that convention. Dr. Shellhous was author of several books widely distributed at that time, *The New Republic*; *Evil, Its Cause and Remedy Considered*; *Problems for the People*; and *Dawn of the New Era*.

He is described at 66 years of age as strong and active, an accomplished swimmer, oarsman, and skater. He was said to be an able orator, a philosopher, yet a practical man of affairs—to be kind hearted, generous, never quarrelsome, genial and witty in conversation. He was a spiritualist and was reputed to have extraordinary powers as a medium of contact with the spirit world.

I recall Dr. Schellhous in Kansas City, Missouri, in 1907, at 86 years of age, a handsome, upright, venerable-looking old man with a flowing snow-white beard and long snowy white hair, a grave face with kindly eyes—to a small boy an impressive picture of a patriarch of old.

Perhaps inspired by the enthusiasm of their leader, California members of Credit Foncier now resolved to wait no longer, but to begin at once the building of this better life. They chartered the steamer *Newbern*, and over the protest of Dr. Schellhous and the directors in the East, in late October 1886 steamed out of San Francisco Bay. From here we read from C. M. Stanley, leader of that group:

> Twenty-seven colonists sailed for the promised land— 2 married and 2 young unmarried women, 6 children and 17 men, most of whom were first class pioneers. With a smooth and pleasant voyage, touching at several seaport towns, they reached Mazatlan [in early November]. Captain Middlestadt was very kind, but had no authority to enter the inner port of Topolobampo . . . not a port of entry [so] with the assistance [at Mazatlan] of the U.S. Consul, Mr. Kelton, they procured a sailing schooner, the "Briza" with captain and crew, to be towed. . . . Twelve hours after leaving Mazatlan the "Newbern" with schooner "Briza" in tow encountered a severe gale which lasted until she anchored, early morning of November 10 [1886] in the outer harbor of Topolobampo.
>
> Passengers and freight were soon transferred . . . with a fair breeze they sailed [the first colonists] into the Straits of Joshua.
>
> The captain [of the *Briza*] did not know where to land . . . he sailed past into the Bay of Ohuira. Discovering some Indians on the shore, four men, Matson, Byrns, Hoelle and a Mexican sailor interpreter, got into a canoe . . . it soon upset . . . Matson swam back, the others clung to the canoe . . . Rolla C. Stanley swam with a rope to their relief . . . the schooner then sailed westward nearer shore . . . dropped anchor for the night.
>
> Seven men went ashore and built a campfire on a rock, the first colonist campfire in Sinaloa [the first of many, many thousands of colonist campfires in Sinaloa!].
>
> Next morning the schooner made her way back into

the Bay of Topolobampo and entered a cove [Schellhous Cove, where the Customs House now stands].

They then searched for the old camping ground of the engineers, the termination of the proposed railroad. Mr. [Joel] Byrns, an energetic and experienced pioneer, always on the alert in difficulties, went out to explore—up the summit of a low, brushy mountain. A vast wilderness presented itself, brush, rock and cactus on every

hand. He perceived a dim trail, followed this—and found the old camp ground. Upon a cactus tree he found the following notice: "We left this camp October 30, 1886. We left 5 barrels of water, 2 boxes crackers and the mast and sail 50 feet to the left of this notice in the brush. Signed [Burt] Pressey."

The colonists were much gratified, this removed all doubts as to locality—they remained in the cove—cut away some brush from around camp, built an oven to bake bread, built a boat, cut a trail to the Engineers' Camp, fitted up the [Railroad Construction] Company's boat which they used for bringing in water from Las

Copas. [Information of this water must have come from the Indian fishermen.]

On the 17th of November a vessel was seen approaching through the Straits of Joshua with passengers aboard. Great excitement prevailed in camp. As she came within hearing distance a band of music greeted her [the Stanley family band].

The vessel was a sloop rented by the Credit Foncier at Guaymas, loaded with lumber, provisions, 10 passengers, one a woman, all in care of Mr. [W. A.] McKenzie. . . .

Cheering news, Mr. Owen was enroute [from Guaymas] with 150 colonists on the steamer "Altata." . . .

Here we leave the story of C. M. Stanley to take up the trail of those 150 colonists he mentioned.

CHAPTER VI

Early Days of the Credit Foncier Colony

Each soul that has breadth of being
Is touched with heaven's own fire;
Each living man is part of the plan
To lift the world up higher.

I HAVE just spent some days visiting with an old friend, once upon a time our able teacher in the community school at Los Mochis, Sinaloa. This very interesting and alert lady was twenty-three years of age when the Topolobampo Colony began in 1886.

We have discussed the colony at length, from the beginnings of the dream of Colonel Albert K. Owen in 1872, through the planning years to the colonization in 1886 and the years beyond. Fair minded, sensible and kindly in her reasoning, still a pioneering liberal in spirit, but tempered by the wisdom of experience, Ida Hoagland Dawkins knows the story of those hundreds, altogether thousands, of persons involved in this enterprise as it could be known only to one sharing in its enthusiasms and its difficulties.

It fell to her lot to function at various times as teacher, storekeeper, postmistress, journalist, and as one of the resident directors for the Americans gathered there. She has preserved written records of those eventful years and remembers much beyond the records.

Ida Hoagland was born and spent her early life in Shelby County, Illinois, attending teachers' college there. Her brother became a Unitarian minister at Greeley, Colorado, where she went to live with him in the spring of 1886. A prominent member of the congregation was Mrs. Lydia Stevens, who was a friend of Louisa M. Alcott, Nathaniel Hawthorne, and others of the "liberal" writers' group in New England. Mrs. Stevens was an enthusiastic member of the "Brooks Farm Movement," an experiment in noncommercial community living being carried on near Boston and recently mentioned in the book *The Flowering of New England* by Van Wyck Brooks. She inspired her young friend, Ida, to share her interest and enthusiasm.

Mr. and Mrs. Alvin J. Wilber and a small son, Lawrence, attended the church of Dr. Hoagland. They became interested in the Credit Foncier Company of Sinaloa, and planned to take part in the Pacific Colony being organized. They offered to take Ida Hoagland under their care, and she left with the Colorado group from Denver about November 1, 1886. Their emigrant train carried them to Guaymas, Sonora.

Owen was appalled by what was happening. The enthusiasms of himself and his fellow planners had carried farther and faster than they had dreamed—like a fire out of control. Completely unprepared for these migrations, Owen hurried to meet the Colorado immigrants at Nogales, Arizona. There was no turning back now. These people had cut loose all ties and staked their future on Owen and Integral Cooperation.

Helping the colonists through border customs, Owen continued with their emigrant train to Guaymas, Sonora. Here he hurriedly rented a large vacant warehouse lying alongside the wharf of the harbor, where the colonists made temporary shelter as best they could, cooking on open fires for ten days while waiting for a ship. First the McKenzie party was sent with the sloop, closely followed by Owen and the 150 colonists on the *Altata*, 100 tons, captain, Charles H. Robinson.

The bay of Topolobampo was so little known that after crossing the bar between the two projecting sandy points, Santa Maria to the north and Las Copas to the south, they could not find the inner channel which follows along Las Copas and the southern shore into the inner harbor. Turning northward into Santa Maria Bay, they anchored off Baviri Island, the colonists waiting on board ship for two days while soundings were made over the miles of bay to locate the inner channel. On entering the inner harbor they found the group of colonists from California, arrived a week before them, on November 10, 1886.

Here the new colonists encamped for about six weeks. There were no houses, no living facilities, no fresh water, no roads into the interior. The dream city was a rocky, rugged group of hills, brush and thorn covered, encircling a beautiful bay, enchanting scenery, glorious landscape, but formidable and completely unconquered by human hands. Around the campfires on the shore of this bay, Owen, the magnetic personality, the dreamer, discussed plans with these colonists, appointing various ones, according to their previous experience, to certain duties in their colony life. At one of these campfire meetings Ida Hoagland was appointed schoolteacher for the group of about twenty children. Under the direction of their leaders, Owen, Schellhous, and Wilber, groups were organized for various tasks. One group cleared brush for tents and campsite and began the planning of more permanent houses of stone and lumber. A few fished for food. A detail was assigned to bring firewood, another to bring water seven miles by sailing launch from Las Copas, a task that must be continued for sixteen long years until 1903.

This country was a treasure place of ocean life, as it still is, and game abounded on its shores. But rather than indulge in reverie, in dreamy contemplation of those waters and shores, we must follow our colonists, escapists from an unpleasing world, from too much commercialism, too much competition with people, now pioneers in a competition with nature, which too is hard and unforgiving, particularly so to those who do not know her moods and ways.

On the low drift-sand points of Las Copas and Santa Maria, as well as on many other such sand peninsulas and islands in the Gulf, there is fresh water, presumably stored by the rains of many centuries. This water may be found by digging a foot or two or three in certain of the lowest places, sometimes within fifty yards of the ocean. This fresh water in some places rises and falls several inches with the movement of the tides; evidently the two bodies of water, fresh and salt, gradually merge near the shore line, the ocean water being kept from intrusion inland by the pressure of the fresh water poured from rains into the drifting sand.

This water the colonists dipped from holes in the sand into casks which were then sealed and rolled aboard their sailing launch. Trips were made almost daily for water. In this instance nature was kind. The early morning breezes were offshore, from the colonists' camp to Las Copas, and the prevailing winds after late morning were from the northwest, so

The Credit Foncier of Sinaloa

Collective Ownership and Management for Public Utilities and Conveniences—The Community Responsible for the Health, Usefulness, Individuality and Security of Each.—*Albert K. Owen.*

Vol. V, No. 18.   TOPOLOBAMPO, SINALOA, MEXICO, JUNE 1, 1891.   Whole No. 203.

Masthead of Colonist Newspaper The Credit Foncier of Sinaloa.

the launch could be sailed eastward for the return trip to camp.

This first home of the two hundred or more colonists, then, was the projected great port of the future, the terminus of a great railway linking the United States and Mexico to vast trade with the Pacific coasts of North and South America and the Orient. Here and extending along the shores of Ohuira Bay, a great city was planned to be built.

Quoting from *Harper's Weekly*, as reprinted in *The Credit Foncier of Sinaloa*, August 7, 1887:

> The Topolobampo colonists are a peculiar people. One cannot visit among them long without coming to the conclusion that they are an educated, steady going race of skilled craftsmen and women with a settled purpose and a fixed determination to carry it out . . . they are mostly persons who have positive convictions concerning religion, government and society . . . they went quietly away to the great Southwest . . . there resolved to build homes and to live in conformity to by-laws which they judge to be equitable. . . . They say "Our principles enjoin upon every member order, industry and courtesy. . . ." If there is one trait of character peculiar to these colonists it is the forethought and method which have been given to their plans and the details by which they are carried into execution. They have not only during several years [before beginning the colony] carefully laid out their building sites, railroads and farms; but even the designs for their houses, wharfs, quays, shops, parks, etc.—have been drawn and distributed so that each member may assist to form the structures and improvements which are to follow . . . these people [are] the most remarkable reformers of whom we have any record. They have surveyed and laid out about 18,000 acres on the north shore of Topolobampo Bay into avenues, diagonals, streets, walks, parks, circles, quays, piers, drives, etc., the public areas occupying about 40% of the whole. This city plan is unique, attractive and thorough in every detail.

The corporation [Credit Foncier Company] holds the title and management forever of this building site, and, in fact of all lands which are used by the colonists, and every member has the use of a building lot or farm or both as long as he or she wishes to occupy the same, and no longer.

Tax, interest and rent are, in fact, entirely abolished by these people; they pay for their houses by exchanging services, not by payments in money. . . . As it is with their dwellings so it is with their factories, shops, hotels, theatres, lecture halls, dry-docks, sailors' homes, schools, etc. There is a place set aside forever for each. . . . All transportation in the thoroughfares will be on tramways moved by electricity, the lights will be electric and so will be the power for factories, etc. The wheelways will be paved with asphalt so that roller skates, bicycles and tricycles can be used by the citizens for quick locomotion. . . . Topolobampo has the only landing on the West Coast of Mexico where a ship can go directly to a wharf and be unloaded. In all other ports lighters are used . . . from the stone pier the colonists have their railroad go north 4½ miles . . . then 31 miles to Vegaton [Fuerte River], then to Fuerte City, across the Sierra Madre mountains about 1,000 miles to Galveston, Texas. . . . All is industry with these people now. They are called to breakfast at six by a tune on a "clarionet," and in the same way they are summoned to begin and stop work, and for discussion and to hear news read. They have gone to Sinaloa to build up a community, a state, if you please, founded upon the development of man. . . . To make homes for every member and to keep the individuality of each person sacred is their purpose. Well may we say with the Pilgrim Fathers, "The right is more than our country."

I have placed here these selected phrases from the quoted article to show the extent of the dream toward which these people were striving, grouped on those rocky shores that winter of 1886.

Alvin Wilber soon led a "miners and sappers" crew in building a road over the harbor hill, thence along the dividing line of an estuary and a hill into the back country, the wooded plain extending to the Fuerte River.

[50]

Ida Hoagland led her group of children in pleasant days of exploration along the bay shores, studying the many shellfish and other ocean life, the rock formations, the vegetation. Leader Owen soon departed to other duties, but Directors Schellhous and Wilber were both well-learned naturalists and were helpful with suggestions. Later Colonel Edward Daniels, a scientist, once State Geologist of Wisconsin, organized the "Academy of Sciences" of Topolobampo, classified the sea life, and sent specimens to the Smithsonian at Washington.

Something had to be done to provide food, water, and more substantial shelter. An American pioneer named Haskell owned land on the river at Sufragio, thirty miles inland. A deal was made for the use of this land. Less than two months after the first landing a road had been cut through the woods and most of the people had moved to Sufragio, and shortly after to nearby Vegaton and Cahuinahui.

The first houses were built in the native style with walls of brush, or of bamboo mats, brush roofs, dirt covered to shed rain, all very much exposed to the open air. Some walls were of wattle—small branches woven horizontally in and out around uprights placed at about two-foot intervals in the line of the wall. These wattled walls were plastered with mud. Sometimes roofs were sharp-peaked and thatched with palm or tavai grass, making with their dirt floors quite cool dwellings.

Women and children made the trip on foot to the new location.

More colonists arrived. Early in 1887 there were over four hundred persons in the colony. Schools were organized at the port and at the three other locations. Miss Hoagland taught at Sufragio in a native corncrib, which was about sixteen feet square and about three feet off the ground. It was built with a floor of hardwood branches bound together with *mescal* (a type of henequen) fiber, with a thatched roof shelter and lath walls some three feet high, access to this odd school room being by means of a ladder. The advantages were privacy, shade, and relief from the fleas abundant in the area of all native villages, where dogs propagated uncontrolled except by the starvation processes of nature.

One who has grown up used to such inconveniences can still comfortably do without them. For persons unused to exposure to fleas, sand-gnats, wood-ticks, mosquitoes, scorpions, Gila monsters, rattlesnakes, and tarantulas, all indigenous to the area the colonists were settling, they bore their lot cheerfully.

A rare sample of this optimism is expressed in this letter dated Cahuinahui, March 15, 1887:

> To all whose hearts are turned to us with interest and anxiety . . . we are asked to give a few facts learned from a residence of nearly three months here. . . . The people in camp are all happy, healthy and industrious; the scorpions, when they sting, which is rare, are harmless and hardly painful; the tarantula has not yet bitten; the spider, such as bites in the states, has bitten, but the same right arm that received the bite is able to write these statements; the mosquito comes along, sings his solo and departs without alighting. . . . Signed Sera E. Wilbur, Maggie Burr, Ida Hoagland, B. F. Burr, committee.

Imagine the embarrassment of our good friend, Ida Hoagland Dawkins, some sixty-two years later on being confronted with that statement! Such are the enthusiasms of youth, and youth shall move the world.

The impetus of the Credit Foncier movement continued. During that first winter of 1886 a steady procession of single persons, families, and groups of families uprooted themselves from city and from countryside in the north to undertake the trek to this new cooperative colony in Sinaloa. These were self-selected by personal desire, not selected by Owen or the other leaders for their qualifications as pioneers to a strange land, and of a new plan of living.

Inevitably there were persons of every physical condition and of every type of mind.

On the night of December 5th there came a vessel with colonists who included two directors elected by groups in the north—Hawkins, an attorney, and Eaton, an ex-minister.

Quoting again from C. M. Stanley:

> Among these were two directors who came against the wishes of Owen, who had protested against moving any more colonists to Sinaloa until he had the way bet-

ter prepared. Notwithstanding, they pushed on, and after landing seemed dissatisfied with everything—found fault with the people, the harbor, the land, Mr. Owen and his plans—stating that he was not capable, but that they would reconstruct the colony and put it on a better footing. Dr. Schellhous, overburdened with responsibility and hard work, was rejoiced to learn of the arrival of these two directors, thinking he would be relieved—but these men added greatly to his burdens.

At first they would not hand over to the commissary provisions bought for the colony at Guaymas, thinking they could control by authoritative ways. But determination of Dr. Schellhous to carry out Owen's plans, and the great majority joining him proved too much—finding themselves foiled in their plans to control the colony by such methods, they turned in such goods as they did not need—by assuming good fellowship hoping to gain favor and lead the colonists, and thus secure their ends.

But the colonists were suspicious of these men and would not be led. Dr. Scally, who came on the same ship with them, warned others. His mild, yet convincing language did much to open the eyes of the colonists. Hearing of the intended return of Owen, under cover of night, without making known their intention to any except their confederates, they stole quietly away to Zaragoza and sailed for Guaymas.

After the departure of this discordant element, through the great efforts of Dr. Schellhous and others devoted to the cause of Integral Co-operation, peace and harmony were once more established throughout the colony.

Returning to the United States, Hawkins and Eaton publicized adversely the whole colony plan, the story carrying widely in the press. To it were added other stories by persons who had gone down expecting some sort of dream world—or expecting to be supported in a life of comparative ease under the new scheme of living. There arose a furious controversy throughout the United States—in fact, throughout the world —between the Credit Foncier groups (and there were many) and what they termed the "capitalistic press."

From this point forward the movement labored under an

extreme handicap from lack of a united support even from its former "followers in the faith."

It is not the function of a historian, even a minor one, to promote conclusions, but rather to give facts which seem evident, and interesting or appealing. As there were many discordant notes from the beginnings of the colony, so were there many manifestations of faith and determination to carry on to success.

Director Dr. Schellhous, after the first critical months, turned northward. He wrote from Guaymas May 3, 1887, "I go to California and perhaps to Oregon and Washington Territory to present before the people the advent of the New Civilization, to purchase supplies for the colony, negotiate for our [railroad] construction bonds and take subscriptions for stock. . . ."

With the general approval of the colonists, Owen appointed Alvin J. Wilber, leader of the Colorado Party, as Resident Director. Wilber was born in Genessee Valley, New York, spent his youth in Michigan and in Ohio, then frontiers of the country—rose to become a captain in the Civil War. After the war he had worked in the Freedman's Bureau on rehabilitation of Negroes in the South. Later he had become a teacher. He was a botanist and naturalist. His wife, Sera Eaton Wilber, was likewise a botanist. Mrs. Wilber was a very bright, cheerful character among the colonists. Wilber was a practical minded man, a forceful leader, something of a driver; too aggressive in his ideas—particularly of work to be done—to suit many of the colonists.

Here is a quotation from him that indicates this quality: "I have attempted to organize the brickmakers group on the city site at *so much per thousand*. Mr. Friend wishes to start the Mochis on the same plan; to pay for clearing *by the acre*, and farming *by products delivered*. Gradually we will get upon the plan of Integral Cooperation—of paying each for what he or she accomplishes."

The other local directors were W. P. "Bill" Friend, a farmer, and Dr. Thomas Young. Friend, born in 1845 in Pennsylvania, had gone to the Illinois frontier at ten years of age, had enlisted in the Union Army at seventeen years. After their marriage he and wife Mary moved to Nebraska, then across the western country to Mussels Slough, near

Tulare, California, being participants in the bloody battle that resulted in the settlers' being evicted from lands that the railroads claimed from the Government. By 1886 they had five children.

Another family, Mr. and Mrs. B. F. Burr and their children, Grant and Maggie, also were in the Mussels Slough settlement and were involved in the same struggle.

These two families resolved to move to the colony overland from California. On November 13, 1886, they left with two wagons—the Friend and Burr families and John Budlong (described as a tall, big-framed old man wearing a fine white beard—another able pioneer, afterwards a useful mechanic in the colony). Crossing San Gorgonio Pass into Coachella Valley, they were caught in a freak snowstorm and only saved their horses during the week of storm by feeding them flour mixed with water made from the snow.

Wherever possible they followed the railroad in order to have water, having sometimes to demand this forcibly from stations of limited supply. Traversing the rough and rugged desert hills of the southwest and of Sonora, and going through the Yaqui country with soldier escort, they arrived in the colony on February 5, 1887, after nearly three months on the way.

The practical abilities of Bill Friend soon made him a director of the colony.

One of the most cheerful, optimistic, and enterprising of the colonists was Dr. Joshua W. Scally, who had arrived December 5, 1886, with his wife, Eliza Clementine, and their children, Joe, Sam, twin girls Hattie and Mattie, and younger daughter Ida—on the same vessel with the insurgent directors Eaton and Hawkins. Besides being the colony physician he was a dispenser of good cheer in those early days.

An extract from a letter written to Dr. Schellhous April 22, 1887, denotes his friendly optimism:

> I called on the Stanleys last night. Mr. Stanley took his violin, Mrs. Stanley her guitar and both sang and played until I was most charmed out of this world into one of heavenly love and peace. I tell you this Stanley family are precious jewels to the colony.
>
> Last night there was a dance—Mr. Faulds called,

"Take your partners for a Quadrille" to begin two hours of amusement. . . .

There are comforts and happiness in store for us in the near future never before enjoyed by any people on this earth. It must be, if we are true to our principles.

The Stanleys were an unusual family. The father, Cyrus Milton Stanley, a man with a long greying beard, deep-seeing eyes, serious, studious, courteous, was composer of various orchestral selections and songs for the colony, and leader of the "Stanley Family Band," himself playing the violin. Married twice, the children of his first marriage were sons Rolla, Lynn, Clair, Milton, and daughter Ella; this daughter a beautiful character, who had unfortunately been confined to a wheel chair by a fall from a horse as a child. The children of his wife Viola were Etta, Lulu (Lutie), Willis, and Fred. All played instruments in this band, and their reputation as musicians has carried through for many later years.

During those first months Owen worked constantly to improve the situation of the colonists. Funds were raised for the purchase of provisions by Dr. Schellhous. These were sent by the steamer *Newbern*. At La Paz, Lower California, the first port of call for customs inspection in Mexico, some over-officious inspector discovered that a case of kerosene had not been placed on the goods manifest, and ordered the entire cargo unloaded and held pending payment of a fine. This was a desperate blow. No quantity of food crops was yet ready for harvest. There were over three hundred persons dependent on this consignment.

The *Newbern* failing to arrive, it was assumed to have been lost at sea. A messenger was sent overland 200 miles on horseback to Guaymas to telegraph for aid. Dr. Schellhous could do nothing by letter or telegraph, so took the first coasting ship southbound from San Francisco. At La Paz he paid a burdensome fine to release the goods, and reshipped them to Topolobampo.

Meantime the situation had become tragic.

The colonists on passing through Guaymas had been exposed to an epidemic of smallpox, had carried it on to the colony, and several had died of it, including Tully Witter,

Credit Foncier colonists water and fishing crew, which made daily trips from Las Copas to Topolobampo for seven years, sailing out at dawn with the land breeze, and returning with northwest wind in the afternoon.

Engineer Corp carrying forward survey for proposed railway from Mid-western United States across Mexican Sierras to Fuerte River Valley and Harbor of Topolobampo. Man with heavy mustache, in dark shirt, seated at lower left of picture is believed to be ALBERT KIMSEY OWEN, *with* EUGENE A. H. TAYS *standing at his right.*

the father of a family of nine children, and Clair, a grown son of C. M. Stanley. There was other sickness as well. Quoting from Stanley:

> My letters would make you sad. On July 1st my son Milton passed to the other life . . . typhoid fever . . . two daughters, Etta and Lulu were sick with the fever . . . waiting and watching for the "Newbern" to bring the saving nourishment.
>
> The three that died (of typhoid) were young and stout. Physical discomforts are nothing compared to the agony of the mind . . . so much depends on the success of the colony that it has become life or death to us, and the great hope or despair of millions of oppressed and suffering people.

On July 16, 1887, according to Marie Howland, ". . . others wrote the joyful news of the arrival of the 'Altata' with our supplies."

Soon after this midsummer crisis the colony gardens up country began to produce in quantity. Enterprising comrades gathered in food from the sea; ". . . the wild fowl and turtles furnish us hundreds of dozens of eggs in their season; the waters abound in fish. . . . The country back of the mountains abounds in game."

The irrepressibly cheerful Burt Pressey, the youngster who had been on the survey in 1886, wrote his sister, Anna, at Hammonton, New Jersey: "After all, corn meal mush, with plenty of good salt, is not so bad as one might think, and then, you know, we vary it in the cooking—one day it is well cooked, the next day it is half raw. . . ." Later he wrote, "I spent last week rusticating at the seashore—Topo and Las Copas. I went down principally to get a taste of the clams, and I did taste them two or three times a day for the whole week . . . we would dig our own clams, then build a fire and cook them. I tell you it is a king's dish!

"The supply is inexhaustible. They are found right on the edge of the surf, about two inches underground. There is a strip of them 600 feet wide and something over 3 miles in length . . . when you use this supply you move to the next island. . . ."

Mrs. Sera Eaton Wilber, a very talented woman, often

wrote to *Credit Foncier*. One of her excellent descriptions of the Fuerte River in the area of their camp is quoted here:

> Aug. 18, 1887. The Fuerte River (the main water channel) is nearly a quarter of a mile wide and from 15 to 20 feet deep. The banks on our side are steep . . . the trees throw their great branches out over the water . . . the vines make a network like the ropes of a ship . . . there is a pretty island, well set in willow trees, opposite

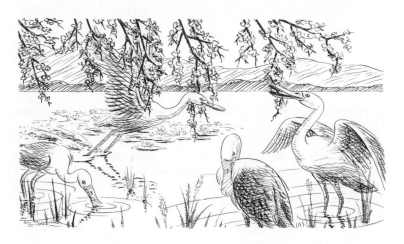

> us about midway of the stream, where at all times may be seen ibis and cranes, spoonbills and gulls, quaint and interesting birds. The spoonbills are the most lovely dainty pink, shaded with rose color. . . . All we have to do in order to have a museum covering forty square miles and containing the most wonderful variety of nature is to keep quiet.

> When our railroad is running through it you may come to make us a visit; we will take a week for the museum. Say on Monday we go down to the bay to see the flocks of sea fowl, the romping porpoise, the leaping fish, the sharks and the spouting whale, and eat clams and terrapin and sea-turtle. On Tuesday we will get into the woodlands to see the birds of all sizes, colors and styles, from the parrot to the humming bird. Another

time will be for the deer, the ant-bear, the ocelot and all of their neighbors, and the wonderful family of lizards, from as slim as a penholder to larger than any cat.

After this will come a day for the trees and flowers, the minerals, lava, obsidian, porphyry, copper and iron —still there are remaining the flamingoes and the pelicans, the roadrunners and many other interesting birds; and all this time we have not given a moment to sampling the fruits, wild or tame.

The wild fruits I have tasted and like are the three kinds of cactus, echo, pitahaya and tuna; the chapote, about the size of a small peach with the taste of a pear. We are now beginning on the guavas which look much like a green butternut and have the flavor of a quince and a strawberry.

Colonel Edward Daniels, the naturalist and geologist, owner of Gunston Hall, Fairfax County, Virginia, was a resident of the colony at this time. He was encouraging to the colonists: "I was on the governmental surveys and saw the great immigration that filled up the new states. I am confident that not over one third of the people who came in, remained—all honor to the heroic band who have braved the hardships of pioneer life in this grand endeavor [in Sinaloa]; they are the vanguard of the true civilization, as the Pilgrims of the Mayflower on the Atlantic Coast. . . ."

It was Colonel Daniels who said, "The chief difficulty with the Topolobampo Colony is that it is top heavy with intellect —too many planners, not enough workers."

The youthful Pressey expressed his mind differently, "Now what about the people coming down this fall? Are all the infirm, cripples and cranks to be allowed to come as they were last year? Last year it was a mistake, this year it would be a crime. We now have 171 persons left—of that number probably 35 working men—it keeps these 35 men rustling to supply the remainder with wood, water, fish, clams, etc."

By the summer of 1887 the impetus of the movement had subsided—and of those who had gone down many had returned disillusioned of any ideas of a quick success.

John H. Rice, of New York, Secretary of the Texas, Topolobampo, and Pacific Railroad and Telegraph Company on

August 2nd wrote to Mexico City to Ignacio Pombo, President of the Mexican Board of Credit Foncier:

> The Government of Mexico, this Company, your Board and the Credit Foncier Company have been disappointed in the results of the years operations.
>
> That the colonization plans were wrought with great industry and with an honest intention stands without question.
>
> However, it should be understood that this Company is not in any way committed to the theories of the Credit Foncier Company.

It is something of an enigma that President Diaz, friend of big foreign capital, should have been so fully behind this socialistic enterprise as events of those years have shown.

On November 22, 1887, Director Dr. Schellhous reports, "President Diaz has sent a letter to the Governor of Sinaloa, requesting him to issue letters of instruction to the Judges of this District to ask the native population to assist and encourage the colonists all in their power. . . ."

A letter from the colony in the summer of 1887 says, "We find the natives to be of a kind, gentle and trusting disposition, taking a deep interest in as well as wondering at our proceedings."

Travelers southbound on the Southern Pacific of Mexico will recall San Blas, the station just south of the railway bridge over the Fuerte River. The colony farms and gardens were located on the Fuerte River a few miles below San Blas at Sufragio, Vegaton, and Cahuinahui.

The Vega family—several branches—owned a large portion of the lands along the river in the area around San Blas.

The junction of the railroad to run over the Sierras with that to be built northward to Alamos, Sonora, was planned to be located at Vegaton, property of Don Martin Vega, who contracted to sell 1,500 acres for a townsite.

Trustees for this proposed city site were Vega, Owen, and Engineer Tays.

Here enters into our story a character known to many thousands of Americans and Mexicans from that time until his death in very recent years.

Eugene A. H. Tays was born at West Point, New York, on

October 24, 1861. His father, born in Halifax, Nova Scotia, of Scottish parents, became an Episcopalian minister, and served as chaplain, as well as teacher of mathematics, at the military academy of West Point. This Episcopalian minister and teacher married the daughter of an English sea captain.

Young Tays was educated at Maysville Baptist Institute, Maysville, Kentucky; Burlington Military College, Burlington, N. Y., and Union College, Schenectady, N. Y., his education including civil and mining engineering.

The elder Tays moved to the South, where the yellow fever so dreaded in those years claimed in death the mother and a younger child. Following this tragedy the father with his two remaining children, Eugene and Joseph, moved to El Paso, Texas. Here the father established a church, and eventually became State Chaplain of Texas.

The tall, slender, blue-eyed, blond-haired young Eugene soon become interested in the promise of pioneer life below the border. He first found employment, during 1882 and 1883, with the Mexican Central Railway then building down the central plateau of Mexico from El Paso to Mexico City, during this employment being promoted from rodman to locating engineer. During this time too he became interested in Sinaloa and the proposed railroad from Topolobampo across the Sierras, and so went with Owen to assist in the original railroad surveys from the Gulf to the Sierras.

He remained to marry in 1885 Señorita Rosaura Vega, daughter of Don Jesus de la Vega y Pacheco and Eloisa Gaxiola y Vega, both families as distinguished as the names would imply, and to become a foremost citizen of the area. He and Doña Rosaura built a lovely Spanish home overlooking the Fuerte River near San Blas, and there reared a fine lot of youngsters, sending them to schools and universities in the United States.

A son, George, has been a specialist in the field of Latin-American affairs for many years, teaching at the University of California; recently he was honored by acting in an advisory capacity at the United Nations Conference in San Francisco.

Another son, Eugene, served as a major in World War II.

The eldest daughter, Eloisa, for many years has accompanied her husband, Dr. S. M. Lambert, on his explorations into the farthest islands of the South Seas in the interest of research on tropical diseases for the Rockefeller Foundation —the trips that made possible the advances in treatment of those diseases so graphically described in his recent book *Yankee Doctor in Paradise*.

The second daughter, Linda, is Mrs. Edward Dunn, whose husband, now Chancellor of the U. S. Embassy at Santiago, Chile, has held important posts in the diplomatic service.

A son, Alejandro, administers the properties of the family in Sinaloa.

Doña Rosaura, now 85 years of age, still graciously receives visitors on the wide veranda of the old home, her bright smile and fine brown eyes, despite the snowy hair, still showing the sparkle of years long past.

Below the home toward the river was their large orchard, including oranges, dates, *guayabas, papayos, mangos, ciruelas*, and other native trees. Beyond lay their lands to the river. Other ranches were owned by them in various places.

Engineer Tays was a close friend and loyal supporter of Owen for many years.

The peak of harvest of summer crops is in the fall. In the fall of 1887 the colonists were preparing their first substantial harvest at Sufragio. In addition to vegetables, beans, and grain, through the efforts of colonist L. A. Gould, a farmer from Auburn, California, they had secured many thousands of trees and cuttings of peaches, prunes, pears, persimmons, nectarines, figs, olives, oranges, and grapes.

Quoting Resident Director Wilber: November 15th—"We had set out trees now in bearing, put up houses, dug wells, cleared land and done other labor."

Then they lost their contract for rental and purchase of some 1,400 acres of this property. There are no clear reasons given, only this excerpt from Wilber: "The loss of the Haskell property was by faulty papers of transfer, not by any neglect of the colony to conform to its contract. . . . We have had to change from preparing the way for other colonists by building houses and roads, to just a struggle for existence . . . a band is making up for the north . . . there are a hundred tried and true here. We shall still conquer."

The midnight hour of December 31, 1887, was indeed a dark hour for the colonists of Sinaloa.

CHAPTER VII

La Logia

*Under every cloud, every adverse circumstance,
he sees this colony with the eye of prophecy;
rich, prosperous, happy, a model for the world
to follow.*

THE NEWSPAPER *Credit Foncier of Sinaloa*, edited by the Howlands at Hammonton, New Jersey, published an appeal for aid. Very shortly contributions began pouring in from many states for the purchase of a colony farm.

Food must be produced not only for the resident colonists, but for those who were expected to come to build Pacific City; to build the first strip of railroad from Topolobampo to Vegaton on the river; to clear land; to build houses; to begin small trades through which the colonists were to supply themselves with most of the necessities of life and to exchange for essentials not produced in the colony.

The 76,000 acres of Mochis lands were seven miles from the nearest point to the river, and were not productive without irrigation. This meant that eventually an irrigation canal must be built from the river and lateral canals from the main canal in order to irrigate these lands.

Resident Director Wilber and Engineer "Don Eugenio" Tays cast about to find land bordering the river, which would grow crops from underground moisture or after being flooded with overflow waters of the river.

Don Zacharias Ochoa, a wealthy *hacendado* of Ahome, had extensive land holdings. Quoting Wilber, "Mr. Tays and I . . . examined and closed a bargain for a fine farm—La Logia (The Lodge) about half way between Ahome and Zaragoza and four miles from the head of the Santa Maria *estero* . . . 150 acres of best river bottom . . . 250 acres good upland—rented . . . with privilege of buying a total of 1,000 acres for $10,000 any time before 3 years."

Soon after the beginning of 1888 most of the colonists had moved down river from Vegaton, Cahuinahui, Sufragio, and from Topolobampo Bay, to the new location, which was forty miles down river from Vegaton. They soon had land cleared. Vegetables and field crops were planted on the moist lowlands. They laid out a central site for residences and constructed their various homes, mostly in the native style.

In the north Owen was making up a new band of adult volunteers, persons selected for the needs of the colony. He laid down strict requirements—each colonist must deposit $100 for assisting to establish himself on a farm, pay $50 additional for each child under twenty years. Colonists must have read the "Principles of the Credit Foncier Company," and must have signed a pledge to abide by these "Principles," to live in accordance with by-laws laid down by the colony directors, submit to fines and penalties for failure to comply with the rules of the colony.

The Colony Concession provided for arbitration of disputes of colonists with the Company or among themselves. Recourse to Mexican courts over disputes between colonists must be only in the event of failure of arbitration.

Colonists must pay their own transportation, take six months' supply of foodstuffs, one year's supply of clothing, medicines, personal goods, and a tent.

Every man or boy over twelve years should take a shotgun or rifle, and a pistol, with 200 rounds of ammunition, this amount being duty free.

There was printed an extensive list of articles needed by the colony for which credits would be given. A request was made for all kinds of livestock—dairy cattle, horses, mules, hogs, goats, sheep, turkeys, chickens. Ostriches were included in the list!

Many, many letters came from supporters of the cause, and some contributions of useful articles, as well as offers of many things not so useful.

I cannot resist quoting from one such letter, dated December 4, 1887, by an old Tartar, Thos. W. Taylor, Homestead, Pennsylvania:

> I was one of the pioneers who started the first cooperative store at Ashton [England], four years previous to

the Rochdale movement . . . disgusted with the rule of
kings, I came to free America, where boasting freemen
rule. . . I found that their degenerate sons were ruled by
thieves and rings. . . I have had a successful lecture tour
in Indiana and Pennsylvania—I gave the people something to think about, I can tell you!

But alas and alas, three score and ten years, with a
frail body, will not admit much exposure. . . .

The old belligerent then expresses regret over not being
physically able to join the colony, and offers two corn shellers
from his farm.

Here is a short note indicating the scope of interest: "The
Credit Foncier Club of Jacksonville, Florida is doing well;
they are to follow the example of the San Francisco Club in
subscribing for stock."

The irrepressible Pressey was cheerful; on December 27,
1887, he writes: "Game is plenty. Today we killed a wild
hog, two deer and four jack rabbits within 500 yards of the
tent."

However, newspaper comment in the United States by the
end of 1887 must have been most critical, to arouse the Government to action. Quoting Director Dr. Schellhous: "Commander Leavy and Lieutenant Norris of the U.S.S. 'Iriquois'
are here in obedience to instructions from the Navy Department, to report as to the conditions of the colony, and to take
away the 'helpless and starving.' He will take none. He tells
those who would go that they are better off here. . . ."

Credit Foncier issue of January 10, 1888, gives a report
from Commander Leavy:

My orders were to visit the Topolobampo Colony and
learn whether the reports of hardships were well founded
or not . . . we were cordially received.

The country is a paradise . . . without irrigation it will
produce two or three crops a year . . . with irrigation
there is not a month when crops cannot be planted or
gathered. The climate is magnificent, never reaching an
extreme temperature.

The harbor of Topolobampo is one of the finest. There
is at low tide never less than 16 feet of water on the bar
and its [the harbor's] capacity is very great.

Agricultural Director Bill Friend guided the farming at La Logia. C. M. Stanley was in charge of the plantings of orchard trees. There was trouble about regularity of work, so that the gardening was put on a contract basis, so many credits for so many vegetables produced. Three colonists, C. M. Stanley, B. F. Close, and T. E. (Ed.) Whitney, did the gardening.

An old miller, John Baumann, took charge of grinding corn, the cheapest and most staple food. For power he walked an ox on a homemade treadmill. Water was raised from a well, by the same method, for domestic use and for gardens. For five years this same ox, "Old Berry," patiently performed on the various treadmills built by the colonists.

Director Friend had his troubles. January 31, 1888, he wrote Owen:

> When we came [to La Logia] we had but 2 plows . . . I traded my shotgun for one—by trading and repairing we now have six . . . have 140 acres already plowed. . . . At present time I am commissary, timekeeper, postmaster, Director. . . .
>
> There are many suggestions in regard to what is proper food—some want meat, others do not—the only way I see is for people to choose their own food.
>
> We have learned much by experience and have much to learn, but by all means let us keep near the earth in the future and have less soaring aloft to sweet Elysian fields.

Later Friend resigned, saying, "Discipline is essential to success; noble natures never hesitate to obey directions by those in charge . . . do your duty not from compulsion but from devotion."

Various camp foremen at La Logia included Hobart W. Brink, a young man from Binghampton, New York, by way of Denver, Colorado, one of the earliest colonists, a hardworking, sincere cooperator, who lived out his convictions during forty years of later life in the colony, and Ed Whitney, a big, fine-looking, energetic fellow who worked hard in the fields by day, and evenings and Sundays played in the orchestra, sang solos, or formed part of a quartette for the Lyceum entertainments.

Another camp foreman, Newell Thurstin, wrote several colony songs and played a violin in the orchestra.

Thomas Doyle and his wife Lucy, a slender, frail person, were among the most steadfast and faithful workers, he farming and serving as a director, she as a teacher, seamstress, cook, or in any capacity where most needed.

The early colonists ate in a community dining hall. They operated a community laundry. A German colonist, Rudolph Koebitsch, was for years the community shoemaker—then tall, slender Samuel Jones, who worked in an open-air shop under a great mesquite tree, turning out, among others, "four-button shoes of undressed buckskin, very nice in appearance." Herbert Patrick was the tinsmith, soon finding his products in large demand from the natives, so adding a little to the income of the colony.

John Foss was for many years the colony blacksmith; his wife Grace was one of the colony seamstresses, also manufacturing stockings on a knitting machine for the women and children.

Dr. Scally extended his practice to the native families, and was in much demand—for a quarter of a century afterwards he traveled constantly over an area a hundred and more miles—driving one of his several fast trotting horses to a light two-wheeled cart, his medicines and instruments in a native woven palm basket suspended under the seat of the little cart —a well-remembered figure, tall, gray bearded, with finely cut features, wearing a straight-brimmed western hat and a linen duster.

In my youthful mind he was completely associated with bitter quinine powders taken with jelly to slightly compensate for the ordeal; with castor oil, calomel, and acetanalid, with steam baths for croup.

Malaria (*calenturas*) was the fate of practically every colonist of those days when there were no screened houses, no protection from the up-ended attack of the malarial mosquito.

Director Dr. Schellhous, to assist in the expenses of the colony and to foster friendly relations, in addition to teaching the higher grades at La Logia, taught an increasing number of Mexican youngsters, children of ranchers and merchants.

Twenty-year-old Joe Scally, son of the doctor, taught mathematics in Spanish at the district seat of Fuerte, besides teaching English, beginning an educational experience of value in later years.

William L. Patten, Director at Topolobampo, in early 1888 wrote Marie Howland, "The wealthy Mexicans here are calling for us to establish the higher grades of schools, where they can educate their sons and daughters; to furnish engineers to teach them how to build irrigation canals, to furnish them with machinists to run their sugar mills, their mining machinery . . . there never was a better opening for men and women who are intelligent and willing to work."

Director Wilber hit upon a major problem in this statement, "We cannot compete with native *peon* labor, especially while we are without appliances for farming."

A strange situation; here was a group of colonists on foreign soil, "top heavy with intellect," with education generally far more extensive than that of the upper-class Mexican families, readily welcomed into the highest-class homes, asked to educate the higher-class children—yet toiling in the fields to produce the bare substances for living; in competition with Mayo Indians and the poorest class of Mexican labor which earned only fifteen to twenty cents a day. The upper-class Mexicans did not work at such tasks as clearing land, plowing, seeding, cultivating, harvesting. They did not become artisans, such as carpenters, blacksmiths, tanners. They did ride the ranges, handle cattle, horses, and mules with their *vaqueros*, or run merchandise establishments.

There were certain lines of social demarcation. For instance, butchers and saloon keepers found it hard to achieve a place in the upper social level.

Yet here was a group of foreigners of superior education, encouraged by President Diaz, setting a strange, disturbing example by toiling like Indians in the tropical sun. Perhaps more alarming, they stood first of all for the rights of the poorer classes, and would no doubt teach their thoughts to the children of these higher-class Mexicans.

It is interesting to note what effect each group—colonists and higher-class Mexicans—had upon each other. This story unfolds through the years with the story of the colony.

Mexicans of all classes were friendly to the colonists.

The small town of Higuera de Zaragoza lay about an hour's

ride down river from La Logia. It was typical of the area. A few *callejones*, country roads, led into town from the farms and ranches. Various *hacendados'* houses were built in the suburbs, with large corrals in the rear.

Farther into town were the stores, most of them facing a central plaza. These stores usually formed about one-half the frontage owned by the merchant, the *comerciante*; the other part was taken up by the front of his home, the home continuing with enclosed *patio* towards the rear or perhaps to the next street.

Without reflection on the hospitality of good friends of any country, I will say that I know of no hospitality quite equal to that of the Mexican people, and generally this is true of all classes from aristocrats down to the very poor families. The story of the La Logia days is filled with evidences of good will. For instance: "One of our delightful treats was a visit to the home of Don Salvador Castro in Zaragoza. The ladies gave every moment to us. They sang for us, played the guitar, led us into their irrigated gardens and loaded us with flowers and oranges, invited us to dinner and danced with us afterwards to the music of the 'autophone.' Madame Castro is a lady of real beauty, dignity and grace of bearing. The other ladies were gracious and charming."

There was this thoughtful bit of advice to colonists going down: "Courteous speech is a talisman with the Mexican people."

There were many young people in the colony. It is not to be supposed that they felt so seriously as their elders the importance of their undertaking. Being young, they easily adjusted their pleasures to fit their new situation. One of their excursions to Zaragoza was on *Cinco de Mayo*, a national holiday, to witness a bullfight. We have a description of this event by the colonist young lady, Etta Stanley:

> May 5, 1889:—In my childhood [she was then 21 years of age] I read of bullfights and saw pictures of them, and I had a curiosity to see this relic of barbarism. . . . In the center of the town is a plaza of two or three acres. In the center of this is about ½ acre encircled with upright posts buried in the ground, and lashed (at the top) one to another with rawhide thongs (the bull ring).

On top of this was erected a staging for spectators and a band for music. When we arrived this space was densely packed . . . [cowboys] brought the bull in tied to an ox. . . . They roped and threw him to turn loose the ox . . . four or five horsemen came into the ring on their gaily decorated horses, riding with ease and grace. Some of them carried red blankets and red flags (capes). The bull eyed them for a moment with glistening eyes, then made a charge, scattering them right and left . . . again and again he would charge . . . would miss his enemy, only hitting the red blanket. (An unusual skill, using a

blanket from on horseback.) How skillful were the horsemen! How gracefully they sat in their saddles . . . it seemed so little effort for them to dodge the furious assault of the enraged animal. How well trained the horses —they seemed to enter into the spirit of the entertainment. . . .

Several footmen came into the enclosure . . . the horsemen retired . . . the footmen advanced. The furious bull would chase them to the fence upon which they would leap for safety. One man lost his sombrero in the fight. The bull caught it on his horns, pinning it to the ground, then tossing it into the air, and seemed to say, "If I can't catch the man I'll spoil his hat, anyway!"

At length he was taken from the ring, another brought in, thrown down, $6 or $7 tied between his horns. It was announced that it would be awarded to the man brave enough to take it off. . . . A horseman rode up, gave the bull a thrust in the neck to make him more furious . . . four of five footmen came forward . . . the musicians struck up a lively tune.

One man, made reckless by his eager desire to win the prize went in advance of the others, shaking his red blanket . . . the angry animal made a lunge at the unfortunate man and, catching him on his horns, flung him up several feet into the air. The moment he hit the ground he was tossed up again. The third time a horseman managed to attract the bull's attention, and the man, badly bruised but not seriously hurt, scrambled to his feet and made his escape.

Several now advanced . . . one attracted the bull's attention by shaking his blanket, another stole behind and seized his tail. The bull whirled around and around in his confusion and blind fury . . . others rushed to his assistance, and by their combined strength and some dexterous pulling and twisting managed to throw him on one side and take the money from his horns. . . . A horseman in uniform on a beautiful black horse—apparently the manager—divided the money among the winners.

We did not stay to the end of the performance. . . . [We] drove to the house of a Mexican friend and put up our horses. [They had stood on the carriage seats outside the arena to watch the performance.]

In the evening we walked up town to the ball, out in the open air on the hard ground under an awning, the place lit up with candles. All around were refreshment stands with coffee, fruits, etc. . . . the music began, all was animation, dancing . . . . [Later] the National Anthem was sung . . . we started homeward singing, laughing, joking as only young people can.

On March 10, 1888, Albert Owen wrote, "With this issue the Credit Foncier moves to Sinaloa that it may be among its people."

Quoting Editors Howland, "We have engagements. We have got to dig clams one day at Las Copas; then we have got to learn to like clams—that will take we should say a week— we will visit the farm at La Logia—the school of Comrade Schellhous—Comrade Byrns, shivering in his flannels up among those orange plantations at Sufragio—the friends at Vegaton—then we want to roam over the sub-tropical wood and watch the lovely birds that Dr. Scally writes so eloquently about."

Joel Byrns, thick-set, rugged, elderly, with blue eyes and dense beard, was one of the ablest, most versatile of the colonists. He raised vegetables and orchard, built houses, tread-mills for grinding cornmeal and for lifting water, conducted classes in astronomy—was an old woodsman, a "compleat" man, to be sure. He had written to his friends, the Howlands, "You say you will not bring your flannel underwear. Now if you do not you will make an awful mistake for sure. This morning I was glad to put on my flannel underclothes, and I am no tender chicken either! But I have more feeling for you who are suffering the rigors of that cold climate than for ourselves in this lovely one."

The first issue of *The Credit Foncier of Sinaloa* at Topolo-bampo, on September 15, 1888, carried at the top of the title page a sketch of the harbor entrance, with a rising sun coming up out of the inland bay, and with a vessel steaming into the harbor.

The first "at home" editorial from the pen of the How-lands at Topolobampo told of a tedious trip, nine days against adverse weather in a sailing sloop from Guaymas, little over 200 miles up the Gulf. However, there were compensations. Writing of their first impressions:

> Topolobampo Bay, as we approached the Straits of Joshua, appeared to us most beautiful in its wild grandeur. As we approached it seemed more stony than it ought, and, we must confess, an awfully lonesome place.
> That same night we slept on one of the wide verandas of Alberton Hall. Friends joined us, and we held high

converse, as the moon rose in glory. Then the wonderful beauty of sea and sky, hill and valley, sank into our hearts never to be erased.

Never in all our travels have we seen so lovely a view. The Alps, crowned with eternal snow, are magnificent, but cold—here all is beauty, warmth and color. Never were hills and dales more green [the summer rains had come]; Never skies more glorious. The sunrises and sunsets are magnificent.

There are many flowers already in bloom. One, a tall shrub somewhat like a currant bush (*buena mujer*) is laden with great blue blossoms; another has a flower like a forget-me-not and foliage like a smilax; another one of the most beautiful trailing vines we have ever seen, bearing long luxuriant sprays of the loveliest pink blossoms. It climbs over the tall cacti; the dead and the living, and robes in beauty everything that it touches.

This is the *San Miguelito* (Antignon in English)—the woods in summer in Sinaloa are covered with its trailing clusters of dainty pink blossoms—each blosson three tiny pink heart-shaped shields fastened about a small round seed-pod. It truly "robes in beauty everything that it touches" and may be seen far, far away through the woods, its trailing clusters covering the higher trees. In the same editorial they wrote:

> We are delighted with our colonists . . . people of earnest purpose and clear intelligence . . . careful in speech, and refined in manner—superior to the ordinary men we meet. We notice that serene, kindly smile. . . .
>
> What it must be to work hard in the broiling sun in their patched and ragged clothing . . . they have no other.
>
> These men might thrown down their burdens as others have done, and go out of the colony . . . they prefer to suffer, to labor and to wait. For high-minded, cultivated men to be subjected to such torture appears to us inexpressibly regrettable. Yet most of these appear to have profited by what they have endured—we are surprised, we might say amazed, to find their faith as strong as our own.

[73]

The Howlands wrote of their first visit from the newspaper headquarters at Topolobampo Bay to the colony farm
of La Logia:

> Our vehicle was a buggy or buckboard with a span of
> our own horses . . . first the *estero* bordered by a dense
> growth of magnolia (mangroves) . . . then the tidelands
> along the hill; on the hill masses of luxuriant vine, laden
> with the sprays of pink flowers . . . lagoons of fresh
> water, water lilies white and blue . . . strange beautiful
> wading birds . . . cows grazing upon the luxuriant grass,
> or standing in the water ruminating! Mountains every-
> where seen, and miles of plain covered with huge cactus
> and mesquite . . . clusters of blossoms of purest white
> beauty—(the *vara prieta* bush) . . . and most of the way
> the long pink sprays . . . water lilies, lantana, morning
> glory, scarlet salvia, clematis, and the cypress vine . . .
> large plants, trees, cacti (*pithahaya, cardon*), lignum-
> vitae (*guayacan*), banyan (*macapule*), century plant
> (*mescal*) . . . the nearer the river the more lush and
> dense the vegetation . . . finally clematis and morning
> glory disputed possession of every cactus, every shrub
> and tree. . . .
> We entered the Hacienda of Señor [Don Ramon]
> Castro. . . . Señora Castro kindly took us all around her
> beautiful gardens, and gave us fine cut flowers. In the
> bouquet were many rare tea roses, exquisite jasmins, and
> the royal flower, corona imperialis—a huge bunch of
> purple and white lilies . . . the lady was most kind, most
> gracious, to a stranger, and we shall not forget her, nor
> the pretty daughter who accompanied us around the
> garden. . . .
> La Logia is a lushy labyrinth of flowers . . . even the
> squash vines climb trees in company with the wild
> clematis. . . .
> The cottages of adobe or of cane or reeds, thatched
> with straw, are so cool and so comfortable, and the roofs
> so raintight . . . some (colonists) have made a clay floor,
> raised four or five inches . . . many lay down the native
> mats (of woven palm) and spread carpets over these. . . .
> We took tea in one of the houses, table set with snow-

iest napery, good dishes and fare excellent—brown beans, fried sweet potatoes, white corn hominy, syrup, cakes of Egyptian corn and graham flour, coffee and stewed peaches. Among those most picturesquely situated, Miss Hoagland's tent, one of the loveliest niches imaginable . . . and Comrade (Dr.) Young's, which has four giant cacti in front . . . the vistas through them (the tents and houses) as lovely as a dream of Eden. . . .

We shared the tent of Miss Hoagland . . . after breakfast made calls . . . admired Dr. Scally's drug store . . . had an hour at the Stanley home . . . enjoyed a musical rehearsal by the Stanley band—a rare treat! We got lost among the bowers in looking for the schoolhouse . . . the thatched schoolhouse, a credit to Dr. Schellhous. . . .

In the evening attended the regular entertainment under the auspices of the Lyceum Society. . . . We were indeed well paid for the journey . . . the sweet smiles of welcome that greeted us, the warm clasp of the hand . . . the deep conviction among people there, as here, that nothing can swerve us from our purpose, made every hour spent with them a lasting pleasure.

William Slocum, the printer who went down from San Francisco to assist the Howlands, was soberly enthusiastic:

Everything looks better than represented—climate good, bay commodious, scenery magnificent, the colonists much better than average people.

Whether the Credit Foncier is a success or failure, this country will not be a failure. It is rich in natural resources, requiring only intelligent industry and development.

In a score of years there will be hundreds of thousands of progressive people in Sinaloa, and this part of Mexico will be esteemed, as Southern California now is, one of the best countries on the face of the globe.

Capitalists stand ready to pay the Mexican Government in cash for franchises granted to co-operators on promises—promises as yet unfulfilled.

To verify the last statement of this colonist, in October 1888, "Don Eugenio" Tays wrote that Luis Huller, a "Capitalist," had a concession for a railroad from Guaymas, 219 miles to Topolobampo, thus proposing to provide the harbor with railroad transportation from two sources, from over the eastward Sierras, and southward down the west coast from the United States. By May 1889, Tays was one of the engineers running surveys for this road, and 300 men were employed on grading.

CHAPTER VIII

Christian B. Hoffman and
the Kansas Sinaloa Investment Company

*Fortune is always conquered by such men—we
see the signs of her favor in raising up such powerful friends for him, friends like C. B. Hoffman,
complementary in powers and qualities, not less
admirable in character, rich, influential, and
thoroughly acquainted with business methods and
with the hearts of men.*

DURING THIS early period of the colony Owen had worked
unceasingly. We learn of him at various times in New York,
in Mexico City, and in the colony.

In a letter from Hotel Iturbide, Mexico, D.F., to Dr. Schellhous he pours out his feelings:

> Not for one moment have I hesitated in my purpose to
> assist the colonists by every means in my power. The
> difficulties, the indignities, the miseries I have suffered
> in trying to extricate them and myself from the engulf-
> ments which the over-enthused majority got us all into
> I have kept to myself.
>
> My intention is still to push ahead by every means at
> my command. I have no end in life except to make our
> cause a success.

Owen was a poor man, but his dreams, his ambitions, were
not limited. He revealed great ability to enlist large resources
in his behalf.

Evidently the Texas, Topolobampo, and Pacific Railroad
and Telegraph Company no longer represented in the mind
of Owen his means for building the railroad, for in 1888 he
met with the Kansas City Council, propounding to them the
desirability of a "Kansas City, Presidio del Norte and Topolobampo Railroad."

At about the same time he seemed to have persuaded the Pathfinder, General John C. Fremont, and his associates, Vice-Governor Dorchimer of New York and John C. Ford of Tennessee, to unite their line, extending from Shreveport, Louisiana, to Presidio del Norte, with the projected road to Sinaloa. However, this proposed combination was never carried into effect.

With the proposal to build the railway beginning at Kansas City, interest in the colony increasingly centered in the midwest United States.

In midsummer, 1887, almost in its darkest hour, there came into the life of the colony a character second in importance only to Owen himself. Christian B. "Chris" Hoffman was, to quote him, ". . . the owner of large flouring mills and machine shops" at Enterprise, Kansas. Practical minded enough to become a wealthy mill and shop owner, he was essentially an idealist. At the time we first hear of him he had been a member of the Kansas Legislature for several terms. His character is well pictured in phrases taken from his letters. The first is on August 9, 1887:

> For years I have worked in the political arena for the enfranchisement and emancipation of the masses, but with evergrowing conviction that nothing can be accomplished by political methods or parties. . . .
>
> I am tired, very tired of the never ending conflict between man and man, which brutalizes and demoralizes us. . . .
>
> I have studied these questions. I believe I know on what lines a satisfactory solution can be reached. It is Co-operation, Integral Co-operation. . . .
>
> I want information, reliable, exact information as to financial soundness. What if colonists fail to make payments on lands, to maintain controlling interest in the railroad? How soon can the colony be self supporting? How soon can it export? What products? Are there mineral lands? What danger of change of policy by the Mexican government?

From a second letter dated September 18, 1887, we choose the following:

> I have carefully studied every plan and detail of the

[78]

Visit of Mariano Martinez de Castro, *Governor of Sinaloa, to La Logia colony.* Governor Castro *is center figure with beard and felt hat. Seated, at left of picture,* George L. Page *(above him),* Dr. J. W. Scally *(third from left),* Don Patricio Robles, *(fourth),* Don Zacharias Ochoa *(to right of Governor Castro),* Don Francisco Orrantia, Don Ramon Castro *(near extreme right, with large straw hat and flowing beard),* Dr. Edwin Schellhous.

American colonists at La Logia, Sinaloa, November 17, 1889.

Credit Foncier. It has been an ever present thought. . . .

I realize the difficulties to be removed. I know what hardship pioneering entails, having come to Kansas in 1858; passed through chills and fever, drought, grasshoppers and Indians, and living for months on milk and corn bread. . . .

Yet . . . I have come to the conviction that success is absolutely certain. It is the combination and application upon a grand scale and upon an adequate basis, of business principles and methods, with the avowed purpose, guaranteed by the very charter of the association, to justly and equitably distribute among its members the wealth produced by it.

We can only imagine the meeting of Owen and Hoffman between the dates of those two letters, and the inspired, far-flung discussions that were had. Owen was then about forty years of age, tall, with straight-cut features and black mustache—a handsome man. Hoffman was perhaps five years older, shorter, heavier built, with studious, serious face, also adorned with a mustache, as was the custom of the day. Each was a strong, distinct personality. Each was of mature experience. They had one deep interest in common, the building of a better social-economic order. Owen was the dreamer idealist, Hoffman the practical idealist. Hoffman soon was supporting the colony by purchase of stock and by interesting others in the enterprise. On March 1, 1889, he arrived at the colony with a number of Kansas families, including George L. Page, a civil engineer, wife Susan, young sons Chester, Ross, Ray, and Cecil. George Page soon learned Spanish, became a colony leader, ran surveys, was active for many years. Mrs. Page was a fine character, friendly, hard working, helpful in domestic life of the colony. The sons grew up there.

Hoffman was immensely pleased with the natural resources of the area. In addition to farming, he suggested the starting of more small industries such as wagon making, fish canning, a soap factory, gristmill, sawmill, woolen mill.

Interest and support in the north were increased. Other parties arrived in the colony from time to time, some by schooner or sailing ship to Topolobampo, others overland from the border or from Guaymas.

The guide for these overland parties was John Whitney, a character who well rates description. An extremely tall, slender, weatherbeaten old Texan from Atascosa County, John Whitney moved into and out of the life of the Colony like a soul from another world. He seems to have had no special interest in the project of the colony, did not live there, but appeared now and again, out of the mountains from

Chihuahua, or down the plains from Sonora, a dusty, white-bearded old frontiersman, always riding an old flea-bitten gray roan horse. Apparently fearless, he moved alone through and about the dangerous Yaqui country at his pleasure. In the colony he was a welcome guest who brought bits of news, remained awhile, then departed to visit other places or friends.

He seemed to be on hand as a guide when needed, at other times drifted away on the dust-colored horse back to Texas, to Chihuahua—somewhere—wherever it was, it would have been interesting to have followed along with him on his travels. I like the picture of the tall old white-bearded man riding down through that west-coast country in advance of a wagon train, using his knowledge of, no doubt even his contacts with, the Yaqui Indians to see them safely through, "calculatin'" the journey to arrive at waterholes and stock-feeding places; where to stop over; where to push ahead; where to carry feed; where to depend on the country; where to camp away from sand gnats and mosquitoes, or of cactus patches bad for man or beast—taking a wagon train through, keeping stock and people in fair condition—all this depended on the experience and versatility of their guide.

The last we hear of old John Whitney he was back in Atascosa County, planning to guide a hundred young Texans, single men, on horse back over the plains and through the mountains of Chihuahua to join the colony. This suggested group never appeared. Perhaps they did not start. Or we may speculate that they decided to start a new Republic of Texas among the Tarahumara Indians in the Sierras of Chihuahua!

Hoffman wrote, "We can get 500 first class families every six months from Kansas. We are going to get the land. Owen will hold the railroad. We will buy a boat . . . after awhile we will have our own factories. . . ." Times were hard in the United States in 1888. Quoting Hoffman, "There is an anti-interest and anti-rent movement forming, and should another hard year come upon us, the farmers will refuse to pay rent and taxes. What then!"

By the fall of 1889 Hoffman had organized the Kansas Sinaloa Investment Company with capital stock of $100,000, for the purpose of raising capital to push forward the work of colonization. The Kansas Sinaloa Investment Company, represented in Sinaloa by Tays, Wilber, and C. J. Lamb, a Kansas friend of Hoffman, purchased several thousand acres of land between the river and the Mochis lands held by the Credit Foncier Company by virtue of the power-of-attorney of Owen from the owners, Carman and Ibarra, and by means of Owen's own 20% interest.

In Mexico City the influence of Owen was as strong as ever. On March 8, 1890, the Government extended to Owen personally, new concessions for colonization.

By June 7, 1890, Owen had succeeded in getting government approval of his detailed plan for Pacific City (Topolobampo), and in having his concession renewed for the railroad, with telegraph and telephone lines, 1,200 miles, aided by a subsidy of 12,900 pesos a mile in Government bonds bearing 6% interest. Quoting from a Mexico City dispatch to the New York *Herald*, "Probably Mexico never granted to another man what has in this instance been given to Owen."

"Owen has left for Topeka, Kansas, to start another party of colonists. He then goes to New York to meet the managing director of an English syndicate which has contracted with him to build the railroad from Topolobampo to the Texas frontier."

By August 1890 the Mexican Investment Company, with two and a half millions capital, was being organized in London.

Quoting *La Revista Financera* of Mexico City, June 6, 1890, "The Topolobampo Railroad like a new Phoenix arises from its ashes."

CHAPTER IX

On to the Mochis

Onward, brothers, march still onward
Side by side and hand in hand
Ye are bound for man's true kingdom,
Ye are an increasing band.

Though the way seem often doubtful
Hard the toil ye may endure
Though at times your courage falter
Yet the promised land is sure.**

THE LATEST concessions to Owen were most complete, for railroad building, for colonization, for building the harbor city, for water from the Fuerte, and incidentally, the Sinaloa, Rivers. Owen concentrated on plans for building the railroad. Hoffman enlisted increasing support for the building of a canal from the Fuerte seven miles to the Mochis lands. His Kansas Sinaloa Investment Company sold interest-bearing stock to the general public. This Company took as security for money spent in the colony a lien on Credit Foncier lands.

The Credit Foncier Company sold its land at $5 per acre, but to no one except persons who became members, so that the new social-economic order might be preserved.

Proceeds from land sales they paid to their financing organization, the Kansas Sinaloa Investment Company, to redeem the land under lien, being credited with the purchase of an acre of land for each $2 paid.

Kansas Sinaloa Investment Company proposed to pay for its stock and to meet interest payments to stockholders through proceeds of these land sales. Credit Foncier proposed by the land sales at $5 per acre to redeem its land and to secure that land with water for its future colonists. For money, materials, food, or labor furnished by colonists in

*From "Onward" by Henry Havelock Ellis.

building the ditch, the K.S.I. Company issued "Improvement Fund Script," redeemable at double its face value by July 1, 1895.

Credit Foncier "units of account"—script—continued to be issued to its member colonists for their products and services, as in the years past.

Summing up, funds for the increasingly large enterprise were to come temporarily from two sources, sales of interest-bearing stock to the public and from payment by persons becoming colonists. Eventually the colonists were to repay all borrowings through production of farm crops, of small industries; by profits from operation of the railroad, and from sale of lots at the harbor.

Quoting Hoffman, "Ditches must be dug, land cultivated, homes built for our people . . . men and women with clear heads, warm hearts and steady hands are coming to the aid of our cause . . . whose cardinal principle is equity, its bond of union love."

New life surged into the colony. The paper, *Credit Foncier of Sinaloa*, with Marie Howland now editing due to the continued severe illness of Edward, published messages of encouragement from everywhere, even from correspondents in other countries, such as Sweden, Germany, France, England, Italy, Switzerland. At La Logia houses were crowded to overflowing. The old institutions were reinvigorated—the weekly Lyceum with young people's dance following, the Garden Club, the Pomological Society, the Ladies' Social Culture Group.

Don Mariano Martinez de Castro, Governor of Sinaloa, paid a visit to the colony, being given a reception including a speech of welcome written by Director Wilber, read by Joe Scally in Spanish, and was serenaded by the Stanley Band.

The Russian Jew, William Cotter, who had been the colony mail carrier, packing the mail on one burro and riding another, making weekly trips through the woods from Topolobampo to La Logia, was soon overburdened with business and gave way to the caustic but versatile old Joel Byrns, who drove a round trip seventy miles by wagon with passengers, mail, and colony products, Topolobampo to La Logia, then a round trip 140 miles from La Logia up river to Fuerte and return.

[84]

The ditch survey party rode in to La Logia over the week-end by burro to attend the Shakespearean play *Richard III* with the talented young John Shoop taking the lead.

Colony note, "The young folk are having ox-cart picnics about every Sunday. Sometimes they go to the lakes south of La Logia, sometimes to the banyan trees below San Jose, and they enjoy themselves greatly." Where in the world would happy young Americans have gone for oxcart picnics under great spreading banyans but in Sinaloa!

A young chap, William Groves, walked all the way from Dallas, Texas, to join the colony. Two young Germans walked all the way from Chicago, became lost in the coast Sierras, and "we were soon dead," as one of them expressed their plight.

Charles Heath Cheyse of London, a prospective colonist, wrote: "I am very glad to know that the tarantula's bite is no worse than the sting of a wasp. I had gathered, from a tradition connected with a waltz named 'La Tarantella,' methinks, that the bitten party is seized with an irresistable desire to dance, and gradually, as the poison works, quickens his movement until he falls from sheer exhaustion produced by his frenzy, and dies in maddening pain." Relieved of his anxiety about the tarantula, Cheyse eventually became a resident in the colony.

Marie Howland wrote, "Confidence is being restored. We have most to fear a 'boom' that will bring a crop of weak, uneasy beings—their fate is ever the same, the deprivations of pioneer life take on gigantic proportions, and they soon go, leaving no regret behind."

Edward Howland, increasingly a sufferer from arthritis, lived only to witness the beginning of this regeneration of the colony. The dampness of the sea air was thought to aggravate his condition, and he was removed to La Logia where he was attended with every care. During his last days at Topolobampo, August 15, 1890, he wrote this verse to Marie:

> "Out on the rampart that overlooks the sea
> I take my lonely way to think of thee;
> Still in the west the flush of dying day
> Gleams as it pales and slowly fades away.
> There is no motion in the evening air,

Without a wave the sea lies calmly there;
I leave the city to its gathering gloom
And here, alone, to think of thee I come."

Edward Howland died at La Logia on Christmas morning,
1890. Marie, learning of his extreme illness, drove from
Topolobampo:

> . . . we left the other teams, pushed on, driving all night
> . . . a light was burning in Edward's cottage. . . . Mrs.
> Lutton and Miss Hoagland watching . . . the cactus
> burned low in the fireplace, casting fitful lights. . . . Coy-
> otes howled in the woods . . . cocks crowing in the early
> morning. . . . I stood with feelings no tongue could utter
> beside my beloved dead.
>
> Mr. Hoffman at the grave spoke eloquently and ear-
> nestly of the life and character of our lost friend, and of
> the lesson taught by his noble and useful life.

Parties continued to arrive from the north. The "November Party" of 200 men, women, and children arrived on December 17, 1890, coming in sections, by land and by sea.
These new colonists were filled with enthusiasm. Docking
the *Romero Rubio* at the wharf, they greeted those on shore
with the chorus of a new colony song, "Topolobampo Bay,"
written by colonist Lon Hoding, and rendered with instrumental accompaniment.

Director Wilber met them, during the first evenings discussed with them the principles of the colony and its pros-
pects. Quoting: "He paid high tribute to the bravery and
steadfastness of the women of the colony, upon whom the
burdens of pioneer life fall heaviest. This party brings great
supplies of goods, horses, cows, plants for orchard, garden,
vineyard—and warm hearts and strong hands to help us—
for the accomplishment of our dearest hopes in the land of
our adoption."

Director Wilber discussed these new arrivals, "They came
in upon us at La Logia in grand procession of teams and
people. They came by sea to Topolobampo. They swarm upon us and outnumber us from all sides. We are uplifted and
carried forward; nor voice nor paper can express our emo-

[86]

tions—and besides, we can already hear Briedenthal (of K.S.I. Company) bringing up the reserves."

Ida Hoagland wrote, "A pretty sight it was to see the long procession wending its way across the green verano [river bottom] land, the sunlit mountains for a background."

Chris Hoffman describes their departure from Enterprise, Kansas, November 15, 1890, and their journey:

> Amid sobs of parting friends, tender goodbyes and a rousing cheer by the large and sympathetic crowd, the November party departed for their homes in far Sinaloa. At Newton, Kansas we overtook the Chicago, eastern Kansas and Texas contingents, at Kinley the McPherson and Ellinwood families joined us, at La Junta the Colorado group.
>
> At Deming, New Mexico the Mexican Consul, Señor Salvador F. Maillefert, Governor Ross and leading citizens gave us an enthusiastic reception—quoting from the speech of Governor Ross, "You are a State on Wheels, you have the stuff that builds empires."

The line for the canal to irrigate the Mochis lands was

determined. Some of the new families stayed at La Logia, others went at once to the head of the proposed canal, at Los Tastes, on the river. These people brought 62 scrapers, and plows and teams. On January 4, 1891, the first ground was broken for the big canal, which must be an average of 18 feet deep and twice that width for the first mile from the river.

Hoffman wrote to Briedenthal:

> Everybody old and young, newcomer or old pioneer, talks ditch, works ditch, dreams ditch. It will take another six months of uninterrupted work to put water on our lands—then another six months until we can begin to harvest crops—for one year we must depend for the sinews of war, to some extent, upon friends of our cause in the north. . . .
>
> Upon these fertile plains, my friend, brave hearts and sturdy arms will found prosperous communities. . . .
>
> The women, God bless them, patient, brave women, standing in the broiling sun over a camp fire, cooking, washing, making the men comfortable, taking care of the children, ever hopeful and cheery; again, God bless them, and may they find recompense for their uncomplaining devotion. . . .

We quote from Ditch Notes:

> The camp is as busy as a humming western town. . . . At the river bank are massed the corral, the commissary, the corn grinder, the harness shop, blacksmith shop and charcoal pit. Back of these are the "messes," Lamb, Wolf, Butler, Drake, Baldwin, Wilcoxon, Hopkins. The sound of the anvil, of grinding corn, pumping water— men leading horses and driving oxen to and from work, harnessing, unharnessing horses, yoking, unyoking oxen. Then there is the coming and the going of the Mexicans—some working, some curious to see—things are lively from early morn to late at night. In the evenings, calm, delightful evenings, the air is resonant with music of violin, guitar and flute. . . .
>
> The darkness is lit up with numerous camp fires . . . wood is plentiful. . . . Huge fires blazing in front of many tents—around them chatting groups of men dis-

Colony leaders: left to right, ALBERT KIMSEY OWEN, CHRISTIAN
B. HOFFMAN, HENRY A. HART, JOHN BRIEDENTHAL.

The Stanley Family Band.

cuss ditch, politics, religion, science until bedtime. Residences of the camp are among mesquites and cottonwoods, with trailing arches of wild vines; a delightful location.

These colonists' wives were of the world's best cooks, sometimes under most limited and trying conditions. Quoting, "I had for breakfast this morning wild duck, baked sweet potatoes, squash, boiled rice, wheat flour biscuits, corn bread,

panocha syrup, baked beans, pumpkin pie and coffee! For dinner, boiled beef and the regular menu of vegetables; for supper, a dessert of fresh strawberries."

Newsnote: "A wagon load of beets, carrots, rutabagas, turnips, sweet potatoes and beans arrived Thursday from La Logia—photographer Ira Kneeland, teamster. A large consignment of strawberries arrived Wednesday morning."

Local Mexicans were interested, friendly, helpful. Don Jesus Cruz, Don Manuel Borboa, Don Patricio Robles and Judge Don Victor Padilla, *hacendados* and merchants, subscribed substantial blocks of Improvement Fund stock, to aid the building of the ditch, and to secure the privilege of buying land and becoming colonists.

Groups of colonists going for Sunday picnics were entertained in the gardens and home of Don Francisco Orrantia y Sarmiento, the *Jefe Politico* of the district. Mexicans were already accepting colony script for fodder, corn, cattle, and merchandise.

A band of twenty picturesque Mayo Indians, clad mostly in loin cloths, wielded mattocks and *machetes* clearing the brush and stumps from the line for the ditch. What they thought of this new invasion of their ancestral property is not recorded. There probably was no concerted discussion among them on the subject—they were working and being well treated; receiving a little better pay and many small favors from the colonists.

The new colonists were in the majority. They were furnishing the means, the equipment, livestock, and most of the labor for work on the big ditch. They soon deposed Wilber from active charge, he remained as Resident Director of the colony, but canal affairs were in charge of a committee, J. S. Payne, John Dowling, and Jacob Dockter, with a very practical man, "Uncle Billy" Porter, in charge of camp management and ditch construction.

There were other changes in leadership. Dr. Schellhous moved to Zaragoza to conduct a school for Mexican pupils. A new colonist, Tom Whitzel, farmer, and once a member of the Nebraska Legislature, became the new Director of Agriculture.

There were many records of marriages, births, and deaths. Ella Stanley, the crippled girl, now about twenty-six years of age, who was much loved in the colony, died at the new camp. The sermon at her burial was given by Dr. Schellhous, who had been a constant close friend of the Stanleys.

Many of the new colonists contracted chills and fever, dysentery, diphtheria, typhoid—the result of exposure to mosquitoes, polluted water, and other causes. The summer season in the tropics is terrific for northern men and women who are working directly exposed to the sun. It is no easier for large draft horses from the north. Many died that first summer on the canal work. By midsummer there were numbers of deaths of people at the ditch camps.

Some who fell by the way were of those who had arrived young, healthy, vigorous. This tragedy of death entered into the lives of many families. Tom and Maggie Whitzel lost two young children by diphtheria. A few months later Maggie Whitzel died, leaving a family of five children in the care of the oldest sister, Irene, only fourteen years of age. Irene seems to have been a much-loved character, at her age already a fine musician. She was, too, a conscientious little mother to the family, the youngest a baby sister, Marie Sonora, born at Guaymas, Sonora, while the November party was waiting there for transportation to the colony.

Colonists from the earliest days had imported dairy cattle, principally Jerseys and roan milking Shorthorns. These had almost all died within a few months of their arrival; no one knew the cause. The large groups coming during construction of the ditch brought many cows, which suffered the same fate. This was a real tragedy, especially for the many families with smaller children. It was finally determined that tick fever contracted there had caused their deaths. It was observed that young calves apparently had immunity or suffered only moderately from the disease. From the calves saved and other young cattle shipped from the north the milk cows for the colony gradually increased, and from this stock, renewed from time to time through the years, there gradually was developed a superior lot of milk cows in the Fuerte River valley—that is, superior to the longhorn native variety.

Work slowed during the hot summer. Excursions were taken to the seashore, where there was relief in ocean swimming, in boating, fishing, digging clams, and other diversions. "Dancing on the broad verandah of Alberton Hall by the light of the moon is much enjoyed by our young people."

An interesting, and to us from Sinaloa, a familiar touch is this, "Outside the veranda [at the dance] a fringe of quaint, silent, Bedouin-like figures in white, listening and watching. They were our Indian laborers."

A fishing scene at Las Copas told of by K.S.I. Director Charles E. Smith of Colorado describes pulling of a 400-foot seine along the sandy beach, the vast quantities of mullet, Spanish mackerel, and other fish leaping through the water, and the great haul taken.

There was social culture, too. At the Camp Catwood Opera House, by all odds a great brush shed with perhaps a tent or two for dressing rooms, John Shoop, handsome, tall, moustached, always nattily dressed in a suit and derby hat, produced the tent scene from *Julius Caesar* before a packed house. There was music by an enlarged Stanley orchestra. At the H.O. (*Echo*, the giant cactus) Opera House at Ditch Camp, the talented Shoop took the lead in the Shakespearean plays, *King Richard III, Othello, King Lear, Hamlet.* Between times Shoop was commissary man and colony statistician. How he was able to do all these things, with a reputation for seldom being quite sober, is a wonder. It seems that he was lucky in everything. Years later the expression "Shoop's luck" was applied to many things, like a narrow escape, or getting a lucky break at cards. His luck extended even to marrying the very popular young lady, Etta Stanley, who with great devotion followed him through those trying colony years and a long and apparently happy life thereafter.

With the close of summer, work on the canal was undertaken with renewed vigor. Behind the timetable planned by Hoffman, nevertheless making steady progress, from mile to mile, from camp to camp, went first the twenty or so Mayo Indians, clearing, burning brush, and grubbing stumps. Next came young George Drake, cracking a long bullwhip over eight yoke of oxen dragging a great plow to break the hard sod. Then came the scrapers, moving the surface dirt by driving the team over it, filling and dumping the dirt to both sides; later, when the canal deepened, pulling the slip scrapers down into the canal as the horses above backed to the bank, then at the word from the driver heaving out the heavy loaded scraper attached by a cable to the eveners by which the horses pulled.

It was time the work should be done. By February 1891, it was known that Charles (Don Carlos) Conant had secured a concession to take out two-thirds of the waters of the Yaqui, Mayo, and Fuerte Rivers, for the purpose of selling land with water to settlers—a capitalistic enterprise, possibly to compete in the same valley with the members of Credit Foncier. Fortunately for the pioneers of Sinaloa, Don Carlos began his development in Sonora. The Credit Foncier held a previous water right, but it must be put to use—the cooperative colony had been trying to make a real start now for five years, and for it the sands of time were running out.

CHAPTER X

With Owen through the Sierras

I say it in the meadow path
I say it on the mountain stairs
The best things any mortal hath
Are those which every mortal shares.

The air we breathe, the sky, the breeze
The light without us, and within
Life, with it's unlocked treasuries
God's riches, are for all to win.

The grass is softest to my tread
For rest it yields unnumbered feet;
Sweeter to me the wild rose red
*Because she makes the whole world sweet.**

IN MARCH 1891 the *Credit Foncier of Sinaloa* announced the death of the Honorable William Windom, formerly Secretary of the United States Treasury, once President of the Texas, Topolobampo, and Pacific Railroad, a good friend and supporter of Owen in the railroad project, although not a believer in the use of "greenbacks" or in the socialist-cooperative colony idea. We know that Windom had also traveled to London in the interest of the proposed railroad.

We read, ". . . the death of Mr. Windom is unfortunate for us . . . but Colonel Owen never loses heart for a moment. . . . Owen has just made a deposit of $30,000 in the Mexican Federal Treasury as a guarantee of speedy construction of the railroad."

By July 15th the railroad building project was no longer being planned by British interests, but by the "Mexican Western Railroad Company," an association of American business men incorporated in Colorado.

This company planned to issue ten million dollars of bonds bearing 5% interest and secured by a mortgage on the rail-

*From "Shared" by Lucy Larcom.

[93]

road, interest on the bonds being guaranteed through a cash deposit by the organizers of the company. Owen was given the contract for surveying, and for construction of the road. Construction, as well as later operation, was to be by labor from the colony.

In August 1891, Owen visited the colony. Engineer "Don Eugenio" Tays, who had been in charge of the Los Tastes Canal surveys, was named Chief Engineer for the projected line. In September Owen and Tays rode with a party over the proposed route. Owen describes this mountain country through which he proposed that the peoples of the Atlantic and the Pacific were to travel in the future years.

> In August 1891 . . . I left Topolobampo Harbor . . . traveled mainly along the route reported by Engineer Holbrook for the Mexican Western Railroad Company over the Sierra Madre to Chihuahua City . . . accompanied by Mr. E. A. H. Tays, Chief Engineer of the Company, Mr. Kneeland, photographer for Credit Foncier, Messrs. Thornton and Patrick, representatives of the colonists who are digging the irrigating canal. . . .
>
> Five Americans, a mozo, six riding animals, two pack mules, a local guide.
>
> Bayside to Chihuahua City is about 450 miles. Examination of the line was from Vegaton to Carichic, the latter about 130 miles west of Chihuahua City.

The difficult terrain Owen stated to be from Agua Caliente de Lanphar to Sisoquichic, a distance of 155 miles.

> A supply of jerked meat, *pinole* [corn parched and ground, the staple food of the countryside for travelers], groceries and bread were procured at Fuerte. . . .
>
> When in the Sierras it is policy to rest beside campfires on the borders of the running streams, rather than near the habitations of man [to avoid hogs, dogs, fleas, flies, and pollution of drinking water].
>
> What impressed me most in the Sierra Madre of Southwestern Chihuahua; the stillness which reigns upon the higher altitudes—quietness crystallized. . . . Among the pines, one great impressive hush. It is God's presence . . . the inner light of one's consciousness, ask-

ing for a higher plane, which one feels under the influence of solitude. . . .

The vast beauty of the vistas . . . the *cumbres* of Ubalama, from the rocky crests overlooking the Valley of Guaza. . . . Two thousand feet below lies the river of Chinipas. The Sententrion River came out from its canyon to the right of the village—Chinipas—joined the

Chinipas River, went with it to join the Fuerte and San Miguel Rivers at La Junta. The Canyon de Huites stood guard at Agua Caliente [de Lanphar].

The heights surrounding Guadalupe y Calvo [State of Chihuahua] rose prominent to the eastward . . . the peaks of Alamos [State of Sonora] were at the westward, and over 120 miles in far away Sinaloa, on the coast lands—towards Heaven's Rest, Topolobampo—was the cone shape of Chahuinahui, the mountain pyramid of the lower Fuerte. It is the first grand view of the Western Slope.

[Later.] I was impressed by the first extensive panorama from the height of the western slope, facing eastward—that which embraced the Valley of Sisoquichic, the plains of Carichic, the mountain cones of Cosihui-rachic and the plateaux of Southwestern Chihuahua.

I was impressed by the Tarahumari, the Indians of the well traveled trails, the number and height and steepness of the ridges one has to climb, up and down; the depth of the valleys, the ruggedness of the arroyos, the grandeur of the barrancas in this mother range of mountains.

[Later.] I was impressed, standing at midnight in the moonlight on the rocks overhanging the Barranca de Tarerecua, at a point where the trail comes in between Tepunapachi and Los Ojitos. It is a solid rock mesa, over 8,000 feet above the sea, with a precipice wall dropping 800 feet into the barranca, then from the base of this precipice wall the sides dropping at 90°, 80°, 70° and on for a drop of 4,000 feet, half the rise gained in 200 miles of travel from the Gulf of California into Urique Canyon. . . .

Urique Canyon, the lofty palisades of which are in full view, but of whose depths there can be at this time only conjectures, for white man has not yet, probably, looked down upon the Urique River from this vicinage.

[Still at midnight.] Pitch pine fagots were burning in Pomachi, a large pueblo of the Tarahumari, far away on the heights beyond the canyon of Urique, and the cave fires of the cliff dwellers were burning dimly out of the dark fastnesses of the great walls of rock, here and there, far and down, and up high on the sides of the Tarerecua, which means in Indian language "the bottomless arroyo."

What a night! What a panorama of ruggedness and awful depth!

I was impressed by the Tarahumari, the Indians of the Sierra Madre; by their straight and agreeable features, their shapely and naked forms; by their shyness, by their industries, their agriculture; by their superior cattle, short horned, short legged and thick shouldered—fat, pretty, Jersey like oxen, cows and bulls. . . .

I was impressed by the activity of the people . . . the many silver mines being worked in spite of almost insurmountable difficulties of getting to and from them . . .

[96]

by the immense mineral resources of silver, gold, copper, lead, iron, fine building stones . . . all of which only await the coming of the Mexican Western Railroad to spring into action and usefulness.

I was impressed by the apparently inexhaustible supplies of pine timber, straight and clean trunks, 30 to 60 feet high, without a limb, one to two feet in diameter . . . and with the many oaks, and good cedars.

I was impressed by the frequency of the streams and the abundance of sweet, clear waters, the ease with which they could be stored into lakes or reservoirs for manufacturing or for horticultural purposes.

I was impressed by the evidence of the mildness of the climate [mid-September]. Precipices were covered with ferns, mosses, lichens . . . by the growth of indigenous grasses on lower ridges and levels . . . by the flavor of peaches, quinces, pears, apples, wild strawberries, English walnuts, grown at various little ranches . . . by the rich and rare colors of flowers, the ferns, mosses, dahlias, daisies, begonias, asters, primroses, honeysuckle . . . the large red and purple dahlias found in profusion in the Canyon of the Sententrion . . . the most superbly beautiful of the wild flowers we have ever met with. . . .

I was impressed by the few difficulties to be met in the construction of a railroad through the Canyon of the Sententrion from Guaza to Bocoyna. . . . Tunnels will not be necessary; light grades, little cost compared with east and west trunk lines already across the same chain, the Rocky and Cascade mountains of the United States.

From Chihuahua City Owen turned south to the National Capital, no doubt on matters pertaining to his plans for the railroad.

CHAPTER XI

The Silver Stream of Life

But there was a path he must tread alone
Through a fiery furnace of seven fold heat
Whose secrets of pain may never be known
To the weary ones waiting his coming feet.*

QUOTING from *Credit Foncier of Sinaloa,* July 2, 1892:

At 8 A.M. Engineer Tays raised the headgate of the Los Tastes Ditch, and the water of the Fuerte started on its way to the lands of the Mochis. In ten hours the nine inches [depth] of water turned in as a test reached the end of the ditch, seven miles.

It is a pretty sight to stand on one of the bridges at twilight and view the silver stream of life. . . .

Eighteen months of labor, bringing hope for some, despair for many others, had completed the building of this canal that was so vital to the life of the colony.

Before the work was well under way there had been dissension, begun over the fundamental, inescapable issue of community ownership, community production, and community living, as contrasted to private ownership, individual production, and separate living.

The original colonists formed the nucleus of a group determined to own, to produce, to distribute, to live in the closest possible cooperation, allowing only for the proper privacy of family life—they being proponents in this respect, to be sure, of the highest type of idealism, of brotherly love. Through all the years, through all adversities, Owen continued stubbornly steadfast in his original purpose of creating such a cooperative commonwealth.

The new colonists were cooperative-minded also. How-

*From "Topolobampo" by Derrill Hope.

ever, the majority of them, together with some supporters from the older colonists, disagreed with Owen and his supporters. During the progress of construction of the great canal they had experienced the difficulties attendant upon carrying through such an idealistic plan for living. Perhaps they were influenced too by the prospect of greater gain, better living through their own initiative. They were no doubt honestly concerned over their possible future as mere shareholders, not owners, in a project where land titles, water concessions, railroad concessions, even colonization concessions, were vested in a single individual, Owen.

With such considerations in mind, these colonists made demand upon Owen and Hoffman (1) that they be given legal ownership of the lands that each should occupy by virtue of cash paid in or credits earned; (2) that the railroad interest be completely divorced from the Credit Foncier Company; (3) that, quoting a resolution directed to their two leaders, "We desire a commonwealth here in Sinaloa wherein all laws shall be made, and all questions of social order be determined by the popular voice of the people, and whose charter shall be broad and liberal enough to guarantee to every man, woman, and child the greatest amount of personal, social and economic freedom, not inconsistent with the rights and liberty of others—we pledge our support and endeavors to that end. . . .

This resolution in effect demanded the right by the colonists to rewrite the Owen plan of Integral Cooperation under which they came contracted as members of the Credit Foncier Colony.

Owen refused to concede this. Hoffman took the part of the objecting colonists. Months of dissension followed.

A site for the first settlement had been surveyed, 1,700 acres, to be divided into tracts 2 to 40 acres, and 7 miles of lateral canals were constructed for this area. The Owen group, soon titled the "Saints" by their rivals, settled largely in an area of 150 acres called the Engineer Farm or Public Farm (*El Publico*) at the lower end of the main canal.

Here they built a community store, blacksmith shop, harness shop, corral, and a community kitchen and dining hall. At distances permitting families two to ten acres each there were built homes, of native materials.

These homes soon were picturesque in the fashion of the country, usually clad with climbing vines of light blue or purple morning glory, or some other attractive native climber. Vegetable gardens were planted by various colonists. Presently a community farming project was begun.

Those opposed were dubbed the "Kickers." In line with their demand for individual ownership they settled on "Plats" of 5 to 40 acres each, scattered over the 1,700-acre area. The two areas were for fifty years thereafter known as the Farm and the Plat.

Thirty-eight farmers settled here, most of them heads of families. Some leaders of this group were Henry A. Hart, Treasurer of K.S.I. Company; Dr. J. W. Scally with his two sons and sons-in-law, John Newton and Grant Burr; Tom Whitzel; C. J. Lamb; Julius Echart; and Cyrus M. Stanley.

The great canal, completed at the beginning of the summer rainy season, flowed an abundance of water for whatever clearings had been made in the dense woods. With the end of the rains in fall, the stream lessened; by the following spring the canal was dry, the water in the Fuerte River running lower than the entrance to the canal.

Here was trouble indeed for those dozens of families living miles from the river, dependent on this one stream not only for crops but for drinking water imperative for existence. Dissenting colonists submerged their grievances long enough to hurry with teams, plows, scrapers, and hand tools to the canal entrance, where they built a temporary diversion dam of brush, silt, and sand out into the river, to turn back into their canal a part of the life-giving stream.

Another unforeseen problem—there was so little fall to the canal that the alluvial mud of the river water would not flow in suspension, but began filling the seven miles of canal.

Disputes over the handling of the colony water system and the allotment of water were added to those over what social-economic plan for living should be carried forward by the colony.

The divided, disheartened colonists faced the necessity of installing a large pumping system at the head of the canal and of constant dredging of silt from the canal. This was beyond their poor means to do.

In a tragically short period life for those adventurous colonists changed from one of inspired enthusiasm to one of bitter disappointment.

Owen and Hoffman, both earnest, able, inspired men, long united in purpose, now became alienated as leaders of two bitterly opposed groups.

Reluctantly, step by step, they were drawn apart, as many good men have been, by forces within themselves, as well as pressure from their followers. As a compromise, on March 15, 1892, Owen came to a friendly agreement with the colonists, gave them the right to select their local leaders, and agreed to a permanent reorganization of Credit Foncier in February 1893.

Quoting, "One of the never to be forgotten events in our history as a colony is the masterly way in which he united all factions by his clear and bold interpretation of principles that had come to be misunderstood by many . . . he acceded to nearly all our wishes . . . gave not a few gentle rebukes . . . never has there been such a revival of confidence, of faith. . . ."

During all those years socialistic groups from many countries had watched with interest the Topolobampo Colony. Leaders included Hurzka of Germany, Mueller of Sweden, J. Bruce Wallace of England, and a multimillionaire, Michael Flurschiem of Lugano, Switzerland.

In April 1892 Flurschiem contributed $1,000 to the colony, during this period carrying on a correspondence with Owen and Hoffman in an attempt to reconcile their interests.

He proposed to build factories for the colonists, which they should purchase from him by working in these factories and paying a part of their wages as the purchase price. He was essentially with Hoffman in his beliefs. "It will never do to make people happy against their own will . . . compel them, and you enlist against you the most powerful elements for success."

Hoffman, still trying to reconcile his ideas with those of Owen, wrote reassuringly to Flurschiem, inviting him to the reorganization meeting, and met with Owen in New York; following this meeting the two leaders wired their colonists that all differences had been adjusted.

Hope rose in the colony as it awaited the proposed meeting which finally took place on May 27, 1893, with Owen, Hoffman, and Flurschiem present.

The "Kickers" demanded title to their land, water right to follow the land, and a majority rule management in the colony.

The "Saints" proposed to operate under Mexican law through a resident board, but adhering to the principles of Integral Cooperation, which were a set of rules too rigid to permit majority rule in colony affairs.

Owen clung tenaciously to his plan. He insisted on holding the land, the water rights, the colony concession. By this insistence he again divided the colonists, lost the support of Hoffman, and convinced Flurschiem that he was determined to maintain leadership at all costs.

Regretfully Hoffman withdrew from participation in colony affairs, selling his Kansas Sinaloa Investment Company interest to a notable character, Colonel A. J. Streeter, a prominent labor reformer, once candidate of the Union Labor Party for President of the United States.

Flurschiem went to Mexico City, discussed colony affairs with President Diaz, found Owen completely in the confidence of the President, and so faded out of the life of the colony, leaving an unanswered question as to what his interest and support might have accomplished.

Streeter in his turn attempted to persuade President Diaz without success, so retired from the scene as owner of a large tract of land purchased, but without concession for water.

With the colonists embattled over the right to water, and facing a mounting water shortage in the years to come, Colonel Streeter had offered to provide a pump adequate to irrigate several thousand acres, and to sell water to the colonists, in return for a share in the water concession. Although in desperate need, the "Saints" refused, standing by their leader Owen to the bitter end during those trying years.

An interested observer of the affairs of the colony was Edward Lycan, a sugar producer from the Hawaiian Islands, and more recently resident of Washington Territory and California. He first visited the colony in 1890, talked with colonists enthusiastically of the possibilities for profits from growing sugar cane. Don Zacarias Ochoa, owner of La Logia, was also owner of *El Aguila* lands and a *panocha* (brown sugar) mill. Lycan entered into a deal to reconstruct this mill for a daily capacity of 100 tons of cane, 10 tons of sugar. He secured options from Ochoa and others for purchase of 97,000 acres of land. Colonists' sugar cane was to be processed on a cooperative, profit-sharing basis.

By the fall of 1892 small plots of cane, from which to cut stock for larger plantings, were being grown by several colonists.

Lycan began the building of his mill in the late fall.

On November 1st the steamer *Dora Bluhm* appeared at the entrance of Topolobampo Harbor laden with lumber and parts for the mill.

A *chubasco* (tropical hurricane), not uncommon at that season, struck the gulf with such force that the *Dora Bluhm* in attempting entrance was stranded on the bar, pounding violently and threatening to be dashed to pieces.

Captain Walton, the crew, and the customs officer on board abandoned the ship to the sea. Putting into the harbor in small boats, they met Lycan and a partner, Ruggles, gathered with numerous colonists at the wharf. The captain, acting for the insurers, offered to sell the ship and cargo, as salvage, for the sum of $1,000. Lycan and Ruggles offered to pay the sum, and to share salvage proceeds with the colonists in exchange for their help in salvaging.

Manning the colonists' fishing sloop and water boat, colonists Alvin Wilber, William Patten, W. W. Green, Fernando Pasquette, Irving Smith, M. George Desmond, George L. Page, and Messrs. Bragg, Wilson, Ruggles, and Townend made their way through heavy seas to the stranded vessel, by now leaking badly and well waterlogged.

They hastily made rafts of some lumber, threw other lumber and further cargo into the towering seas, plugged leaks, pumped ship, and finally, after riding out the storm, towed the lightened ship to a safe anchorage inside the point of Las Copas.

Consider their consternation when three weeks later there arrived at Topolobampo a District Judge with the officers of his court and a detail of policemen to place under arrest the colonist salvage crew, charging them, upon demand of Don Zacarias Ocha, with committing an act of piracy.

The astounded colonists were kept jailed in separate rooms

and subjected to the most rigorous questioning. They were then removed, still under arrest, to Fuerte, the District seat.

Here Don Francisco Orrantia, the main Jefe Politico of the District, immediately put up bail and secured their release. For six weeks their trial continued, finally ending in acquittal of the charge of piracy, but with the ship and goods reverting to the owners.

It became evident during the trial that the action by Ochoa, instigated by the insurers of the ship and cargo, was for the purpose of avoiding payment of salvage to the colonists.

This was a bitter experience but not without its certain retribution for the accused.

A year later the steamer *Guadalupe*, laden with lumber and machinery to complete the mill, encountered bad weather and was stranded on the same bar. This time there was no help to be had from the colonists, and the ship pounded itself into the shifting sands, its masts standing for many months above water as a grim reminder to the owners, and a source of grim satisfaction to the colonists.

The losses incurred by Lycan, even though insured, resulted in his retiring from the sugar business.

Another misadventure of importance overtook the colonists.

To supply the need for lumber for homes, warehouses, and other buildings, the colonists purchased a sawmill. In the spring of 1893 Directors Amos L. Miks and Albert Law organized a party to cut logs in the high mountains 200 miles up river. By June, before the first floods, there were 1,075 logs cut and made ready to start downstream with the rising of the river.

Will Bentley with a crew of men started the logs downstream. Miks went up river with a second crew, leaving two men 70 miles below the starting point in the Choix River, at Agua Caliente de Vaca, to watch the progress of the logs, and to travel to the colony and report, so that the logs in passing could be secured with canoes and drifted down the canal to Mochis.

While the logs were being moved several dozen a day into the river, a quick rise carried down most of those still on land, except for some lodged fifteen to twenty feet high in trees or on steep banks.

The crews of Miks and Bentley hurried after them downstream. Arriving at Agua Caliente de Vaca, they were stunned to learn that the two men in camp had seen no logs, had not moved to send the word to the colony. Sheer indolence seems the only explanation. Heartsick, Director Miks continued downriver by canoe, to learn that the logs had passed by the head of the canal unseen and into the Gulf. Director Miks, one of the really most competent and hardworking of colonists, paddled sadly down the Los Tastes Canal to his home towing one salvaged log behind his native dugout canoe.

There is real pathos in the long article by Miks telling of this fateful expedition, and there must have been real sorrow in the hearts of many men and women of the colony who dreamed of American-style homes from those logs now drifting about the Gulf of California.

To the credit of Amos Miks it is that he persisted, next year supervised cutting and drifting 400 logs down to Altillo, near Fuerte, where the colony sawmill, hauled up with ox teams by George Drake and Charles Hays, was put to work getting out lumber not only for the colonists but for sale to secure funds for the colony.

An enthusiastic letter, Will Bentley to Ida Hoagland, February 20, 1894, from Altillo says, "The sawmill is a daisy . . . a great sight to the Mexicans . . . always a crowd of natives watching . . . the native ladies bother us a great deal as they always have to thank us and shake hands all around before leaving. It is quite amusing to see Miks trying to control the saw lever, shake hands, lift his hat and talk Spanish all at the same time."

CHAPTER XII

Life among the Saints

We speak with the lip and we dream in the soul
Of some fairer and better day
And our days meanwhile to that golden goal
Are gliding and sliding away. *

THOSE COLONISTS who had stood with Owen at the meeting of May 27, 1893, lived either at the Public Farm or at Topolobampo. Quoting: "The Farm issues daily an average of 142 rations. . . ."

At Bayside (Topolobampo) there were thirty-five "Saints"; Marie Howland, John Dawkins, and Ida Hoagland printing the *Credit Foncier*; George and Willis Matson, sometimes others, bringing in firewood and fresh water by boat; the Townend brothers, Wilk and Jim, living at Las Copas and providing fish for the colony. The fish were sent in with the water boat.

The Townends were famous hunters, always keeping their camp well stocked with venison or young peccary.

The water boat crew, in the spirit of true cooperators, often removed the venison or peccary left hanging by the Townends, taking it to the colonists in port.

The Townends, finally annoyed by this free sharing attitude, killed a coyote, skinned it, removing head, paws, and tail to conceal its identity, and hung it in camp, thoughtfully staying away while the boat crew arrived, loaded up with water and the carcass of the coyote.

Next trip the boys questioned the crew, found the coyote had been cheerfully devoured. They then told the crew what they had done. Needless to mention, their game was never disturbed again.

Mr. and Mrs. George Desmond built a little native-style house on the shores of Mumicahui Island, which lies in the

*From "The Voice of the Heart" by Schiller.

bay about a mile from port, here raising a flock of chickens for the colony, feeding them largely on fish.

On this picturesque cactus- and brush-covered island, only about a half a mile across, there were several of the little whitetail deer, which soon became so tame that they were often seen in the cove where the Desmonds lived and raised their little garden. The chickens ran loose about the slopes of the island.

A mysterious plague affected the chickens there—they would suddenly be taken with staggering, wander dizzily about, and finally perish. A curious colonist finally dissected one of the victims and found a scorpion lodged in its craw, scorpions evidently supplying the poison that caused their mysterious deaths.

Turtle meat gave a change from a fish diet. Mrs. Agusta Matson, in charge of the community kitchen at the port, soon learned to dry the turtle meat in strips, also to prepare it as smoked meat. Fish too was dried. The turtle and fish were often sent to add to the commissary supplies at the Public Farm.

Turtle fat was rendered into lard to be used when lard or tallow was scarce, much to the discomfort of the boarders, as it has a most strong and rancid odor. Many a brave colonist was known to shudder at the sight of the cornmeal hotcakes fried in turtle grease by the thrifty Mrs. Matson.

At the port the colonists kept a goodly herd of milch goats, which fed thriftily from the brushy, rocky hillsides, under the care of an Indian goat-herd who received as pay $6.50 (pesos) per month plus two *almudes* (about 40 pounds) of corn for his family *tortillas*.

At the Public Farm, despite the overall disillusionment over results from building of the canal, and despite the intensity of feeling between the rival Farm people and the "Kickers" on the Plats, the residents shaped their living, poor as it was, into something of a permanent pattern.

On their small home acreages the "Saints" had planted gardens. On other acreages they attempted to grow crops by community effort. This attempt ended in failure—the cooperators were not equally competent, nor equally interested.

An item by the Farm Correspondent, R. J. Kendall, to *Credit Foncier*, entitled "A Frank Confession," illustrates

humorously the problem involved. "I find tomato plants coming up all over the garden, evidently from the seeds of last
year's crop. This suits me, for I am fitted by nature to swing
in a hammock, smoke cigarettes and drink lemonade while
my crops grow. At this I am an undoubted success. I can
talk as well as most people about the 'dignity of labor' when
some other fellow does the work."

So the field crops were grown by "contractors," Leon
Green, Hobart Brink, Festus Ward, Peter Peet, Henry Korfhage, George Drake, and Charles Hays among others. Being paid script for their work, they soon accumulated so
many "credits" that they became an object of criticism by
others not so employed.

Community living presented other problems:

> There is too much of the *stockholder* idea and too
> little of the *employee* idea in this colony . . . the conse-
> quence is that things go on loosely, ends are not gathered
> up and tied, profits depart. . . .
> Another trouble with the stockholder idea is that each
> man begins to feel that the place and all in it belongs
> to him . . . he takes a little thing here, another there . . .
> his neighbor, seeing him, does likewise . . . there has to
> be reform in these things.

The Public Order Committee lacked authority: ". . . something has got to be done, or we are going to find ourselves in
a state of anarchy. . . . The Committee has posted a notice
that $3.00 fine will be imposed for each offense where chick-
ens stray to public or private crops . . . $3.00 for leaving a
gate open . . . watchmen have been employed to report cases."

Supplies for the colonists were purchased through their
commissary, and exchanged to colonists for credits (script)
or money.

Products of colonists were received by the commissary,
credits being given to the producers.

Products sold for cash never seemed sufficient to provide
cash for purchase of products needed but not produced in the
colony. Products delivered by colonists to the commissary
were not always saleable, yet the producers demanded credits
that they could exchange for other goods.

Quoting, "Instead of giving credits on the basis of a service for a service, we have given them upon the communistic principle of 'to each according to his needs' . . . we have got to conduct the Colony on business lines; we cannot afford to make it a charitable asylum where there is free food without labor."

How to balance the needs of colonists against their earnings became a subject of much controversy. Single men earned as much as the heads of families—yet families must be fed in a cooperative commonwealth. This issue was resolved by allotting a five-day ration per week to nonproducing members of families.

Single men maintained that as they worked all day in the fields in exchange for credits, same as the family men, and helped provide food for the families, they were entitled to have their clothes washed and mended, and their bachelor quarters cared for.

At this point many of the women balked, although some energetic souls among the women toiled long and patiently in the cause of complete Integral Cooperation.

Securing of cooks for the community kitchen was a paramount problem. A group of the women insisted that in a commonwealth of equals, men should cook and help with domestic work.

Down through the years there had been sometimes men, sometimes women cooks and assistants in the community kitchen. Usually these had quit because there were so many ideas by the boarders as to how the food should be prepared.

The incredible fact, for it is a fact, is that the community kitchen was carried on for about ten years, with practically all the colonists, single men and families, sharing a community table. Three stalwart souls, Mrs. Emerick, Mrs. Drake, and Mrs. Korfhage, served long turns at feeding the colonists.

The women of the colony, with their children, suffered most the privations of pioneer life in a foreign land, but with the pioneer spirit shown by women the world over they created homes and gardens, rearing and educating their children in the manner of their own upbringing.

Five women teachers taught sixty children.

There were always women's social culture groups, card parties, dances, Lyceums, and musical entertainments. There was usually a Sunday School but no church. There were too many nonconformists to secure cooperation in building a church. However, group services were sometimes held in homes.

Here are a few notes reflecting the life of women in the colony:

Mrs. Herring decorated the long open community dining room with the trailing San Miguelito which grows everywhere in such profusion.

Mrs. Thurstin is the most perfect housekeeper. Her new home is made of mat sides, with shingle roof, and has vine clad shades over windows and doors; oleanders in bloom.

Mrs. Heliot sometimes sighs for the conveniences known in the home of the Parisian.

At Mrs. Morgan's door, I asked about her husband, long gone to the States. "Times are hard," she said, "he may return in the spring." [He never returned.]

Mrs. Hallan related her experience moving 30 miles by wagon from La Logia in the rain, with all her household goods.

Grandmother Thatcher is devoted to her flowers. She never fails to remember a birthday with a floral tribute of one rose for each year—Mrs. Young received seventy-four roses.—Leota Irelan seven roses.

Mrs. Hays has a vine clad little house next door to Mrs. Thatcher.

The Drakes keep a cow and some fine Leghorn chickens.

Mr. and Mrs. Dewey keep the colony apiary.

Mrs. Brian and her four daughters sat in their front dooryard at twilight enjoying the cool autumn air.

Miss Grace Moore has been engaged to teach Mr. William Lanphar's family ... one of the Americans who

holds large and valuable properties [at Agua Caliente
de Vaca, on the river above Fuerte] . . . has lived here
nearly thirty years . . . has extended many hospitalities
to colonists enroute for the mountains . . . Mrs. Lanphar,
a fine looking Mexican lady . . . several daughters, young
ladies . . . on her way Miss Moore was entertained in
the home of Dr. Hubbard at Fuerte . . . he, too, an American with an interesting Mexican family whose warm
reception of "the little foreigner" made her feel like a
native.

Mrs. Marie Howland left on the 13th of August
[1893] with many Godspeeds and good wishes. The *Rio
Yaqui* upon which she embarked lay against the pier for
early morning sailing—we said our last goodbyes that
evening. Her words as we clasped hands for the last time
were "Ida, do not suffer anyone to say I am not coming back."
—And like those waters rushing among the
    wooden piers
  A flood of thoughts came over me that filled
    my eyes with tears.

She never went back. After preaching the gospel of the
colony for some time in the north, she turned to writing for
The Youths' Companion and other publications. During the
cold northern winters she would write to her friend Ida
Hoagland, now publisher of *Credit Foncier*, with longing to
return to "Sunny Sinaloa among the Roses."
  She finally went to the socialist colony at Fairhope, Ala-
bama, and stayed until her death.

Derrill Hope, endeared to those who love our cause by
her fearless writings, is a lithe, frail little Southern woman, with blue eyes that dance and sparkle under merry
moods—become penetrating under serious thought. During her early life she has ever been about the world on
voyages of discovery and missions of peace, and finally
has come here to become a working member of this
colony. She lives much as any other colonist—has her
own writing table, cot, hammock and little stove. She

[111]

keeps a goat, gets water from the ditch in front of her house, and despite her primitive surroundings, enjoys her work and every breath of our balmy air.

Derrill Hope, the poetess, was an unusual character, so unusual that she belonged in such an environment. Deeply religious, she was an ardent advocate of rights for women. She led a revolt in dress in the colony by appearing everywhere in brightly colored, Oriental-type bloomers, soon acquiring a following of this fashion, especially among the girls—much to the annoyance of the more conservative members of the colony.

There are many of her poems in *Credit Foncier*. Perhaps because I lived some of the tragedy of those days, I am inclined to choose this writing, after the death of Emma Sattler Hampl, to reflect her mind.

> The miracle of ever recurring blooms of flowers with which tender hands had covered the coffin; the glory and the marvel of the yellow sunlight flooding the green fields; all the bright and solemn mystery of life face to face with the deep mystery of death, spoke to the soul of other hopes which not time nor death may blight, and the vision arose of a New City indeed, of which the fairest earthly plan may be but a type and shadow, and through the sorrows and uncertainties of human years sounds a deep still voice saying softly, "If our earthly house of this tabernacle be dissolved we have a building in God, an house not made with hands, eternal in the heavens."

One of the kindliest, sweetest characters I have known was Mrs. Marie Klueber, wife of Dr. Emil H. Klueber. She was said to have been a governess in the family of Abraham Lincoln. How well she caught the feel of that country in that time is shown by her account of a trip, Topolobampo to Fuerte—*Credit Foncier*, May 15, 1894:

> We lay over at the Farm, enjoyed the hospitality of our friends. . . . Mr. [Ira] Kneeland was our fellow traveler, Mr. Schleuniger, our driver. [They drove along the Los Tastes Canal.] As we neared Camp Catwood we gave a loving thought to those brave men and women

who sleep there—their last sleep—in the shades of the *mesquite*, having laid down their lives in the pursuit of a noble idea. . . .

After a dusty ride of seven miles we reached the river . . . started for Mochicahui—paid a little visit to Mr. and Mrs. Hampl, regaled ourselves with *tamales*—stopped at La Constancia sugar factory and beautiful nearby *hacienda* and home of Señor [Don Francisco] Orrantia. Oleanders, covered with blossoms so full as to hide all the leaves, stood 20 to 30 feet high. . . . The garden was full of amaryllis, heliotrope and roses, and was cooled by jets of water irrigating them all . . . this place is one of beauty and joy. . . .

The sun had gone down as we reached the beautiful lake, Laguna Camajoa. A fine mesquite cast its picture in the limpid water. . . .

There we saw some Indian water carriers—a feast to the eye to see the grace of these women, dark eyed, clear dark complexioned, straight as an arrow, with large *ollas* balancing on their heads and walking as if on springs. What a contrast they present to our generation of women, round shouldered . . . and these Mexican women feed on nothing but *tortillas* and beans. . . . The water vessels (*ollas*) I suppose are of the same shape as those Rebecca bore to the well of Beersheba when Abraham's servant man had his thirst quenched by a drink at her hand. . . .

This was the spot where our late lamented colonist, Herbert Patrick, was killed . . . no wonder that with his intense love for the beautiful he should select this camping ground. The full moon with its silver light turned night almost into day . . . we could not think of sleep, preferred to travel in the night . . . reached Charay, a Mexican village of some size. . . . Mr. Wilber came along with his team, persuaded us to go further. . . .

We were able to enjoy the grand scenery of the mountains skirting the river . . . from one of these our Editor was named the "Rose of Cahuinahui." . . .

The road being quite narrow and oxen very obstinate, in one place our team locked with an ox team, fortunately without injury.

We reached Vegaton and lay down to sleep . . . I could not sleep . . . recalled the stories . . . contention, strife, greed for mastery, and abandonment of Vegaton. The house built as a Familistere is fast crumbling to pieces . . . but here still is a place of pristine beauty resting among the mountains, quiet and peaceful as if just from the hand of the Creator . . . Before sunrise we were on our way . . . needed all our wraps to keep us warm . . . welcomed the sun's golden rays as they filtered through groves of large *mesquite* trees. . . . We had no idea they reached such a height [30 to 40 feet in Sinaloa]. They were in bloom and their blossoms remind one of willow blossoms used as so-called palms on Palm Sunday in the Catholic Church of northern countries. . . .

These *mesquite* groves alternate with desert like stretches, with the peculiar bluish gray tints of desert plants, the *echo* with its shafts straight as Norway pine, the *pitahaya*, stretching its uncouth arms into the air. . . . Cacti that remind one of snakes intertwined, fighting to the death, seeming hillocks of lions and tigers' paws . . . leaves all bristling with spikes that say "touch me not." . . . An ever varying scene . . . a glimpse of the river . . . a snatch of the melodious sounds of soft music, floating up to us from some Indian women who, kneeling on stones at the river's bank, amid continual laughing and singing, wash their family clothes. . . .

All along the river, acres and acres of corn and bean fields . . . we reached Tehueco, where we had to stop owing to the heat and the weariness of the horses . . . enjoyed a bath in the Fuerte, at present not over two feet deep . . . feasted on boiled potatoes . . . went on . . . gradually the sun sank behind the hills . . . the tints upon the mountains deepened to violet and at last to dark blue . . . night is upon us . . . sleep sits upon the eyes of the stranger admiring the beauties of this southern landscape. . . .

Again a golden spring morning . . . the road becomes more traveled as we near Fuerte. . . . We are received by Señor Don Francisco Alvarez, introduced to his family . . . we feel at home immediately, for the spirit of hospitality seemed to hover around us, so cordial and gracious was the reception. . . . The ladies of the house vied with each other in rendering our stay pleasant. . . . We had ample opportunity to test the culinary skill of "Dona Refugio.". . .

The Mexican houses with their peristyle and the garden back of it bring back the childhood days when see-

ing Moorish pictures . . . one feels as if one might enjoy heavenly bliss living in one of these houses!

There was a fiesta . . . we were led to see it by Señor Alvarez . . . Mexican etiquette forbids the ladies, who are in mourning . . . we saw the people at the gaming table . . . a large amount of money spread out . . . I asked whether a man ever staked a dollar on anything like that. He, the *cicerone*, replied, "Not one, but thousands.". . .

We saw more than the average of women of stately figure, with unspeakable grace; pure wax pale complexion and large dark eyes. The city itself is not large or busy . . . about 2,000 inhabitants . . . several small factories. . . . In the center of the town is a Plaza with pretty flowers and shrubs, at which we wondered, knowing that all the water used is brought from the river (in leather or canvas bags) on burros and sold at 3 cents a sack. Opposite the Plaza is a fine Catholic Church which forms a pleasant contrast to the dilapidated condition of some houses of worship we saw along the way. [In the smaller *pueblos* churches were supported only by Mayo Indians and poorer natives.]

We had no time to spend in school . . . passed through as it was about to close.

The city is very old, having been founded by the Spaniards as early as St. Augustine. It was destroyed by the Indians, but rebuilt by order of the Viceroy, Marques de Montes Claros in 1610. In 1810 it became capital of the *Estado del Oeste* (Sinaloa). The first Congress held its session here. In 1826 the capital was removed to Cosala, owing to a rise of the tumultuous Yaqui Indians who are forever trying to throw off the Spanish yoke.

We have forgotten all the hardships of our journey and have remembrance only for the days of unalloyed happiness we have been permitted to enjoy. . . .

CHAPTER XIII
Life among the Kickers

*Once to every man and nation comes the moment
to decide,
In the strife of truth with falsehood, for the
good or evil side. . . .
Part the goats upon the left hand, and the
sheep upon the right,
And the choice goes by forever 'twixt that
darkness and that light.**

THE KICKERS, who had demanded land titles and water rights, made the mistake of settling below the Saints on the canal. For several years they engaged in bitter altercation, demanding water which was often refused—sometimes having to go singly by night, or by daytime in groups to open check gates against the orders of the Saints in control up ditch. Control of water has been cause for strife and often bloodshed as far back as the history of man. Of strife there was no end, fortunately in this case of the colonists it stopped always short of bloodshed.

The Kickers sued for possession of their chattels such as horses, wagons, and implements, and a settlement was reached.

Wresting a living from that brush country was tough. The Saints planted their small gardens and their "contracted" crops on a small scale, and talked and dreamed of a brighter future in the making.

The Kickers ambitiously marked out plots up to forty acres each, cleared land as they could, dug lateral canals to their plots, threw up brush fences and planted corn, wheat, beans, or other field crops.

The open, unfenced country carried numerous native cattle. When grazing was scarce, these cattle filtered through the colonists' brush fences, or were assisted through at night

*From "The Crisis" by James Russell Lowell.

by solicitous owners. Damage became so serious that the colonists were compelled to adopt drastic methods. Presently it became a common event for quarters of beef to be hung on various neighbors' doors, spikes being driven conveniently to receive them. This was a real blessing to the hard-up colonists, until the intrusion of cattle sharply declined, and so the meat supply also.

What a turmoil there must have been in the minds of those staunch early supporters of Owen—Dr. Scally, B. F. Burr, and their families, Dr. Schellhous, the Stanleys, and the Stanfasts—these latter who had gone down with the Howlands—before resolving to cast their lot with the Kickers on the Plat.

A Mexican colonist, Judge Don Victor Padilla, he of the obstinate mules at the river crossing, who had followed the fortunes of the colony with keen and friendly interest, and had sent his children to the La Logia schools, now cast his lot with the Kickers. Worse still, he farmed with hired labor, for which he was criticized, and became the owner of a small mill for processing sugar cane into *panocha*.

The Scally family soon installed another *panocha* mill. These small mill owners bought sugar cane of various colonists, so beginning the sugar industry at Los Mochis which has since grown into the largest of Mexico.

What strenuous times those were for the Kicker colonists; digging canals; clearing land; fighting over water rights and land titles in the Mexican courts.

In that early period they were represented by Henry A. Hart, a former member of the City Council at Stockton, Kansas, and Treasurer of Kansas Sinaloa Investment Company.

Hart was the jeweler and watchmaker as well as a farmer on the Plat. *El Corazon*, the heart, as he was called by the natives, had a bright mind and a keen sense of humor.

During the years of litigation he often traveled the *Camino Real* 75 miles up river to the district seat at Fuerte. Colonel Streeter, the very dignified ex-candidate for President of the United States, during his stay in the colony made the trip occasionally with him. Hart had observed during his trips that native Mexicans seldom rode saddle mares—almost always horses, so he persuaded Streeter that to while away the tediousness of their long journey by buckboard they should bet a dollar each on the gender of the animals being ridden along the *Camino Real*, Streeter to choose mares, and Hart horses. Streeter accepted and lost about a hundred dollars on the trip.

At Fuerte one day Hart, encountering an organ grinder, sent him to the hotel to play for Colonel Streeter, taking care to be there with the Colonel, to explain that this was a tribute from the citizens of the *pueblo* to the distinguished citizen of another country.

The Colonel was gratified at first, and tipped the organ grinder handsomely—a bad mistake, as he continued to grind out the same old tune until the Colonel became frantic. "Hart, get that damned thing away from here!" raged the Colonel.

"Colonel, you do not understand," soothed Hart, "these poor people are doing the best they can to honor you—you must not possibly do anything to offend them." —and so the Colonel was obliged to listen until Hart chose to send the man away.

The ex-candidate for President was a prohibitionist, an embarrassing fact in his meetings with local dignitaries, when prolonged discussions inevitably called for the hospitality of offering drinks.

Several meetings were held with the *Jefe Politico*, Don Francisco Orrantia, a wealthy *hacendado*, and of very dignified manner. The matter of the Colonel beeing a teetotaler was successfully bridged during the meetings, until a day when Orrantia was invited to the Colonel's room at *Hotel Diligencias* (Stagecoach Hotel).

Hart had gone to a saloon, secured numerous empty liquor bottles and some partly filled, and had them well strewn about the room when the distinguished Colonel ushered in his equally distinguished guest. The expression of amazement on the face of Orrantia was only equaled by that on the face of the Colonel.

To have been drinking in private while holding out on his company would have been an ungracious—an unforgivable act indeed.

After the first shock of surprise had been thoroughly enjoyed by Hart he squared matters with Señor Orrantia, of course, and the ice was broken for perhaps more cordial relations than before.

There comes to mind another incident told by Hart of the Mexican boarder at *Hotel Diligencias* who used a pair of sugar tongs, exclaiming in compliment to his American table mates, "Ah! What ingenious people you Yankees are," as he picked up the tongs, with his free hand inserting in their jaw a cube of sugar, and so transferred it to his coffee.

A sister of Henry Hart, Rosella Hart Bunker, and children, Bessie, Willie, and twins Clyde and Chloe, went to the colony in 1891 during the construction of the canal.

Soon after, she married the widower Tom Whitzel, whose daughter Irene, his 15-year-old housekeeper, had died a short time before, leaving him with daughters Cozy, Maud, and the baby Sonora. Mrs. Whitzel's oldest daughter, Bessie Bunker, sixteen years of age, married Rolla C. Stanley, then forty, a marriage of two people of very determined will which soon terminated.

An incident startling to the colony was that before this marriage the Stanley family revealed themselves to be of the name Schellhous, Cyrus M. Stanley being a younger brother of Dr. Edwin Schellhous, having changed the name and moved to California when relatives opposed his second marriage.

Dr. Schellhous lost faith in the colony and moved to Kansas City, Missouri, where he lived and taught for many years.

Cyrus and Viola, his wife, with three children lost to them by death in the colony, with Rolla and the two sisters Etta and Lutie married, and a son Lynn gone from the colony, decided to move to the new canal and colonization project on the Yaqui River with their two small sons Willis and Fred. After a period there they departed by wagon for the United States, had a breakdown, traded their outfit for passage on a steamer to Guaymas, continued by train to Nogales, where they chanced to meet a "medicine man" conducting open-air exhibitions in the cure of warts and infections, this man outfitting them with a team and wagon in exchange for their services in playing—an instrumental quartette—at his medicine shows. This kindly man, head of a large family which moved about with him, seems to have been a most successful healer, and shared his income with the Schellhous family until their travels took them to Kansas City, where the Schellhouses established themselves, Dr. Edwin and Cyrus M. teaching. The sons grew up to become high-class musicians,

[120]

eventually moving to Hollywood and playing solos for moving pictures and for radio.

Viola, now past ninety years of age, lives in Santa Monica, California, with a widowed daughter and her grandchildren. So passed from the life of the colony a family who had done much to cheer during the dark and trying days, with their beautiful music and their kindly spirit and earnest endeavor.

CHAPTER XIV
The Dreamer
Is Gone and the Dream Is Done

*I know of a land where the streets are paved
With the things which we meant to achieve,
It is walled with the money we meant to have saved
And the pictures for which we grieve. . . .*

*And Oh! this place, while it seems so near,
Is farther away than the moon,
Tho' our purpose is fair, we never get there
To the land of "Pretty Soon."*

*The road that leads to that mystic land
Is strewn with pitiful wrecks,
And the ships that have sailed for the shining strand
Bear skeletons on their decks.*

*It is farther at noon than it is at dawn
And farther at night than at noon
O! Let us beware of that land down there
The land of "Pretty Soon."**

ALBERT OWEN never returned to the colony after the fateful meeting with Hoffman and Flurschiem in May of 1893. For two years after, the *Credit Foncier of Sinaloa* recorded his efforts to promote the cause of Integral Cooperation and of the loyal colonists—printed lectures given by him to varied groups in the United States, in Mexico City, and in England, and articles by him directed to the colonists.

Colonization efforts continued, largely from Colorado, where Dr. B. A. Wheeler had been the colony agent, while his family lived in the colony.

As his representative in the colony Owen appointed Joseph Hampl, a young German-American draftsman and engineer who had kept an office for Owen at Guaymas for several years.

*From "The Land of Pretty Soon" by Ella Wheeler Wilcox.

Quarreling over the land and water rights and use of water continued, varying in intensity; in summer when there was ample water there was comparative peace, in spring when water became scarce there was quarreling, when water ran out Saints and Kickers together moved to the mouth of the canal at the river and worked like beavers to build a diversion dam to secure water. Meanwhile fate was building a new future for the colony.

Associated with Edward Lycan and two other Americans in his deal with Don Zacarias Ochoa in 1890 to build a sugar mill to grind the Ochoa cane and that of others was a young man recently of the Northwest, but of eastern background— Benjamin Francis Johnston, in 1890 about twenty-five years of age.

For the first few years little was known of him except that he had become the principal in the mill deal with Ochoa, through the death of a partner from malaria, and the return north of Lycan and another partner.

B. F. Johnston was the very antithesis of Albert K. Owen —as brilliant as an individualist as was Owen as a cooperator. His personality was dynamic, ultra-forceful, with a marvelous capacity for adjustment to events of the moment. He could be kindly, considerate, gentlemanly in his attitudes, or a veritable devil in a business quarrel, according to his convenience.

With proper modesty I can say that I have known in various degrees of friendship various prominent men, some generals, some governors, four presidents of Mexico, some men high in national agriculture and marketing in the United States, and that I have never met another man of that certain personality of B. F. Johnston—yet for two reasons he failed of being a great man. First, that for all his brilliant mind he was a driver, not a leader of men; second, that he had not except on rare occasions that certain magnanimity in business which places a select few business men in the class of the great.

From the first there was a business duel between Johnston and Ochoa, which, omitting the ample hearsay of the time, ended in Johnston's becoming owner of the mill, and of the plantation of El Aguila.

From the scene of his sugar mill activities at El Aguila

Johnston cast appraising eyes on the Mochis lands, the Los Tastes Canal, and the situation in the colony.

Within a few years he had secured a part of the Streeter-Kansas Sinaloa Investment Company lands, and acquired other colony lands from John H. Rice. Rice, once Governor of New York, was president of a company which held in trust, for payment of debt, the Carman and Ibarra lands which Owen represented by power of attorney and by twenty per cent ownership.

While the colonists quarreled and sued each other their house was burning. Johnston secured a Federal concession for water from the Fuerte River and for building a canal from Los Tastes to Mochis over the same general area as the colonists' canal.

On a part of the lands purchased by Johnston were the two groups, Kickers and Saints. Desperate for water, a large number of these colonists contracted with Johnston to pay him 25 pesos an acre for their holdings, and to grow sugar cane on contract for his Aguila mill, he to furnish them water pumped through the colonists' canal. This move gave Johnston temporary possession of the canal.

There was a bitter struggle. Owen contended that neither Rice nor Streeter, nor Johnston for them, could have been assigned the water concession, which had always been in the name of Owen, not of the colony or its creditors.

Some colonists, refusing to compromise, from their meager resources raised enough cash to send Joseph Hampl to Mexico City to fight their case.

Perhaps Johnston was embittered by the fight with these colonists. Perhaps he felt that he could not afford to allow them a foothold. Whatever his thoughts, he was a hard adversary, and began court proceedings for their eviction. It was a sad, shameful proceeding for American colonists in a foreign country first to fight so bitterly among themselves, then to be thrown into a struggle for survival against a common enemy who was an American.

Out of the years of litigation many colonists either were evicted or were left with a very few acres each, and the colonists collectively with 35% of the water right of the Los Tastes Canal, with the administration of water use in control of Johnston, but subject to review by representatives of the colony and to adjustment by the federal *Departamento de Fomento.*

The amount and nature of charges for water administration by Johnston were subjects of lively and continued controversy for 40 years after, with Joe Scally, well educated in Spanish and versed in Mexican law, usually representing the colonists in their fight.

The *Credit Foncier of Sinaloa* was published until July 1895. In an earlier issue under the editorship of Marie Howland had appeared this item: "Comrade Dawkins house of mats and thatch is finished and is quite artistic and cozy. Lying in his comfortable hammock reading, rocked by the breezes from over the bay, he is a picture of enjoyment. We think he should have a housekeeper."

Soon after suspension of the paper John Dawkins and Ida Hoagland were married, and remained at Topolobampo to follow the fortunes of the colony, Dawkins becoming a customs broker and commercial printer.

At about the same time Owen married a widow, Mrs. Marie Louise Bigelow of Baldwinsville, New York, whom he had met on an excursion to see some Mayan pyramids in Mexico.

We know that his interests in the Carman-Ibarra lands and in the Los Tastes Canal were transferred to Mrs. Owen.

In 1897 his railroad concession was renewed, and in 1899 he made an arrangement with Enrique C. Creel, Vice-President of the Chihuahua and Pacific Railway, by which Owen was to extend that line to Topolobampo, with Mexican government subsidies.

Owen was in England and Holland when the Boer War broke out, so ending his plans for securing building materials from there.

In 1900 he interested Arthur E. Stilwell and a group of Kansas City bankers, held conferences with them, Governor Ahumada of Chihuahua and President Don Porfirio Diaz, which resulted in organization of the Kansas City, Mexico, y Oriente Railway.

Although he took an active interest in plans for construction of this line, beginning in 1903, over the route planned by him thirty years before, he never afterward figured in colony affairs.

I hesitate to sum up the career, the case, of Albert Kimsey Owen; perhaps the pages of this narrative have sufficiently told his story.

Although I was reared among people who were his bitter critics, a study of his youth, his education, his associations, his aspirations, and his actions have convinced me that he was a noble character, perhaps with a certain personal egotism that carried him too far in his planning to make of him a true cooperator. No doubt he had too much impractical idealism, and not enough judgment of the true desires, ambitions, and, most important, the limitations of his fellow men.

His inspired planning for the good of the world brought much of misery and disillusionment. He and his followers in a movement of worldwide interest of that time, have left a record that might serve as a guide, or as an object lesson, according to the point of view, for the planners of our future.

In Sinaloa he left, whether for or against him, a group of American men, women, and children practically without resources, to either leave the country or undertake to fit themselves into an unusual and uncertain future.

Of these people and of the country of their adoption we will treat in a separate story. The story of Albert Kimsey Owen and the cooperative colony ends here—regretfully it is set aside, for it has been fascinating to consider, although difficult to condense from the wealth of material, written or told by the pioneers remaining from that distant day, without some slight to many who were for long years members of the colony.

At the turn of the twentieth century there remained from the vast colony perhaps fifty American families in the Fuerte River valley, the larger number of them on farms cleared from the tough tropical woods of the Mochis plain, each family with perhaps a pair of horses, a milk cow, a wagon, a plow—just those essential aids to living symbolic of pioneer life since the beginning of the development of the Americas by those who stayed on the land.

APPENDIXES

Topolobampo Colonists

Names of Topolobampo colonists and persons associated with the colony, together with approximate dates of their arrival in the colony, and other data relating to them, largely based on the publication *Credit Foncier of Sinaloa*.

1872

ALBERT KIMSEY OWEN, civil engineer, founder of the colony; began explorations and surveys September 1872; from Chester, Pennsylvania.

EUGENE A. H. TAYS, civil engineer, and chief engineer for Sinaloa division of projected railways; also for the Los Tastes ditch built by the colonists. Married ROSAURA VEGA. Children: JOSE, CAJEME, (Eugene), ELOISA, GEORGE, LINDA, ALEJANDRO, CLEMENTE.

FRED G. FITCH, civil engineer, employed by Dr. Carman and Don Blas Ibarra to survey Topolobampo Bay and Mochis lands; one-time owner of 5% of said lands, settled at Fuerte, married a Mexican wife, died at Fuerte.

JESSE R. GRANT, vice-president, Mexican American Construction Company; son of General U. S. Grant.

1886

BURT PRESSEY, chainman for survey, later a colonist, a "bright, pleasant young fellow," from Hammonton, N. J.

JOHN W. LOVELL, New York publisher, socialist, wealthy philanthropist, friend of Owen, treasurer of Credit Foncier, from New York.

DAVITT D. CHIDESTER, secretary of Credit Foncier, close friend of Owen, from Ohio.

IGNACIO POMBO, Credit Foncier representative at City of Mexico.

EDWARD HOWLAND, scholar, writer, socialist, president of New Jersey Grange, and his wife.

MARIE HOWLAND, writer; after

death of Edward at La Logia, became editor of *Credit Foncier of Sinaloa*; both from Hammonton, New Jersey.

Members of California Party, 27 persons, who arrived by steamer *Newbern*, Captain Middlestadt, from San Francisco, via Mazatlan, on November 10, 1886 (date given by Ida Hoagland Dawkins) in Topolobampo Bay, and encamped in the cove near present Customs House, then named Schellhous Cove. (DR. EDWIN J. SCHELLHOUS, Colony Director, in charge of the party, scholar, musician, teacher, physician,

[129]

spiritualist, medium, arrived very soon after the first party.)

CYRUS MILTON STANLEY (Schellhous), farmer, musician, spiritualist, with his wife VIOLA, and family, all from Turlock, Calif. Children by first wife: ROLLA C., CLAIR, MILTON, LYNN B., ELLA, ETTA. Children by wife Viola: LUTIE, WILLIS, FRED. Died in Mexico: Clair, Milton, Ella.

JOEL BYRNS, from San Francsico.

WILLIS MATSON, wife AUGUSTA, no children, from San Francisco.

GEORGE MATSON, brother of Willis.

MICHAEL GEORGE DESMOND, wife VINNIE, from Laramie, Wyoming.

CHRIS HOELLE, from California.

DR. THOMAS C. GLENN and three sons, WALTER, RALPH, AND WILFORD.

T. E. WHITNEY, mechanic, farmer, soloist at Lyceums in the Colony; married ANNIE BALDWIN; their daughter, MABEL WHITNEY MICHEL.

ROBERT CUMMING, well-driller, poet.

CHARLEY HALLIN, wife, and small son, from California.

L. A. GOULD, from Fresno, California.

J. M. LOUDERBACK, from Riverside, California.

RUDOLPH KOBITSCH, from San Francisco, California.

GEORGE SEVENOAKS, from California.

DR. JOSHUA W. SCALLY, his wife, MARIE CLEMENTINE; their children JOSEPH P., IDA, SAM, twins HATTIE AND MATTIE; a daughter ANNIE came later from Texas with her husband JAMES W. JORDAN and their ten children ALBERT, MINNIE, ERNEST, JOHNNIE, ORA, CLEMMIE, MAMIE, JESSE, MAGGIE, TOM.

JOHN H. NEWTON, son-in-law of Dr. Scally, whose wife died in the U.S.A., and who later married MATTIE SCALLY in the colony. Their children born in the colony, LILLA, WALTER, IRVING. Lilla married Ralph Hale.

PAUL A. SMITH, a visitor, from Ferndale, California.

S. R. PRATT, wife, and mother.

THEO W. CURTIS, wife, and son, from Greeley, Colorado.

J. A. KENDRICKS.

— POWERS.

—· NICHOLSON.

— MCQUARRIE.

HERBERT PATRICK, wife, and daughter NELLIE, from Seattle, Territory of Washington.

WILLIAM L. PATTEN, tentmaker, wife, and children, from San Diego, California.

BENJAMIN WOODRUFF, wife EMMA.

— PREECE, wife and children. (MARIE HOWLAND PREECE, the first child born in the colony, at Topolobampo, February 24, 1887.)

Colorado Party, about 150 persons, which came by train from Denver over the Santa Fe Short Line Railway, Benson, Arizona, to Nogales to Guaymas, Sonora, then by steamer *Altata*, Captain Charles H. Robinson, to Topolobampo, arriving November 17, 1886. ("Santa Fe Short Line" is now a part of Southern Pacific of Mexico Railway.)

ALVIN J. WILBER, Colony Director in charge in Sinaloa, and wife SERA E. WILBER, their son LAWRENCE. Both Mr. and Mrs. Wilber were highly educated, particularly in botany, mineralogy, and natural history; from Greeley, Colorado.

IDA HOAGLAND (DAWKINS), teach-

er, Shelbyville, Illinois, and Greeley, Colorado.
ANNA J. NORRIS, teacher, Unitarian minister, Fort Collins, Colorado.
W. J. LEAVY, Greeley, Colorado.
CLEMENT GRIGYUMS and J. W. NICHOLS left colony in January, 1887.
ISSAC B. and SARAH RUMFORD, from California.
WILL J. STREET (married widow

Whitehill, the mother of "Goldie"), from Vineland, New Jersey.
W. A. McKENZIE, writer and poet.
L. H. HAWKINS, attorney, and W. F. EATON, ex-minister. (These latter two men tried to create dissension and take over leadership upon arrival, did not succeed, and left at night for Guaymas.)

1887

(By April 19, 1887, there were 410 persons reported in the colony.)

HOBART W. BRINK, Greeley, Colorado (lived with us in later years).
C. L. SNYDER, went north to work in Government Office at Washington, D. C.
THOMAS W. DOYLE, his wife LUCY T., and children MARY, LIZZIE, ELLA, JOHNNIE; returned to California.
EDWARD LOVELL, nephew of John W. Lovell, New York.

CALIFORNIA OVERLAND PARTY

W. P. FRIEND, leader of party, his wife MARY, their children RALPH, CLAUDE, PEARL, JOSIE, and FRED.
B. F. BURR, his wife, their children GRANT and MAGGIE.
JOHN BUDLONG. These twelve persons left "Mussels Slough," Tulare County, California, November 13, 1886, with two wagons, and traveled across deserts of California, Arizona, Sonora, through Yaqui country, through smallpox epidemic in Sonora, arrived at colony February 5, 1887 after being nearly three months on the way.

BURNETTE G. HASKELL, settler at Sufragio on Fuerte River before colony days, rented land for first colony plantings. Sons by American wife: AUGUSTINE, WILLIAM. Married in Mexico to Asuncion (Chonita), widow of a Mr. Wiley, their daughter Melinda (Ysabal Batiz), son John (Juan), a bright boy educated in colony, good friend to colonists. Children by Mr. Haskell: ROSA and CHLOE. After death of Mr. Haskell, his widow married W. W. (Will) Green, colonist, so Dona Chonita had three American husbands.
THOS. YOUNG, his wife, and son THOMAS, JR.
LEON GREEN, MORRIS FREE, WILLIAM COTTER, Russians from Northwest.
W. W. GREEN, Ottawa, Kansas.
DR. S. A. MERRILL, wrote poetry for colony.
STEPHEN YOUNG, old man, died in 1887.
W. A. GARRETT, from Colorado, later lived in San Diego, California.
ROBERT W. BEALE, from California.
GEO. A. APPEL(heim), from California.

F. M. Campbell, colony representative, San Diego, California.

H. W. Faust, colony representative, San Francisco, California.

Capt. A. P. Bunker, of *Romero Rubio*, his wife Ella S., and three children.

(By May 10, 1887, there had been three colony marriages.)

MEXICANS INTERESTED IN COLONY

General Carlos Pacheco, Minister of Public Works in Diaz Cabinet, who signed concessions to Owen.

Governor Francisco Canedo, of Sinaloa, then Governor.

Mariano Martinez de Castro, of Sinaloa.

Governor Luis E. Torres, of Sonora.

Eduardo S. Herrera, colony agent in Mexico City.

Don Aurelio Sandoval, agent at Guaymas.

F. K. Blue.

W. F. Romine.

Tully L. Witter (who died of smallpox), wife and children Zada, John, Allie, Walter, Julia, Sam, Roselle, Tully, and May.

J. W. Redd, Alamos, Sonora, Mexico.

James L. Waller.

E. L. Ingham, wife, and seven children.

J. Q. Henck, wife Mary, children Josey and Walter.

C. E. Shafer.

H. M. Shory.

Jack Faulds, married sister of Will Street, moved to Nogales, Arizona, became R.R. engineer on run Nogales to Guaymas.

William Windom, U. S. Secretary of Treasury, President of Texas Topolobampo and Pacific Railroad and Telegraph Company (organized by Owen).

John H. Rice, Secretary and Trustee of same company, once Governor of New York.

Don Martin Vega, a friendly *hacendado* at Vegaton, early colony settlement near San Blas on Fuerte River.

Alexander Willard, American Consul at Guaymas.

Dr. William C. Crooks, Director, Credit Foncier Company; an Army medical officer, political reformer, organized Political Reform League, Philadelphia, with Owen, Henry C. Carey, Carey Baird, E. M. Davis, General Brindle.

Governor Alexander R. Shepard, owner, Batopilas Mine.

John G. Dawkins, Braceville, Illinois, printer of *Credit Foncier*, married Ida Hoagland, later editor of *El Gazetero* and customs agent at Topolobampo.

Benjamin F. Close, his wife Mary, daughter Vernie, from San Francisco, California.

— Potts, resident at Fuerte.

— Williams and wife.

Job Barry, brother of Mrs. Mary Henck.

— Dows.

J. Allen Alcorn, from Colorado.

— Childs.

Stephen Spencer, from Greeley, Colorado.

O. C. Smith.

(All above names mentioned before June 28, 1887, issue *Credit Foncier of Sinaloa*.)

Topolobampo Colonists

WILLIAM LEE, died in early 1887.
CAPTAIN BRIGGS.
— MOORE.
— LAWRENCE.
Left the colony June 6, 1887, on Mexican sloop:
W. P. BOSWELL, wife, and four children.
R. H. FLETCHER, wife, and two children, from Pueblo, Colorado.
I. OYLER and wife.
H. WARRINGTON.
W. ROGERS.
HANS MADSON.
W. E. COONS.
F. YERBES.
S. SANDS.
E. DOOLITTLE.
I. FARDEN.
H. HILLAND.
THOMAS DICKERSON.
W. D. SOUTHWORTH, of Mt. Vernon, N. Y., separated from colony living June 7, 1887 at Fuerte.
C. B. HOFFMAN, flourmill owner, Congressman, political reformer, philanthropist, assisted the colony, organized Kansas Sinaloa Investment Company, to refinance colony and build ditch; was from Enterprise, Kansas.
WALTER HOFFMAN, son of C. B. Hoffman.
JOSEPH BURGHER, printer, *Credit Foncier*, in New Jersey.

INTERESTED FOREIGN CORRESPONDENTS

BRUCE WALLACE, London, England.
WILLIAM SAUNDERS, London, England.
J. MULLER, Upsala, Sweden.
GEO. EDGAR FRYE, Halifax, Nova Scotia.
MICHAEL FLURSCHIEM, Lugano, Switzerland.

JOHN H. LUTTON, wife, HANNAH M.; drove team of bay horses, bringing provisions to La Logia.
D. B. STANTON, from Greeley, Colorado.
THOMAS EBDELL, and son from England.
W. A. LANGHAM (Englishman), wife, and children CORA, DORA, TOMMY, WILLIE, from Texas.
EDWARD ASKREN, wife, and children MARTHA, DAVID.
J. H. SUTTON.
MR. and MRS. JOHNSON, from England.
FRANK YOUNG.
DR. PEET (family), ANNA W., Denver, Colorado.
JOHN FOSS, wife GRACE, and children ED and LILLA, from Texas.
F. M. BOLIN, wife, and children ZADA, JOHN, MAY.
E. G. KELTON, representing colony in Mazatlan.
DON JUAN ACOSTA, of Ahome, became colonist.
DON PATRICIO ROBLES, of El Porvenir, became colonist.
SR. JOAQUIN REDO, Senator from Sinaloa.
COLONEL EDWARD DANIELS, naturalist, scientist, engineer, correspondent of Smithsonian Institute, organized science club in colony. Made gas flame from pitahaya cactus. Owner of Gunston Hall, Virginia.
W. J. RICKABAUGH.
— SHEPPARDSON.
J. T. SPENCE, wife, and children MINNIE, MATTIE, and SAM.
HENRY STANDFAST (Englishman), wife HARRIET (went down with Howlands).
JAMES E. GRAHAM, Hillsboro, Colorado.
A. E. SELMER.
W. STUFFT.

Left colony November 3, 1887, on sloop *Guerrero* for Guaymas:
M. W. EARP and three children.
W. J. RICKABAUGH, wife LIZZIE, and three children.
W. A. SAMPSON, MRS. E. M. SAMPSON, and two children.
MRS. S. J. WILLIAMS and four children.
MRS. MAGGIE YOUNGBERG and three children.
CHAS. L. SNYDER.
THOS. EBDELL and son LAWRENCE.
JOHN B. ROSS.

Left colony November 8, 1887, on schooner *Sol* for Mazatlan:
DIRECTOR S. T. PEET.
MRS. E. L. INGHAM and seven children.
CAPT. A. P. BUNKER, MRS. E. S. BUNKER, and three children.
C. D. READ, MRS. A. M. READ, MISS ELFIE READ, MISS MYRTIE READ.
CHAS. WILLIAMS.
GUS MICKE.
MRS. H. P. DONALLEN.
MISS MAGGIE MICHNER.
Left in colony, 138 persons.

Beginning September 15, 1887, when Howlands renewed publication of *Credit Foncier of Sinaloa*, from new office at Topolobampo.

MRS. LILIE WHITEHILL and little daughter, "Goldie."
S. ARMS.
SENORES PIEMBERT and GONZALES, customs officers.
W. N. SLOCUM, printer, San Francisco, California.
JOHN LOFLEY and son JOHNNY.
FRED HALLER.
HENRY POTTER, Oleander, Calif.
C. J. LAMB, Kirwin, Kansas.
FRANK SMITH, musician in Stanley band, Greeley, Colorado.
JOHN BAUMANN, old man, miller, mechanic.
CLARENCE FRANK CLOSE, born at La Logia.
FRANTZ SCHLEUNIGER, cabinet maker, San Francisco, Calif.
OTTO SINZ, did clock repairing.
— FEYGERT.
JOHN P. WHITNEY, tall, white-haired, white-bearded Texas frontiersman, rode through the Yaqui country alone on a gray roan horse; from Atascosa County, Texas.
Left for California: HORACE BARTRAM, J. SINNETT, G. SELMER, DR. THOMAS C. GLENN, WALTER GLENN, RALPH GLENN, WILFORD GLENN, W. C. MEDBURY.
E. W. HASLAM, JOHN BELL (retired sea captain), Oakland, California.
H. H. CRAGG, gone to Mines.
L. H. SHAW, — JEFFREY, J. W. RYAN, CARL RENZ.
ESTEBAN and JOSE ZAKANY, who attended school at La Logia.
DON SALVADOR CASTRO, Zaragoza.
DON VICTOR and DONA PLACIDA PADILLA, children ALBERTO, VICTOR, GENOVEVA, ROSARIO, ANITA, PLACIDA, LUPE, CARLOS.

1889

H. FIGARD left.
— MOTT, — SCHNABLE.
ALBERTO ARMENTA Y VEGA married ANNIE GATES, girl of the colony.
Party from Enterprise, Kansas:

CHRIS B. HOFFMAN.
GEORGE L. PAGE, wife SUSIE L., children CHESTER, ROSS, RAY, CECIL, Salina, Kansas.
N. THURSTIN, HENRY PAGE, J. M. LIMBOCKER, C. L. BINKLEY, Tampa, Florida.
MRS. ANGELINA WILSON, Oleander, California.
SAMUEL and AURELIA JONES, children CARRIE, CHARLES, Oleander, Calif. RESCUE B. PAGE, Oleander, Calif.
W. R. WILLIAMS, England.
Arrived from California April 7, 1889:
EUGENE L. FISCHER.
MR. and MRS. SVEN SVENSON and three children.
MR. and MRS. MEINECKE; EDWARD MEINECKE and two children.
MR. and MRS. CARL WERNECKE and two children.
In the OVERLAND PARTY from Kansas by railroad to Guaymas, guided in by John Whitney:
W. H. BENTLEY.
A. DURAND.
WM. C. PAGE.
C. E. SHAFFER.
M. B. WILLIAMS (English nobleman).

JOHN BUDLONG returned to colony.
MAY PARTY from Strong City, Kansas, in charge of CAROL J. LAMB:
E. H. G. STARK, wife, and son HARRY.
FRED DREWIEN and children EMMA, WILL, FRED, ROSE.
GEORGE COTE.
HENRY SEVEREIN (all above from Chicago).
B. C. REMLEY, wife, and four children, Chanute, Kansas.
MISS CLARA HOAGLAND, Shelbyville, Illinois.
C. J. LAMB and son, Kirwin, Kansas.
W. A. BROWN, Agra, Kansas.
IRA D. KNEELAND, Boulder, Colorado.
A MR. ICHENLAUB joined the party.
From Santa Ana, California:
DR. J. A. THATCHER, his wife PANSY, and foster daughter DOROTHY A. LANGLEY (actress, married William Sherman Felt, later John Mulkey); and MR. S. FINBOW. (Dot Langley Felt's favorite song, "When the Robins Nest Again," was popular in the colony.)

1890

FEBRUARY

JOHN S. SHOOP, accountant, Shakespearean actor, Chicago, Illinois (wore a derby, and had a black mustache), married Etta Schellhous.
MRS. E. THURSTIN, Hope, Kansas.
G. S. TAPPAN, MRS. I. M. TAPPAN, daughter A. L. TAPPAN, Broken Bow, Nebraska.

W. S. FELT, printer, Monte Vista, Colorado.
WM. GROVES, mechanic, Galveston, Texas.
CHARLES T. ROBINSON, captain of steamer *Altata*.
REVEREND NAPOLEON HOAGLAND, Greeley, Colorado.
A. G. ANGELL, Wisconsin.
S. M. TALLMAN.

NOVEMBER PARTY
(Arrived December 17, 1890):

JOSEPH K. BENNETT, wife MARY, children MARY B., J. J., WILLIAM P., and ALICE, Ellenwood, Kansas.

WM. BALDWIN, wife MARY, children EMMA, FRANK, ALBERT O., ANNIE, and NELLIE (Hultz), Horton, Kansas.

A. BUTTERFIELD, Boyne, Kansas.

JOHN BENNETT, M. J., J. L., M. E., and J. H.; H. O. BENEDICT, FRED BENEDICT, Bennington, Kansas.

WM. BUTLER, EMMA R. BUTLER, JAMES BUTLER, MARGARET A., HENRY W., SARAH L., NINA, MARY, all of Enterprise, Kansas.

S. H. BLACK, Miltonvale, Kansas.

MARY C. and CORA CRANE, Satank, Colorado.

DANIEL W. COLE, Big Bend, Kansas.

EZRA, WILLIAM, JAMES, HERBERT, SARAH J., EZRA F., WINIFRED, ALBERT, MARY E. and LAURA COMFORT, Poe, Kansas.

CHARLES HEATH, Cheyse, London, England.

MAYVILLE DRAKE, wife JULIA, children GEORGE, ROSE, IRENE, WILLIAM, DOT, JULIA, BERTHA, MARY, of Enterprise, Kansas.

MARSHALL DAVIS, Delphos, Kansas.

WILLIAM DELAMETER, Geneva, Nebraska.

JACOB DOCKTER, Hiattville, Kansas.

WELLER EMERICK and wife SAMANTHA, children JAMES G., HENRY H., DORA ETHEL, V. W., Seeley, Kansas.

JULIUS ECKHARDT, Chicago, Illinois.

M. J. L. FRANK, McPherson, Kansas.

H. L. GARVER, Florida, Mo.

JOHN and SARAH J. HEASTON, children DELLA, EVA, JOSIE, JOHN, EDWARD, JULIA, Dallas, Texas.

CHARLES N., CHARLES D., and MARY HOPKINS, Enterprise, Kansas.

ROBERT B. HUNTER, Enterprise, Kansas.

CLARK HULBERT, Chester, Nebraska.

CHRISTIAN B. HOFFMAN, Enterprise, Kansas.

SAM IRELAN, Geneva, Nebraska.

JOHN JACKSON, Dallas, Texas.

JOHN KING, Poe, Kansas.

OLE KNUDESON, Richland, Kansas.

CHARLES W. LOCKWOOD, Parsons, Kansas.

CLAYTON J. LAMB and wife CAROLINA V., children GLADYS (later Ernest), Kirwin, Kansas.

C. F. LINDSTROM, wife ALICE O., daughter HAZEL, Chicago, Illinois.

T. R. MCBRIDE, DANIEL MCBRIDE, Fort Collins, Colorado.

J. H. MULKEY, Garden Plain, Kansas.

LUCINDA, CLARENCE, MILDON, LEVI, VICTOR, and ARTHUR MORGAN, Downing, Wisconsin.

W. (Bill) H. PORTER, Oswego, Kansas.

PETER PEET, his wife NETTIE, her son GEORGE HARTEN, EDNA M., GRACE, CORA, MILLIE, Delphos, Kansas.

J. J. PAYNE, JULIA, his wife, children ORPHU, LEO (and later Edna), Cadmus, Kansas.

S. ROHWER, ELIESE, JOHN, ALICE, Cucamonga, California.

MAURICE and PERCY POWELL

(nephews of Celia Page), Salina, Kansas.
MALCOLM ROBERTSON, Lincoln, Kansas.
FRANK C. ROWE, Lane, Kansas.
WILLIAM and MARY E. Ross, Wichita, Kansas.
A. R. RHODES, Winfield, Kansas.
DENNIS, MARTHA, MELISSA, CHAUNCEY, EMERY E. SIMMONS, Kimball, Kansas.
L. R. SALE, M.D., Lafayette, Indiana.
O. C. and R. K. SMITH, Greeley, Colorado.
J. W. and LORENZO D. SCOTT, Kensington, Kansas.
D. S. STRANG, Glenwood Springs, Colorado.
R. S. THIRSK, children ROBERT, JESSIE, DAISY, Winfield, Kansas.
WILKINSON and JAMES TOWN-
END, Sandusky, Ohio.
E. E. THORNTON, Pipestone, Minnesota.
EVENS TAYLOR, Salem, Utah.
TOM J. WHITZEL, wife MAGGIE, children JESS D., IRENE J., COZY, MAUD H., MAGGIE, MARIE SONORA; JESS D. WHITZEL (Uncle Jess) and MABEL M., all from Geneva, Nebraska.
M. J. WINTER, EVELINE, M. J. (Jr.) and N. K. J. WINTER, Chicago, Illinois.
J. G. A. WOLF, CATHERINE and GRACE, Almena, Kansas.
RANDOLPH WILCOXON, FRANCES, GEORGE W., JESSIE S., PEARL, and ETHEL, Enterprise, Kansas.
JOHN WICKERRINK, Prairie View, Kansas.
ROBERT WHITE, Rosette, Kansas.

Died, at La Logia on Christmas morning, 1890, EDWARD HOWLAND, age 58 years, Editor of *Credit Foncier of Sinaloa*.

1891

MAY PARTY
(Arrived May 1, 1891):
J. ALLEN ALCORN, Greeley, Colorado, returned.
AUGUST, KARL MARX, ERNESTINE, and VICTOR HUGO BOSSHAMMER, Millheim, Texas.
GEORGE W. BECK, Havana, Kansas.
CASSIUS M. BROWN, wife HANNAH P., children ROY F., KENT, OLIVE (KATE born in colony), Guilford, Kansas.
WILLIAM COULTER, Hull, Kansas.
HELMIT M. DAWSON, wife MARY, sons Ross and GEORGE,
Oak Hill, Kansas.
JOHN DOWNING, wife SARAH A., ANDREW J., ABRAHAM LINCOLN, MARY ISABEL, and CLAUDE L., Dell, Montana.
DWIGHT L. FILLEY, Auburn, Nebraska.
MORRIS P. FRENCH, Elk Falls, Kansas.
ANDREW M. FIX, wife, SAREPTA E., son, JOHN R., Dell, Montana.
OTTO and PAUL FEUERBACHER, Austin, Texas.
MAY A. GRIGGS, THOS. W., WM. P., JAMES H., LON V., Watson, Colorado.

Minnie Hogue (Eckhardt), Guilford, Kansas.

Thomas Ashbury Hays, wife Delphia Mandell, and son Charles Page Hays, Stafford, Kansas.

Henry Latty and wife Mary C., Salina, Kansas.

Julius Mentzel, Milwaukee, Wisconsin.

Alexander McDonald, Oak Hill, Kansas.

Alfred C. Pagett, Beloit, Kansas.

Charles A. Petersen, his wife Ella M., children Christopher, William, John, Mary, Oak Hill, Kansas.

Frank Ransom, Minneapolis, Minnesota.

August Sailer, Sealey, Texas.

Henry Travelute, Hull, Kansas.

Edward C. Wilson, Zurich, Kansas.

Ebenezer P. C., Frank S., and Rollin W. Webster, Marysville, Kansas.

LITTLE MAY PARTY:

Thos. Bernard Manning, wife Ora, and children Cora and Albert Owen; Messrs. Carl Amsel and John James Markham (all from Rockvale, Colorado). Later arrivals: Holbrook and Black.

June 21, 1891, married at Mochicahui, Jonathan Mulkey and Rose Drake.

June 6, 1891, died of diphtheria, Maggie F. Whitzel, 5 years, and Mabel W. Whitzel, 2 years, children of Tom and Maggie Whitzel.

Died about July 12, 1891, at Ditch Camp, Ella Stanley, a crippled girl in her middle twenties, a beautiful character who appears many times in the records of the early colony. Touching tributes of her friends appear in *Credit Foncier* issue of August 1, 1891.

Arrivals in colony by S.S. *Romero Rubio*, July 12, 1891:

Wm. A. Burford, Jacksonville, Florida.

Henry A. Beach, Crow, Kansas.

Ezra Brown, Flora, Kansas.

John Everson, Alma, Nebraska.

J. H. Edwards, London, England.

Wm. W. Green, Greeley, Colorado, returned to colony.

John A. Gishwiler, Almena, Kansas.

Chas. H. Hawley, Oklahoma, Oklahoma Territory.

James E. Larkin, Ulysses, Nebraska.

Amos M. Miks and Victor C. Miks, Baxter Springs, Kansas.

Rilla Emerick McClung and child Daisy Virginia, Winfield, Kansas.

Frank Newnham, wife Frances E., children Frances E. and Frank John, London, England.

Albert K. Owen, New York City.

Irving W. Smith, Fort Garland, Colorado (married Lutie Stanley Schellhous).

Stephen Spencer (returned to colony), Greeley, Colorado.

Christian A. Saylor, Myersville, Pennsylvania.

Kansas Sinaloa Investment Company (organized to assist Credit Foncier Company to build canal and carry forward the colony): Chris B. Hoffman, President, John W. Breidenthal, Secretary, Henry A. Hart, Treasurer, James Butler, General Agent. Offices,

Enterprise, Kansas, Chetopa, Kansas. Authorized capital, $100,000.

Born at La Logia, August, 1891, to JOHN H. NEWTON and MATTIE SCALLY NEWTON, a daughter, LILLA.

Born at Camp Catwood, Friday, September 11, 1891, to JOSEPH P. and MAGGIE BURR SCALLY, a daughter, FLORA.

Born at Camp Catwood, November 8, to GRANT H. BURR and HATTIE SCALLY BURR, a daughter, MABEL.

Died at La Logia, Tuesday evening, October 13, 1891, MRS. MAGGIE WHITZEL, age 37 years (wife of Tom J. Whitzel).

Died at Camp Catwood in November 1891, AUGUST SAILER, age 19 years; WILLIAM COULTER, 20 years.

MRS. BURR, wife of B. F. BURR, died during spring of 1891 (could not locate exact date).

THE NOVEMBER PARTY

In charge of J. M. LIMBOCKER (K.S.I. Co. official), by S.S. *Romero Rubio,* November 25, 1891:
DR. LUCIUS A. BUMSTEAD, wife CELINDA A., children LLOYD G., ROYAL E.
ARTHUR and HATTIE E. GREEN.
WILLIAM A. WOTHERSPOON.
DANIEL ROPER SUTTON.
HERBERT S. BERGER.
WM. EDMOND HAIGHT.
CHARLES PIERROT.
CHARLES EDWARD DEWEY and wife.
MARY ANN BAKER.
JACOB HEY, wife ROSALIND LILLIAN, children DENTON CLARENCE, FLORENCE CECIL, ANNIE MAUD.

CHARLES HOXSEY ROBINSON.
HORACE GREELEY SCOTT.
CHARLEY SCOTT.
FRED HOWARD VAN DYKE.
EDWIN KREAMER, wife SARAH S., sons CHARLES OLIVER, EDWIN CHESTER, LOUIS TENNERY.
ROSA HART BUNKER, children BESSIE (ELIZABETH AURELIA), WILLIE (WILLIAM SAMUEL), twins CLYDE and CHLOE.
DAVID M. SMITH, wife MARY LENA, sons ERNEST D. and RALPH M.
EDNA PAYNE (parents in colony).
FRED DOUGLAS MULKEY.
WILLIAM TEVERBAUGH.
CARRIE EMORY HAIGHT.
LOUIS LUDLOW HAIGHT.
THOMAS FRANCIS BURNS.
JAMES EDWARD DAVIS.
HERBERT ARTHUR DAVIS.
DANIEL RUNYEN.
FRANK D. HULSE.
NELLIE BALDWIN HULSE.
CHARLES EDWARD SMITH.
CHARLES DEWEY BLAIR (married Della Heaston).
MISS M. L. JENNER.
JOSEPH MILTON STROUT.
SARAH ADELAIDE STROUT.
WESLEY H. STROUT.
QUEEN DOCKTER, JUDGE DOCKTER (a Dockter already in the colony).
SPOFFORD family consisting of JOHN WHITNEY, EMILY ALBERTINA, CHARLES ALFRED, MAUD AMELIA, HENRY AUGUSTUS, SAMUEL, and BURNAL.
RUTH A., LAURA V. and JOSIE CHAPMAN.
EDWARD LYCAN, nurse, and two children.

November 29, 1891, by S.S. *Ahome:*
WM. H. PATTEN, wife CORA A., children CORA B., ADELE H., REX H. and HELEN M.
GILBERT ARNOLD.

LAURENT MANGUETTE, MARIE MANGUETTE.

December 3, 1891 by S.S. *Romero Rubio*:

JOHN W. BREIDENTHAL.

WILLIAM and ANGIE KLUGE.

J. W. and ANN SCOTT.

AARON, JOHN A., SARAH E., BLANCHIE C. and CLARA C. GARDNER.

ALBERT M. MEAD and ALBERT M. MEAD, JR.

MYRON MILLER, wife SADIE HART, children BERYL BISHOP and MYRON HART.

ALBERT LAW, wife SARAH, son GEORGE C. LAW.

R. N. CUNNINGHAM, wife JESSIE MAY, children NETTIE E., NORA, and baby boy.

MILLARD F. DRESSER, wife ALICE J., children LEONARD R., ALICE A., FLORENCE E., and baby boy.

THE OVERLAND PARTY of the same November:

G. W. DANIELS, wife NANCY J., sons CHARLES E., HENRY F., BERT D., and FRANK A.

SAMUEL and MARY PROUTY.

MANLEY C. CHASE, wife SARAH L., daughters NELLIE B., STELLA F., LUELLA M.

G. ROWLAND MINSHULL.

JAMES STURTON.

A. VIRGIL ROSS.

FESTUS WARD.

A. R. C. SLOAN.

F. F. INGERSOLL.

FRANK, FRANCIS, and CARRIE P. INGERSOLL.

MILLARD COLYER.

WALTER G. and AURILLA E. KIMBALL.

LEON E. RUGGLES and ALICE E. RUGGLES.

LEON A KIMBALL.

DENTON C. HEY.

GEORGE B., PHOEBE RUGGLES.

Married at Camp Catwood, December 20, 1891, JOHN S. SHOOP and ETTA B. STANLEY (Schellhous).

1892

MR. and MRS. J. FAULDS living in Nogales. Mrs. Faulds is sister of Will Street.

ERNEST EBEL and PETER LASSEN, two young Germans, speaking neither English nor Spanish, arrived on foot from Chicago, February 10, after being lost in the mountains and nearly starved.

February 17, 1892, arrived by S.S. *Mazatlan*:

JOHN C. DRAKE, Homestead, Pennsylvania.

JULIAN O. FRENCH, Crown Point, N. Y.

W. H. THOMAS, Gladbrook, Iowa.

W. F. BRAGG, Eureka Springs, Arkansas.

C. S. HAMMOND, Argonia, Kansas.

PETER LORING, Cosmopolia, Washington.

CHARLES F. BERRY, wife HELEN B., daughters MARY E., BERTHA I., and ALICE, of Gering, Nebraska.

MARY A. INGERSOLL, of Clay Center, Kansas.

February 18, 1892, married on S.S. *Mazatlan*, chartered for the purpose, EDWARD LYCAN and MISS LOUISA KELLOGG (nurse for his children).

February 29, 1892, by steamer *Mazatlan*, E. H. G. STARK, wife FREDERICA, son H. A. H. ("HARRY") STARK.

March 9, 1892, from England:

Topolobampo Colonists

JAMES ALFRED KINGHORN JONES, his wife JANE, their nine children ETHEL, FRANK, ANNIE, BRUCE, CHRISTINE, GORDON, HOWARD, IVOR and KATHLEEN-DOUGLAS (10). He, tall, slender, fair complexion, and she, short, good-natured. (Mother's description.)

March 9, 1892: WILSON H. HAWKINS; JOHN ELPHINSTONE.

From Portland, Oregon: CLYDE and PEARL WEST; SARAH E. CORPE and three children BLANCHE M., FLOSS F., and GEORGE R.

From Kalama, Washington: IDA E. WEST and JAMES M. MASON. (Mason died of fever, May 9, 1892.)

From Virginia Dale, Colorado: DAVID B. SHAW.

From Eureka, Nebraska: R. S. STEVENSON, wife, and daughter ESTHER.

April 18, 1892, by steamer *Mazatlan*: JOSE HAMPL, EMMA HAMPL, and two children MARGARITA and MARTA; ANNIE SATTLER. (Margarita married German baron.)

April 28, 1892, by steamer *Mazatlan*: JAMES GLARDON; LOTTIE GLARDON; LIZZIE EVERSON GLARDON; ROBERT HOUGE; NICHOLAS MURPHY; HARVEY J. HOBBS; HARVEY MOORE; GRACE G. MOORE; CHARLES W. MOORE; ANNA C. MOORE and four children.

By steamer *Mazatlan*, May 29, 1892: NIELS C. DAHL, LOUIS ROBERTSON (DAD), LEROY F. AUSTIN, JONAS GAMALIELSON and PETHER JOHN REHN. (Mr. Dahl was Chicago friend of Louis Robertson, only down to visit.) MRS. HICKS joined her son, Mr. Wadhams.

FALL PARTY OF 1892

J. H. BUTLER.
S. H. KIMBALL.
T. HANKS.
COLONEL EDWARD DANIELS (returned).
JOHN HALES, wife LYDIA.
L. D. SCOTT, wife MARY C., children OLA, OSCAR, FRANK, and RAY.
HERSCHEL M. HEILIG, wife ANNIE.
AIME HELIOT, MRS LOUISA HELIOT, children ELMER, CLARA, LOUIS, MATTIE, and LEON.
WESLEY MAULDLIN, wife IDA L., children NANCY, WILLIE, and ROY.
PATRICE CHAUDET and MRS. M. CHAUDET.
WILLIAM BRIAN, wife ELIZA, children MARY E., ANNIE J. (Sattler), GEORGE E., CAROLINE, and LILLIE.
MRS. F. A. WHEELER (school teacher from Colorado), children MAUDE L., ERNEST, IRENE, and LUCIUS.
SUMNER BANCROFT, MRS. M. A. D. BANCROFT, OWEN, ALBERTINA, and O. N. BANCROFT.
M. R. SMELTZER.
MISS ELEANOR GIBSON (artist and sculptor friend of Marie Howland. Married William Cotter).
GEORGE HOEPPNER (young German).
HENRY WISE (young Russian).
DR. EMIL H. KLUBER, wife MARIE, daughter ADELAIDE, (son EDMUND KLUBER arrived after 1900).
ELIAS SLOAT.
W. A. MCKENZIE (returned).
H. W. DAVIS, MRS. A. A. DAVIS.
MRS. M. J. VAN DYKE and three children (joining husband).
MARSHALL F. DAVIS.
JOHN BAUMANN (a miller).
IRA SOUTH.

[141]

IRA E. CORPE.
THOS. STRAIN.
E. J. THORNTON (returned).
CHARLIE BLUMBERG.
ROBERT DUFF, living at Yecorato,
Sinaloa (copper mining area).

PROFESSOR GILBERT E. BAILEY, lec-
turer from northwestern U. S.,
visited Batopilas Mine in
mountains east of colony and
came to colony.

1893

March 1, 1893: CHARLES A. BAIL-
EY, piano tuner from Los An-
geles, California, visitor to
colony.
April 15, 1893, by the schooner
Ahome, arrived March 6th:
ROBERT J. KENDALL, wife
FLORENCE, and son GEORGE
(WILLIE KENDALL born later).
DR. S. A. MERRILL (poet).
F. J. and FENNA DUINTZIN-
GER (Holland).
J. H. SHARMAN.
H. A. HART (Treasurer of
Kansas Sinaloa Investment
Company), brother of Rose
Hart Bunker Whitzel and of
Sadie Hart Miller, both in
colony.
March 25, 1893, by steamer *Cor-
sario*:
DR. JESSE W. MOORMAN,
ANNIE MOORMAN, JESSIE V.
MOORMAN.
HENRY C. KORFHAGE, wife
MARY, sons HENRY W. and
HUGO (it is not clear whether
Hugo Korfhage came before
above date).
CLARENCE FOREMAN (friend of
Bragg family).
WILLIE STEWART, Fort Mad-
ison, Iowa.
May 27, 1893, by steamer *Rio
Yaqui*:
ALBERT K. OWEN, DR. B. A.
WHEELER, Denver, Colorado.
MICHAEL FLURSCHIEM, Lu-
gano, Switzerland.
C. B. HOFFMAN, WALTER C.

HOFFMAN, Enterprise, Kansas.
MARTHA BETHUNE JONES
(Derrill Hope), Norcross, Va.
BRAGG family consisting of
WILLIAM F., NANNIE E., AR-
THUR V., BLANCHE P., and
RUBY, from Eureka Springs,
Arkansas.
DOUGLAS family consisting of
ROBERT J., NELLIE A., VERA,
and RAY, from Raton, New
Mexico.
HERMAN A. FARLEY, Law-
rence, Kansas.
HENRY SHELDON, New York.
CLARENCE E. FOREMAN, Green
Forest, Kansas.
CARL ZWICKER, Kansas.
At Agua Caliente de Vaca, for
over 20 years before begin-
ning of colony, WILLIAM V.
LAMPHAR, large *hacendado*,
with Mexican wife and large
family, very friendly and
helpful to the colony.
At Fuerte, DR. HUBBARD, who
came many years before the
colonists, had Mexican wife
and many grown daughters,
very friendly to the colony.
Born at Topolobampo, October 23,
1893, a son (Willie) to Mr.
and Mrs. R. J. KENDALL.
At Engineer Farm, October 27,
1893, a daughter was born to
Mr. and Mrs. J. J. HALLAN.
R. M. SANDYS, chief engineer of El
Aguila sugar mill, Englishman, 40 years of age, died,
October 15, 1893.

THE OCTOBER PARTY

Arrived by steamer *Rio Yaqui*, November 3, 1893:

WELLER EMERICK, LOUIS KRESS, MARY E. THIRSK and children GUY and VINCENT (to rejoin family).

FRANK D. THOMPSON, wife IDA KORFHAGE THOMPSON, their children BLANCHE N., NOEL W.

MRS. MARY KORFHAGE and children LAWRENCE W., ONA W., FLORA L. (joining family in colony).

ALVA D. PRESTON, MARY E. PRESTON, children MARIE E., EMILY ROENA (Hays), FLOYD, CECIL.

By steamer *Romero Rubio*, November 11, 1893:

PROF. J. H. KERR of Mexico City (friend of Owen).

W. M. BRODIE and GILBERT GEISELHART of Batopilas.

By steamer *Corsario*:
OTTO E. SALZMAN.
HERBERT E. GARCKEN.
WILLIAM CHALMERS.
GEORGE H. BRIGGS, wife, and child.

March 15, 1893: J. P. WILLIAMS, THOS. T. REDDING, and J. CLAUSSON.

April 16, 1893: WALTER H. GIBSON and wife EFFIE M., a young couple from Tampa, Florida; on steamer *Carmen*: C. GOFF, carpenter from Denver, Colorado; ROBERT REID, a Florida nurseryman, sent many seeds and plants to the colony; H. MORGAN.

1894

Born at Topolobampo, January 25, 1894, a daughter, to MR. and MRS. J. S. SHOOP.

March 5, 1894, Overland (Kneeland) Party:
GEORGE S. KNEELAND, wife MARY E. M., son IRA D., daughters ALTHEA M., FLORA I., CLARISSA A.
JOHN C. STODDARD.
JOHN WETTENGEL, EARL WETTENGEL.
GEORGE D. (Dal) THOMPSON.

Up to March 5, 1894, a total of 1189 persons reported to have come to the colony, probably a good number not reported.

The May Party of 1894, by steamer *Carmen*, May 18th:
FRANK LINDEMAN.
JOHN KRESS.
GUSTAV THUMM.
CHAS. M. BROWN.
CARL MUELENTHAL.
WALTER HAGUE.
MILFORD B. HUTCHINSON and MRS. MAMIE HUTCHINSON.
MRS. MAY GARRISON, ANNIE E., JENNIE, LYN, and WILLIAM

FULLERTON GARRISON.
MRS. ANNA REED, IDA, and BESSIE MARIE REED.
MARTIN R. GWYNN, JOHN GWYNN, JR., S. A. GWYNN, MARIE CAROLINE, and MARJIEKO GWYNN.

Departed, NEWELL THURSTIN and wife, the song writer, for Hope, Dickinson County, Kansas, expecting to return.

[143]

1895

Born, at the Farm, March 1, 1895, a daughter, to Mr. and Mrs. F. D. THOMPSON.

March 8, 1895, Overland Party escorted by C. S. Hammond, colonist: MR. and MRS. MILO C. DAVIS, and four children, from North Platte, Nebraska; LOUIS WETZLER, Denver, Colo.

Topolobampo Pioneer Songs

I DREAM OF A CITY*

by

CYRUS M. STANLEY (1886)

In a beautiful land, as I dream
Is a palace and city, all new.
Prophetical vision! I deem
This mystical city most true.

CHORUS

Home of the free! Home of the free!
This beautiful land by the sea;
Home of the free! Home of the free!
This beautiful land by the sea.

2ND VERSE

From dream land, O city, arise!
For shadows, the substance must be;
And he who has faith and who tries
This beautiful city will see.

3RD VERSE

The noblest of cities we'll build
In the sunset land of the west
As our brothers and sisters have will
For a weary haven of rest.

4TH VERSE

Behold, the grand work is before us;
Come with us who wish to be free.
We'll join our glad voices in chorus
And build our sweet homes by the sea.

* Printed Sept. 1, 1891

[145]

"I DREAM OF A CITY."

Words and Music by C. M. STANLEY.

Allegretto.

1. In a beau - ti - ful land, as I dream, Is a pal - ace and ci - ty all new. Pro-phet - ic - al vis - ion!—I deem This mys - tic - al - ci - ty most true....
2. From dreamland, O ci - ty, a - rise. For shadows the substance must be, And he who has faith and who tries.... This beau - ti - ful ci - ty will see......
3. The no - blest of cit - ies we'll build In the sun - set land of the west, As our sis - ters and broth-ers have willed, For the wea - ry a ha - ven of rest.....
4. Be - hold the grand work is be - fore us, Come with us who wish to be free, We'll join our glad voi - ces in cho - rus, And build our sweet homes by the sea......

CHORUS.

Home of the free, home of the free, This
beau-ti-ful land by the sea, Home of the free,
home of the free. In this beau-ti-ful land by the sea.

IT WAS THREE YEARS AGO*
by
NEWELL THURSTIN (1891)

Tune: *"My Mother's Bible"*

It was three years ago and more, that we to Topo came
And landed on its beauteous shore, and camped upon the same.
We left our friends and homes behind, and struck for weal or woe,
To build new homes in foreign lands, 'way down in Mexico.

CHORUS

Our noble leader, Owen brave, we know that he is true.
We trusted him to lead us on, to homes in Mexico!

2ND VERSE

We've worked and toiled there weary years, in sunshine and in rain;
We've suffered disappointment oft, but tried anew again;
But now we see our morning star, arising in the east
We'll take new hope and still work on, and do our very best.

3RD VERSE

Cooperation is our theme, and we shall win the fight
'Gainst Competition's selfish greed, for we are in the right.
With justice for our motto true, we win the heart of each
Who love the golden rule full well, and practice what they preach.

4TH VERSE

Our land is rich, our waters pure, our air salubrious;
Our climate is the best on earth, our sunshine glorious.
With mountain, plain, and valleys grand, and bays and rivers bright,
With many a mile of wave-worn coast, foaming with silvery light.

5TH VERSE

With such advantages as these, why should we not succeed
If we but work in harmony, and not in selfish greed.
If in our workshops and our mills, we work with proper skill
Our orchards, farms and gardens too, and every station fill.

6TH VERSE

And when our steamships plow the seas, and railroads span the land
Then we shall reap the rich reward, a civilization grand.
Then to all people we shall be, a bright and shining light—
A good example—a morning star, to guide them in the right.

* Printed Sept. 15, 1891

CORN AND WINE*
by
GEORGE TAPPAN (1891)

Tune: *"Beulahland"*

I've reached the land of corn and wine, where toil's results are
fully mine
Where endless summer's verdant day, keeps winter's storms and
frosts away.

CHORUS

O, Summerland, bright sunny land, as on this favored spot I stand,
This garden land beside the sea, the modern Eden seems to be
And here on Topolobampo's shore, let Justice reign forevermore.

2ND VERSE

Here noble men and women come, to mold their toil in happy homes
Where free from competition's strife, we'll live a happy, prosperous
life.

3RD VERSE

My fellows come and toil with me, in no driven strife engaged
are we,
Secure from all the robber clan, through Co-operation's glorious
plan.

* Printed Oct. 1, 1891

TOPO-LO-BAMPO BAY

By Lon Hoding

Be-yond the lof-ty peaks of snow, in the sun-ny

land of Mex-i-co where pur-est, sweet-est wa-ters

flow, a-down a love-ly bay — in a valley

where the flow-ers blow and make per-pet-ual May.

CHORUS.

Oh! To-po-lo-bam-po, beau-ti-ful ev-er as

May, the sweet-est place, up-on earth's face, is

To-po-lo-bam-po Bay——!

TOPO-LO-BAMPO BAY*
by
Lon Hoding (1889)

Beyond the lofty peaks of snow, in the sunny land of Mexico
Where purest, sweetest water flows, adown a lovely bay,
In a valley where the flowers blow and make perpetual May.

CHORUS

Oh! Topo-lo-bampo, beautiful ever as May,
The sweetest place, upon earth's face, is Topo-lo-bampo Bay!

2ND VERSE

There government is on a plan, that pleads man's duty unto man,
And tolerates no selfish clan, upon its fertile soil;
And there no modern Shylock can demand the fruits of toil.

3RD VERSE

In our broad land we once could boast, it was the home of Freedom's
host,
The toilers are complaining most, that schemers get their pay
And many a heart sighs for the coast of Topo-lo-bampo Bay.

4TH VERSE

You who obey humane commands, who toil with willing hearts
and hands
Who see your cherished homes and lands, by mortgage swept away,
Go dwell upon the golden sands, O Topo-lo-bampo Bay.

* Printed Oct. 15, 1889

MEXICO*

Warm is the morning light, the sunset glow
That gilds thy mountains as the seasons flow
Like to some blissful dream they thrill me so
    O! Mexico—My charming Mexico.

Perpetual springtime clothes thy hills with green
Perpetual summer tints them with its sheen
Perpetual harvest decks the living scene
    O! Mexico—My lovely Mexico.

* Printed March 15, 1892

THE LAND OF PROMISE
by
NEWELL THURSTIN

Tune: *"John Brown's Body"*

I have reached the land of promise, where the grand Fuerte flows
Where the orange, lime, and lemon and the rich banana grows;
Where the guava and the pomegranate, with the sweetest roses blow,
In the land of Mexico.

CHORUS

O! How happy in this land are we
May there always peace and plenty be
Just and pure may we always be
In our City by the Sea.

2ND VERSE

We will plant our vine and fig tree, grow our cotton, corn and cane
Draw pure water from the river, not depend alone on rain.
We will dig the mighty mountains for the ore that they contain
As we go marching on.

3RD VERSE

We will band the land with iron, from Topolobampo's shore
To the summit of the Madres where is hid the shining ore
We will cross the purple pampas to the Rio Grande shore
As we go marching on.

4TH VERSE

We shall build a model city in this bright and sunny land
And a commonwealth where Justice, may be seen on every hand,
Where our happy sons and daughters, shall unite in Hymen's bands
In our City by the Sea.

PARODY, later:

"We'll hang A. K. Owen to a catwood tree, we'll hang A. K. Owen
    to a catwood tree, we'll hang A. K. Owen to a catwood tree,
As we go marching on."

UP TO THE WORK BRIGHT AND EARLY
by
NEWELL THURSTIN (1891)

Tune: *"Nora Darling"*

Let us on with the Ditch to the Mochis
And to work with spirit and a will
Push the work through the cool months of winter
And work in any station we can fill.

CHORUS

Then up to the work bright and early
Let no time idly pass us all the day
And until the water flows
And onward gurgling goes
From the river, o'er the Mochis, to the Bay.

2ND VERSE

Let us work for our homes of the future
Where want, gaunt and hungry, ne'er shall come
Where the landlord and the sheriff never enter
To drive us from our bright and happy homes.

3RD VERSE

Let us try to be just to our comrades,
With a charity and love kind and true;
Let cooperation be our watchword
And mighty is the work we can do.

PART II

Memories of Sinaloa

CHAPTER I

Don Luisito

IT OCCURS to me as I write this that a life of rugged hardship is not such a bad prescription for attaining a great age. Lajos Michael Amadeus Proschowski in Danish—*Don Luisito* to his friends in Mexico—Dad to me—is celebrating his 82nd birthday today by working in his garden and going fishing on our little lake.

Into Topolobampo Bay in Sinaloa in the spring of 1892, on the schooner *Mazatlan* came a roving young Danish sailor named Louis Robertson, a short husky fellow of twenty-nine years, dark haired, with red mustaches adorning friendly features.

There is in the family a portrait of a handsome, bold, aristocratic, cheery looking gentleman of middle age, wearing a fine wig tied with a ribbon, a velvet jacket trimmed with lace on the collar and cuffs, the jacket giving the appearance of having a light coat of mail underneath. This gentleman was Count and Colonel Proschowski of Poland. There is also his coat of arms—a shield surmounted by the horns of a stag.

It is said that this sire of ours, my great-great-grandfather, was of the Greek Catholic faith, was a born reformer, despite his title, and that he was forcibly removed from the Polish scene in the backwash of a revolution—unsuccessful—for the purpose of changing the monarchy to a republic.

The next generation of the family grew up in Hungary and became Lutherans, then as the aftermath of another revolution—too soon to form a republic of Hungary, my grandfather moved to Denmark, where he seemed to have settled down to a wholesale trade in woolens and the manufacture of uniforms for the officers of the King, while fathering a family of nine children. However, after having this sizable venture well advanced, he left the business and family for awhile to fight for Hungary against the Austrians.

[157]

An early recollection of Dad's is walking with his father through the King's garden and palace on a visit, for some unknown purpose, with the King.

A later recollection is of poaching in the King's private fishing preserve, which, knowing Dad's insatiable love for fishing, is easy to believe.

An older brother, Heinrich, was physician to the King.

Dad's mother, Cecelia Coyet, was said to have been a daughter of a French staff officer of the Prince Bernadotte whom Napoleon made Emperor of Sweden, and to have been a lady in waiting to the Swedish queen.

The Proschowski family were raised in the Danish Lutheran faith, and given an education as professional people—two doctors, some musicians—until the time when Dad was thirteen years of age—then suddenly the family fortunes collapsed by reason of grandfather Proschowski going security for some cargo lost at sea. Dad, together with an older brother, Robert, and younger brother, Frantz, then decided to leave home to avoid being a further burden to the family.

Frantz Proschowski, through savings from hard physical labor, educated himself in art and music to become a world-famous voice master, rating among his pupils such singers as Amelita Galli-Curci, Tito Scipa, Paul Robeson, Virginia Rae, and Elizabeth Lennox.

Some English sea captain objected to having to use the name Proschowski for young "Louie" so changed it to Robertson on his shipping papers—and here we are, the Robertsons. The young Lajos—Louis—sailed the seven seas for seven years, as it were, adding one for good measure, during this time rounding the Horn four times, working aloft in the rigging with icicles covering his beard.

He learned splicing, tackle work, sail making, carpentry, a bit of navigation, and a lot of accordion playing, and ended up with a second mate's license.

In company with a long-time Swedish buddy, Otto Carlborg, he became operator of a trading sloop in the West Indies, with a black crew. For nearly three years—very pleasant years—the boys moved about among the islands, buying principally coffee and bananas in exchange for trade goods and cash. It is my impression that there was a bit of smuggling to avoid local tax on coffee, the native "boys" carrying out the coffee sacks on their heads in the dark of the night to the sloop anchored shoulder deep offshore.

Otto played a violin, Louis the accordion or guitar. They were often taken on mule back inland to play for native dances, sometimes witnessing the native "voodoo" performances. These trips inland gave the boys excellent opportunities for trading.

Eventually tiring of this, Dad landed in New York on his way to explore the United States. Having been told by someone that Arkansas was the wildest part, he took the train for there.

For two happy years he turned trapper, fisherman, and logger on Black River in company with an ex-Civil War veteran named Al who was a keen woodsman and crack shot.

Their furs and fish they sold in St. Louis, Missouri.

They lived in a little cabin high up in some huge cypress trees, their boat fastened with a long hitch for times when the river rose twenty to thirty feet overnight.

They worked like beavers getting out oak ties for the railroad. The tie inspector, despite their best efforts to deliver perfect ties, condemned about every fourth tie, which, however, was taken and used by the company.

Burning with resentment, the partners figured how to get even—they took a contract for cutting log piling, and delivered a lot of *tupelo* gum that could not be told from black oak. It cut several times as fast, and lasted until it went to pithy pieces in not so long a time.

From there Dad got a job as canoe man running logs downstream for building bridges. He presently showed the bridge foreman how to rig his tackle to do a lot quicker job, and so was made rigger at double wages.

With several hundred dollars savings, he went to Danish friends near Lake Geneva, Wisconsin. Soon he was embarked on a dairy business, working almost all the hours of the night and day, one task being hauling of milk by sleigh through all sorts of weather to a depot for delivery to the city.

About three years of this persuaded him of the advantages of a warmer clime. A friend, Niels Dahl, having heard of the cooperative colony at Topolobampo on the Gulf of California, conferred with Dad. Dad sold his business, stopped in Chicago for awhile to work on the planting of trees for the

World's Fair then in the making, and so with Dahl on to Mexico.

At Guaymas Dad found that ruddy, blue-eyed little Captain Robinson of the *Mazatlan* was in need of a quartermaster, and shipped, with the agreement he should drop off the ship, which traded from port to port, upon its arrival at Topolobampo. Dahl also was employed for the trip.

After touching at various ports, including the beautiful Bahia de Los Angeles in the upper Gulf, they arrived at Topolobampo.

Dahl returned north, but the activity of building the Los Tastes Canal for the American colony appealed to Dad, and he worked on the ditch until its completion, turning in some six hundred dollars savings to the fund for the ditch building, in exchange receiving Improvement Fund Script.

Dad was short on theory and long on action. When the blowup came between the "Saints" and "Kickers," he reasoned that there wasn't much prospect for a group that kept so many specialists and so few workers. "There was one fellow with a long sounding title at Topolobampo," said he, "whose only job for a whole week was butchering two or three turtles, still he was paid three dollars a day in script for holding his job."

So Dad became a "Kicker," yet never a violent one; he chose a twenty-acre block, cleared ten acres himself, trading his old accordion and some lessons to a Mayo Indian for clearing the other ten. In the division of chattels among the colonists he got a team, wagon, and plow, and soon he had planted corn, beans, and melons on his little farm.

He and some of the others were so hard up that they ate as the Indians did the *pitahaya* cactus fruit in its late spring season, and the toasted *mescal* heads, as they are before being mashed to distill for the *mescal* drink. No doubt he shared in the division of beef from cattle that were not contented except in the colonists' fields.

He soon made some interesting friends among the young single men: George Beck, a young, tall, and gangling cowboy from Oklahoma; Charley Morgan, a tall young timber man from Wisconsin; Charley Lockwood, his nearest neighbor, a college graduate and a "fine fellow"; Charley Bair, Dad's partner for a while, was a "Suthener" from Louisiana.

Tall and handsome, quite the lady's man—not born to work —Bair's parents were said to have sent him down to the colony to get a problem off their minds—but for all that, as Dad puts it, he was a "mighty fine fellow."

The Yaqui Irrigating Canal System begun by Don Carlos Conant by 1894 was going forward rapidly, with Colonel E. S. Nettleton, former Chief Engineer of the United States Department of Agriculture, in charge. Surveys were being run, canals dug, and land cleared. They had 500,000 acres of land purchased, or under contract to deliver water for.

These young bachelors, including Dad, went with their teams overland about 175 miles to the Yaqui and soon were employed.

From there most of them drifted north. Charley Lockwood moved southward, finally engaging in the banana business in British Honduras. Charley Morgan and Dad were on a survey crew together; Morgan learned surveying and remained in the Yaqui Valley to practice it for probably fifty years, marrying a Mexican *señorita* and raising a family there.

Winters, a colonist, ran the survey; two colonists, Hunter and Koebitsch, the former colony shoemaker, were chainmen. Hunter was city bred, got lost as surely as he stepped a few yards into the woods.

Fortunately they employed a Yaqui Indian, Loreto, who would track Hunter and return him to camp at almost consistent intervals.

Dad's work was camp boss; hustling wood, water, food for men, and feed for animals. He relates that as helper he had a youngster of sixteen years, Sam Spence, whose father had been a policeman in the United States.

Young Spence was a shark at poker, kept the older fellows broke all their time on the survey—except Dad, who doesn't care for cards.

Wherever Dad has been he has fished—and successfully. From their survey camp he sometimes got away for some fishing in the Yaqui River. The woods were infested with wild hogs—*jabalies*. One day returning from fishing he was surrounded by hogs and forced to climb a mesquite tree.

Tiring of sitting idly in the tree, he fixed a hook firmly to the end of a branch trimmed from the mesquite tree, and hooked himself a young porker, which he took to camp for roasting—that is, when the *jabalies* finally tired of waiting for him and drifted away from his tree.

On another occasion when he was bothered by coyotes stealing food from their survey camp at night, he hung up some pieces of venison, first one within easy reach, then another where the coyote must make a slight leap to secure the meat, finally a piece still higher into which was inserted his biggest fishhook attached by a wire to the overhanging limb of a tree.

That night there was suddenly heard the most terrific yowling and howling from a coyote suspended from the hook, an animated ball of agony. There was no more stealing from camp for some time.

Those were troublesome times with the Yaquis. Ranches and even settlements were often raided, and several Americans were killed during the years that followed.

The survey party always left food at their camps when they moved. They fed any Indians who visited camp. They seldom saw Indians, but their Yaqui, Loreto, a splendid woodsman and an able Indian, evidently visited with his people, and gave good reports, as they were never disturbed.

Later Dad was sent down the Yaqui River in a boat to explore its channels into the Gulf and report on possibilities for navigation.

After working for two years on the Yaqui he saved a stake, and engaged passage on the small sloop *Elena* down the Yaqui River to Topolobampo.

The night they left there was a *fiesta* which the Yaqui Captain Flores of the sloop would not forego, so that it was finally a black midnight, with a contrary wind and a falling tide, when they set sail down the shallow winding Yaqui River channel, with their Yaqui captain rolling drunk, sitting on a hatch and singing the old favorite of Sonora—

> *Tu eres mi paloma blanca,*
> *Yo soy tu pichon azul;*
> *Quiereme con tu piquito*
> *Y haremos tu-curru-cu-cu.*

Home of Mr. and Mrs. Herbert Patrick at La Logia. Mr. Patrick labored hard, became colony mail man, also transporting produce and passengers by wagon from Vegaton, Sufragio, La Logia and Topolobampo. He was mysteriously murdered at Laguna Camajoa, a sad event in the colony.

Miller JOHN BAUMAN with ox "Old Berry" used on treadmill for grinding grain.

You are my white dove,
I am your blue pigeon;
Caress me with your little bill
And we shall sing tu-curru-cu-cu.

Taking the helm and posting a Yaqui sailor in the bow with a long pole to sound the channel, Dad tacked through the black night down the stream, listening to the leadman— *"braza y media"*—fathom and a half—*"una braza"*—one fathom—*"y cabeza"*—duck your head—as over went the boom on the other tack—and so out over the bar with the little sloop, and down the coast with a fair breeze bound for Topolobampo.

Soon after the return of Dad from the Yaqui River he married Bessie Bunker, who had separated from Rolla Schellhous, with two children Amelia and Arcie, and built on his twenty acres a little cabin with walls of *echo* trunks hewn by adze— where I was born in November, 1897.

Together with colonists George Drake, Fess Ward, Julius Eckhart, and others, he found work at *El Aquila* sugar mill of Johnston and Ochoa.

My earliest memory is of standing in the mill yard to watch a red-blanketed Mayo Indian gateman swing wide two huge wooden doors to admit the yokes of oxen, two yokes— four oxen—hauling in the great high-wheeled *carretas* loaded with sugar cane for grinding.

Dad was a tremendous worker. He moved through a variety of jobs—carpenter's helper, rigger for setting up the smokestack for the mill, corral boss (a rare job for a sailor), then to open the first farming land for Johnston at Mochis, and so on up to Field Superintendent in the years that followed.

CHAPTER II

Uncle Bill

"Guillermo Loco"

IF, AS SOME of my friends of old Mexico used to tell me, good old *San Pedro* has through the long ages been keeping a faithful record of the deeds of the inhabitants of this strange world in order to determine the time and order of their ascendance into Heaven, the old Saint must have a rare collection of records.

To be sure, the chronicles most to be admired must be those of the straight-laced, strong-willed, meek-spirited souls who are supposed to inherit the earth.

I cannot, however, put aside a suspicion, more, a hope, that after giving proper credit to those meritorious in the eyes of Heaven, he has sometimes relaxed from his labors to pick up the tale of some character so different that the old Saint might well be betrayed into an appreciative chuckle, and now and then the arching of an eyebrow, and that perhaps he has even given the day of such a tale a special mark on his calendar.

Many and many a time might the old Saint have returned to the chronicle of my Uncle Bill. Perhaps the color of his life was helped by its time and circumstances, but Uncle Bill would have given color to any time or set of circumstances.

Let us see him together, as I first recall him down in Sinaloa in the years soon after the turn of 1900—a handsome upright six-foot figure, sitting a fine chestnut sorrel horse— always moving briskly, usually humming a snatch of an Indian, Spanish, or English song—this in a meditative sort of way—an alert meditation that one soon knew could swiftly turn to action.

Looking from the top down, a straw *sombrero* molded in the native cowboy style surmounted a face of ruddy tan; blue eyes, keen and sharp; rather bushy eyebrows, a heavy dark red mustache, widespread in the fashion of the day, a strong chin; an expression between humor and determination.

He would be dressed in a blue denim shirt and well-tailored denim trousers—astride a Mexican saddle, with leather saddlebags that held always a canvas moneybag, his Colts .45, and a red bandana tied full of native *macucho* tobacco and the softest cornhusks, the "makings" for the native cigarette.

On the horse would be a bridle with some silver ornament, suspended from the saddlehorn a riata, thrown over the saddle a pair of *armas*—long leather guards, a half hide of leather on either side, that serve as chaps for the woods of Sinaloa.

Before we could complete this inspection Uncle Bill would be launched on an interesting story, probably rerolling his long cornhusk *cigarro*, one spurred leg thrown over the saddlehorn, or dismounting to loosen and shake the saddle to ease the horse.

In the course of our story he first appears in "Credit Foncier Notes," January 15, 1892: "Little Willie Bunker is working on the ditch."

Big and strong for his twelve years when he arrived in the colony that year with his mother and sisters whom he must help support, he drove a team of horses, loaded dirt scrapers and dumped them like the big fellows—and throve on the work.

When his mother married Grandfather Whitzel he moved into the new family circle very briefly. By this time he had acquired a native saddle pony, which Grandfather loaned to a fellow colonist for a trip to Fuerte without asking permission of young Bill. When the pony was returned gaunt and saddle-sore there was a stubborn argument, and the boy simply moved out, never to return as a member of the family, although he kept friendly relations and was a frequent visitor with his people.

Young Bill first worked at the Scally *panocha* mill for $12.00 (*pesos*) a month and his board, which was mostly cornmeal mush, cornbread, beans, pumpkin, and molasses from the mill. He roomed with several bachelor workers, among them several young Americans. Also there was a rare personality named Butterfield, and old white-bearded John Budlong, who had walked overland many years before with the Burr and Friend families from California.

Budlong was a master mechanic, and the only person who knew thoroughly the operation of the mill. He and the

Scally family were confirmed spiritualists, as were my mother, grandmother and other colonists. Many a discussion was had at the family table tending to prove the return of souls to earth from the spirit world. Budlong insisted to all that after death he would return with messages that could not be mistaken.

The old gentleman did soon die, at a most inopportune time when some machinery was being installed that only he understood how to put together.

Operations were halted, the mill owners in a quandary. Butterfield, a shrewd fellow, studied diligently over the machinery until he knew the answers. At breakfast he related that Budlong the night before had appeared before him in a dream; had described to him just how to proceed to put together the machinery. The family and their young boarders were profoundly impressed as Butterfield, repeating the instructions from the departed spirit, completed the installation.

Pleased with his success as an interpreter of the spirit of Budlong, Butterfield filled the young boys with more stories of the evidences of contacts with spirits. To pass away the evenings the boys played cards in a room which Budlong had planned for storage of molasses, and which had a drain line from its floor through to another room.

One evening Butterfield spoke through the tube from the next room to the assembled card players, imitating the voice of Budlong. "Boys, I've come back! It's me, Budlong, boys! Can't you see me?" The kerosene lamp, cards, and table went flying in all directions, as the boys leapt for the one door.

However, the practical joker suffered one against him that possibly offset all he had done to others. In the United States he had married a girl against the will of her wealthy parents. Wishing to get some of their money, Butterfield and his wife planned a divorce and remarriage after the wife had been given her patrimony. Imagine his embarrassment when, after receiving a substantial sum, she married another fellow.

Of his meager earnings during those first years, and always after, Uncle Bill gave a substantial portion to his mother.

Working at laborer's wages among the Mexicans and Indians, he learned to live as cheaply as they, and he learned their every characteristic, every custom, every superstition. He soon spoke Spanish like a Mexican and Mayo like an Indian. He was full of fun and full of business, both traits admired by the natives, and was soon welcomed everywhere among them.

When he was fifteen, together with several other colonists he left the colony to find work at higher wages on the Yaqui River canal in Sonora. They crossed the Fuerte River with a team of mules and a light wagon, by nightfall were several miles into the woods when they were overtaken by a violent rainstorm.

The men, leaving young Bill to guard the wagon, walked on to find shelter at a ranch ahead. Thoroughly soaked and chilled, and uneasy at being left alone, Bill turned the mules loose to care for themselves, took his big six-shooter in his hand, and started back towards the river. He had to take off his shoes to feel for the wagon track with his bare feet, as he groped his way through the pitch darkness, unrelieved except for an occasional flash of lightning.

Suddenly his head hit against something indescribable—which let out an unearthly shriek, followed by a lot of cackling and flopping of wings. Bill, terrified, sank low to his knees, fired his revolver, turned, and fled, finally finding the wagon and crouching under its wet shelter for the long night.

At first daybreak he started again for the river in search of his mules. At the scene of his escapade of the night before he found several chickens tied by their feet, and a pole on which they had been carried, suspended from either end, over a man's shoulder.

At the river crossing he was relieved to find his mules in a corral next to an Indian house. Upon a bed on the porch, covered with a blanket, an Indian lay moaning piteously.

"What is wrong with that man?" asked Bill.

"A terrible thing happened to him," he was told. "While he was on his way through the woods to the next ranch last night with a load of chickens, the rain caught him. It was so dark that he had to feel his way along by the wagon track. Then he suddenly met *el diablo*, who tried to kill him. He ran away into the woods and was lost until this morning."

The shock of that night was the cause (Uncle Bill insisted) of his hair turning gray before he was twenty years of age.

From the Yaqui River he went north of Guaymas to work

on the railroad. The American construction foreman soon made him assistant for the handling of his Yaqui Indian laborers.

On paydays he acted as interpreter. One payday there was a mixup in which a big Yaqui who had a small amount due was given the cash that should have gone to the man next after him on the list. The Yaqui moved away with his money. When the next man protested being short, young Bill called the big Yaqui back and asked the return of the money. The Yaqui did return the money, but told Bill he would suffer the consequences.

Bill moved north again to Minas Preitas, where he soon had a job going out on the ranches to buy cattle for the commissary at the mine. On one of these trips, coming down a mountain trail, rounding a shoulder of rocky hillside he suddenly met the big Yaqui, face to face and about ten steps away. The Yaqui reached for his knife and moved towards Bill. By chance unarmed, Bill in desperation stooped quickly, lifted a rock that filled his two hands, and as the Yaqui lunged with the knife he flung the rock from overhead full into the Indian's face, then leapt upon him as the Indian hit the ground, beating him into unconsciousness.

He never knew whether the Indian lived or died; it was simply a question of self-defense for survival. Bill returned to the mine, drew his pay, and took a freight train for the border at Nogales. With him went Elmer King, a friend from the colony.

He recalled that on the way he got into a poker game with the train crew and won what money they had along, so that on crossing the border he decided on a room in a hotel for him and Elmer, and a new outfit of clothes.

The hotel had something neither of them had seen before —inside toilets. Elmer gave them one look, said they were too darn nice to be used, and walked all the way out of town.

From Nogales they moved on to the mining camp of Patagonia, where they found a judge holding circuit court. The case being tried was cattle rustling. Some "bad actor" living nearby was on trial, but failed to appear. Looking about him, the judge saw Bill, now seventeen and husky. "Here, kid," said the judge, "put on this badge and a gun, go over the hill to the next ranch, and bring that rustler in."

Not at all happy, Bill mounted a horse and rode away. Near the ranch he met a cowpuncher, arrested him, and took him protesting to the judge, who, disgusted with his new

deputy, turned the cowboy loose as being the wrong man. That move relieved Bill of further service.

The year was dry, cattle were dying, ranchers were in hard circumstances, men were tramping the railroad ties looking for food and work. Railroad camps finally refused handouts—the going was tough.

At one camp the boys found a table all set, with big fresh-baked biscuits, jars of jam being set out to go with the biscuits. The darkey cook was friendly but firm. Retiring to plan their strategy, the boys came back and engaged the cook in a heated argument about the relative abilities of the Negro fighter Sam Langford and Bob Fitzsimmons; Elmer continued the argument in the kitchen while Bill stuffed a lot of biscuits with jam, put them into his shirt, and walked off down the track.

Finally the boys got on as laborers on a construction crew under a foreman named Johnson. Here Uncle Bill made himself useful, soon becoming a favorite with foreman Johnson, likewise with the foreman's daughter, Mary. He really loved the girl and her family, in retrospect regretted that he returned to Mexico, both to accompany Elmer and to take money to his mother, and that, as often happens, circumstances moved him from one event to another so that he never returned.

A rare little story he told of his work on the railroad. He was with an engineer's survey party which moved from camp to camp. To keep in provisions the locating engineer sent Juanito, son of the Indian woman cook, to the nearest village to buy the provisions. Juanito's memory was lamentably bad. A list was of no use, for neither Juanito, nor probably the shopkeeper, could have read the note. One day in exasperation the engineer took from his pocket two *pesos*. "Juanito," said he, "here is one *peso*."—placing it firmly in the boy's hand, with fingers clasped on it—"With it I want you to buy a *peso's* worth of sugar. Now, Juanito," placing a *peso* in the other hand, "with this I want you to buy a *peso's* worth of coffee."

"*Si, señor*," said Juanito, mounting his burro, *pesos* clasped firmly in his hands, "with this a *peso* of sugar, with this a *peso* of coffee."

In a few moments he was seen returning on the burro down the woods path, *pesos* still clasped firmly in his hands.

"*Señor*," he apologized, "I just can't remember which *peso* was for the sugar and which for the coffee."

After his return to the colony, Bill spent some of the busiest years that a mortal could spend. Hiring Indian laborers, he cleared land on contract, dug canals on contract, cut and hauled sugar cane, burned and sold brick, cut and hauled timber, traded in horses and mules and cattle.

Matching wits with Johnston, he took a contract for brush clearing, to be given in payment a block of twenty acres where he chose. He selected the land where he knew a main canal must pass through, and finally worked out of the deal a sixty-acre farm of the best silt-covered land in the area, taking as a compliment Johnston's remark, "Damn you, Bill, you are the only man I have let get ahead of me in a deal."

While serving as Water Administrator he was given permission to keep his cattle in the vast fenced woods below the farming area. Envious of this situation, a chap named Angulo managed to get Bill's cattle ordered out and his cattle in. Biding his time, Bill spent a few moonlight nights catching Johnston calves and placing Angulo's earmark on them. Come roundup time when this situation was discovered, Angulo and his cattle were put out in short order, and Bill's cattle were allowed back in.

His knowledge of livestock was equal to his knowledge of people. His buying and selling put his brand on more stock than any in that whole river area.

He went everywhere, knew everyone, was as generous in lending help and money and good advice as he was keen in figuring his own deals—one of those characters so constituted that he made friends everywhere, and created trades and business from situations that ninety-nine other men would have regarded as barren of opportunity.

His favorite fun was hunting, horse racing, and playing cards. He accumulated humorous stories from real life, retelling them with a drama that drew a group to him wherever he "pitched his tent" for a little while.

One of his first ventures in horse racing became a legend in the community. Every Sunday by noon there gathered on the large "common" outside Mochis the horsemen—ranchers, ranch workers, cattlemen, everyone who owned or could borrow a horse, for the purpose of horseracing. Horses were matched and bets made on the spot, usually with much challenging discussion, and thus racing continued throughout the afternoon.

Uncle Bill laid plans for this. He brought over from Sinaloa River a horse unknown to the local racing group. For a week the horse ran in a pasture filled with cockleburrs, so that his mane and tail were matted—a disgraceful-appearing animal to a horseman of any pride.

He fitted on an old rawhide pack saddle, then hung some native baskets on each side, filled them with cheeses, and put an old Indian on the woeful-looking beast to attend the races and sell the cheeses. Not long after the racing began he tied into an argument with Don Santos Galaviz, owner of the most carefully-groomed horses in the vicinity. Bill was challenged, told to choose his steed for a race. Carelessly he said most any one would do. After eyeing a few, he asked the Indian selling cheeses if his plug could run. The Indian said he didn't know, he hadn't run the animal. "Well, that horse will do," said Uncle Bill, and the crowd gathered in for the kill. Those who hadn't enough money bet their horses, saddles, cattle, even chickens and pigs.

Bill took all bets, won the race "in a walk," and really collected, for he had carefully checked beforehand the speed of his horse with that of his opponent.

Full of fun, and mixing freely with all classes of people, he used his wit to make friends, not to anger people. He recalled an occasion when as a youngster he went to a dance in a village where he chanced to be staying over until next day. The village bully, fired up with *mescal*, was at the dance, and seemed to sense in Bill a challenge to his physical superiority. During a lull between dances the big fellow stepped dramatically to the center of the floor, waved his arms menacingly, and yelled, "If there's someone here who thinks he can whip me, I'm ready for a fight—I want a fight!"

Bill stepped up quickly beside him, exclaiming sympathetically, "Where is that so and so, I'll help you whip him!" The big bully eyed him questioningly for an instant, then laughed with him and the crowd, and throwing an arm over Bill's shoulder, said, "You're all right, little *gringo*, we will be friends!"

The mate of his earlier years was a remarkably handsome *señorita*, Felipa Alvarado, daughter of a poor middle-class family. This young woman was as energetic as he. She ran the household and a dairy, and assisted as she could his various enterprises.

There is a custom in Mexico, far more than with us, of relatives moving in on those who are thrifty—and how they do move in. Calls are extended to visits, and then to permanent residence, until there is no room at table, nor privacy in the home.

Uncle Bill's home presently bulged with Dona Felipa's relatives. He was generous and prosperous, and tolerated the situation for many years. However, on occasion he would rebel, and send one or another off in a hurry.

One old fellow, nicknamed *"El Trompa,"* was particularly indolent and most interminate in his visits. Finally resolved to be shed of the man, Uncle Bill routed him out early one morning, saying, "I have a horse saddled for you. I want you to take to Don Evaristo Mendoza a bull calf I sold him."

Grumblingly the lazy old fellow mounted the horse for the ride to the *hacienda* of Don Evaristo at San Miguel, fifteen miles away. The calf was half grown and strong, and fought his lead rope for most of a long day until they arrived. "Don Evaristo, I have spent the whole day dragging to you this calf that you bought from Don Guillermo."

Don Evaristo, wised to the plan beforehand, took a look at the calf, then responded indignantly, "You take that animal right back to Don Guillermo, and tell him he sent the wrong calf."

Cursing with indignation at Uncle Bill for his careless mistake, the weary cowboy—but not from choice—rode homeward with the calf, far into the night, awakening Bill from his slumber to recount his tale of woe.

"Never mind," said Bill, "by daylight we will have the right calf roped and ready for you to return with."

By morning the old bum had disappeared, and never returned.

A younger brother, Clyde Bunker, grew up in the community, learned Spanish, had many friends, courted a number of *señoritas* at intervals for years, played cards with the boys and consistently lost, finally drifted out to work in the United States, returning at intervals for vacations, staying with Bill until he lost his savings over friendly card games in the town.

Uncle Bill concluded this was no good, so next trip down engaged his brother in a card game before the town boys had a turn, won everything but the clothes he wore, then gave the winnings back to him, a bit at a time, to spend reasonably, until Clyde was ready to return north.

Uncle Clyde owned a fast-pacing little black pony that was a special pride—on this pony he made his calls on his latest heart throb, or for an evening of cards. One dark night while Clyde was engaged in a card game Uncle Bill reversed the saddle on the fast-stepping little pony, horn facing backwards, carefully hanging the bridle on the horse's tail and the reins over the horn. Clyde, who saw poorly at night anyway, innocently hung his tie rope to the saddle, mounted and set his spurs for a quick getaway—and landed in a somersault over the rear of the horse.

The tales of Uncle Bill are too many for a chapter. From

my early boyhood we were the best of friends and frequent companions, especially on trips hunting deer and peccary, and soon we were together in operating timber camps, buying cattle, and other interesting enterprises.

CHAPTER III

A Sinaloa Farm

OUR LITTLE FARM at Los Mochis, at first surrounded by woods, spread into wider fields with the passing years: fields of bright green alfalfa, of fine green rows of sugar cane, of winter vegetables for the markets of the United States.

It never lost that certain air of tranquillity of a farm in Mexico—the leisurely movement of time that comes with living in a tropical country—the plodding of oxen, the patient process of milking a native cow, the pat-pat of endless making of *tortillas* for the families of the ranch laborers— even the hens seemed to cluck-a-cluck with a more languid air, as they rustled their feathers in the warm earth of a Sinaloa farm.

The water in the large irrigation canal flowed gently. Indian women plodded from their little brush houses to the canal, with large round water *ollas* balanced on their heads, to dip with little gourd *jumates* the cool water so essential to their lives. Even the *jumates* cut to form dippers for the *ollas* were a product of patient growth and leisurely manufacture by the water carrier.

The grinding of the native *maiz* for *tortillas*, after boiling in lime and water to remove the hull, was a long and patient process—hours each day of slide, slide of the *mano* stone over the surface of the *metate*, to crush the softened kernels, so forming the wet paste—*maza*—from which *tortillas*, thin, round corn cakes, are patted out to be placed in a wide half-round pottery *comal* for baking.

Sticks for firewood were collected in a leisurely manner; washing was an interminable procedure of beating clothes on a board, adding water dipped with the gourd *jumate* from the stream.

Drying usually was on any mesquite bushes convenient to the site of the laundry. Ironing was with the old flat iron heated over the coals of a wood fire. Irons were a luxury, usually loaned to one or two less fortunate neighbors during the week.

After the household work was done there was a quiet social period. It was a common sight to see several women seated in a circle on the floor, under an *enramada*, the porch of a brush house, each smoking a home-rolled cigarette, searching carefully, hair by hair, over the head of their next neighbor to reduce the tiny livestock gathered there, finally combing out the hair with an *echo* comb, made from the spiny yellow ball in which the fruit is enclosed, these thorny ends being singed to blunt them for safer use.

Not unless you were raised in Mexico, just a friendly and curious little *gringo* sitting around or playing with the poorer Mexican or the Mayo Indian children, could you hope to take in some of the choice bits of gossip of those circles.

Common talk would be the detailed story of the week-end before, when the woman likely had followed her man to the town, stayed about to try to get some of the weekly wages spent for food, perhaps for clothing, before the saloons claimed the unfortunate fellow, then remained near to keep the drunk husband from being robbed of his hat or sandals or blanket, and even more—finally sitting patiently by a roadside while the husband slept off the stupefying effects of the *mescal* for a day or so, she probably whiling away the time by munching on a piece of bakery bread and perhaps a cake of *panocha*, or just sitting stoically hour by hour to protect her own. Fortunate she was if the week-end had not included a beating.

Children were apt to remain at home; usually there was a grandmother or some relative to see that they were fed.

The greatest tragedy of Mexico has been, and still is, the excessive use of villainously strong drink, *mescal, tequila*, and *aguardiente*. The use of *pulque*, the product of the *maguey* plant of the plateau areas, is more stupefying than intoxicating, but the end result is much the same, impoverishment of the health and resources of the man and his family, with collective depressing effect on the welfare of the whole nation.

Living among those poor lower-class people, seeing their turning into beasts when drunk, the half starving of many families, and particularly the children, early created in me an antipathy against drinking that I frankly admit is almost an obsession.

Soon we ran a little store, *comisaria*, on our farm, selling food and clothing without figuring to make a profit; sales were made on account, to be deducted from wages on Saturdays. In this way their wages were apt to be well spent at the *comisaria* by payday. So without the week-end spree they lived better, kept healthier, and passed on a share of improved health and happiness to their families.

The poorest families slept on palm mats on the floor, usually sharing a ragged blanket between two or three members of the household. Those more thrifty built *tarimas*, bed frames with little round pegs set at intervals of about three inches apart, on the under side of the frames; across the frame from end to end and side to side were stretched tightly either rawhide thongs or *mescal* fiber rope, making a rather firm substitute for springs, but quite comfortable for all of that.

On the *tarimas* were placed homemade palm mats, then a piece of leather, a hide, sheepskin, or just a blanket. A sheet under the blanket was a gesture of elegance usually dispensed with. Pillows were for the more exacting; they were of wool or cotton packed to a hardness resembling that of a bag of sand.

Although for most of the months of the year the weather is mild, there are some cold (sometimes foggy cold) nights in winter. Then the families suffered. Yet never did they seem to consider saving ahead to buy several blankets. They would have been marked among their neighbors had they done so and likely would have finished up by giving their extras to some needier person with that charitableness which is perhaps their rarest quality, a quality which has seemed to me more evident in them than we see it among the supposedly more highly cultured and more prosperous people of the world.

On those cold nights they gave proof of a certain cheerfulness that to us demanding many creature comforts, passeth understanding.

In the center of their dirt-roofed porch, which might have a brush-matted wall on two or three sides to protect somewhat from the sun of the day and from wind, they would build a little fire. Here they would sit on their heels, wrapped about with a blanket, holding the forward edge of the blanket tilted upwards, just enough to draw the warmth from the little fire. Snuggled next to them under the blanket would be the little children, sleeping peacefully, often with one of the family dogs lying alongside, each helping the other to keep warm.

To pass away the time there would soon be a song, not usually one of the lively Spanish dance numbers so familiar to us, but on a melancholy note, fitting into the background of their way of life.

The *corridos*, corresponding somewhat to our old western songs, were most common. During the long hours spent around a winter fire many a *corrido* was originated, based on some intriguing event; a courtship, a murder, a scandal, a bullfight, a horse race—anything that occurred to them they would construct into verse, sometimes composed to follow a tune known to them, sometimes to a tune worked out as they sang. Many of these *corridos* were developed on the ranches and farms, taken to the villages on their week-end indulgences and so put into circulation, often to become a part of the national music of the period.

Sometimes more than one family gathered at the fire; at times the best singers from a group of families would spend their evenings harmonizing, and their singing often was truly inspiring. The guitar was commonly used for accompaniment. Finally weary, the singers would curl up beside other members of the family for a brief sleep until the cold drove them once more to sit by the fire.

The Mexican laborers and the Mayo Indians kept separate groups. Each sang their songs in their own tongue. The Mayo's singing is distinctly a chant in which short phrases are sung, followed by a chant without words, and so on without change of tune for a long time.

The Mayos loved their own style of music. They made their own instruments, violins, guitars, and harpsichords, fitting them with gut strings made by themselves. Some of these instruments would stir the mind of a collector of museum pieces. They were well constructed and well played. Another instrument was a gourd cut in two and placed face downward in a large *olla* of water. This they beat upon to produce rhythm with their other instruments.

Almost every Mayo, and every Mexican from boys to old men, possessed a harmonica which was carried about and played whenever there was a pause in whatever they might be doing. M. Hohner no doubt operated with a profit motive but he may be credited with spreading a wondrous lot of cheer among the poorer natives of Mexico.

The Mayos were our most dependable laborers, quiet, self-sufficient, living much to themselves, but unobtrusively friendly to those who proved friends to them. They were distinctly the underdogs in the country. Perhaps from being an outlander too I early developed a special sympathy for them which may have had something to do with their acceptance of a small white boy so freely in their midst. Many a good pottery bowl of beans, many a browned *tortilla*, even an occasional *iguana* toasted over the coals, or a delicious wood-rat stew, I shared with the Mayo Indians who worked on our farm.

In Sinaloa, as elsewhere in Mexico, the lower middle classes constituted much the largest group of people, those of small means in their own business, perhaps owners of a *chumilco* (small store), a *panaderia* (bakery), a small *talabarteria* (leather shop); or those employed in little businesses; or owners or renters of small farms or of a few cattle or horses.

Our laborers came from those Mexicans just a little poorer than this class which meant they had almost nothing; or from the Mayo Indians.

Mexican laborers were apt to stay with us for many years. So were the Indians, except that most of them owned their little brush houses, a small spot of river-bottom land, and a yoke of oxen or some burros and each year took leave to return to their lands for planting season, later for a little cultivation, and again for the harvest. They were likewise off on many of their traditional feast days, even more so than the Mexicans. Too, they were apt to disappear for a few days during the fruiting season of the *pitahaya* cactus and of the *guamuchil* tree pods. They could live with little other food during those seasons.

Besides the regular laborers with families who lived on the ranch the colonists used many Indians who left their families in their homes along the river. Ours was one of the ranches up canal toward the river. On Monday mornings at daylight we would find lined up along the canal bank in front of our ranch quarters two or three hundred Mayos, dark silent figures in native straw *sombreros*. In the winter they were wrapped in bright red blankets that covered their faces to their eyes. From this group we would pick the ones we knew were best qualified as teamsters, irrigators, or cutters and loaders of sugar cane, after which the others moved down the road at a half-walk, half-run, to the next ranch.

Work days were from sunup to sundown. Some of the Indians trotted home seven to ten miles after work each evening. Others stayed for the week until Saturday when their *tareas* (tasks) were done, living all week on *pinole* (parched corn). This they mixed with water in a cow's-horn cup made by cutting the horn evenly across and fitting in a wooden plug for a bottom. A treat to them was a cake of *panocha* (brown sugar) nibbled as they ate from their cup of *pinole*; or to chew a strip of *carne seca* (dried beef), called by our own cowboys "jerky." On this diet they put in long days of labor and kept tough. If this should be doubted I suggest the doubter try to follow them for a day through the woods, or complete the *tarea* of sugar cane cutting allotted to those Mayos in Sinaloa.

I have said that they were a friendly people despite their having been much abused. Many times as a boy I have sat under cottonwood trees sharing the *pinole* and *panocha* of a poor Indian, usually taking care later to make some small gift such as fruit or a cake of *panocha* or a bit of bread.

We colonists inherited a system of accounting for our laborers from the usage of the Mexican *hacendados*. Each Indian carried, carefully rolled and placed inside a bamboo, one large sheet of foolscap paper with his account. The employer kept a duplicate sheet. The bamboo containers were often cleverly carved and ornamented in colors, or woven about with colored yarns. To remove the rolled paper from the bamboo tube, a string also of bright yarn was run through two little holes in opposite sides of the bamboo near the bottom, so a pull on the string would eject the *vale* (account paper) out to where it could be easily withdrawn from the bamboo. Wooden plugs were used to seal the bamboo against losing the *vale*. *Vales* were usually carried tied to the base of their straw hats, on top side. Their hats were also often adorned with bright yarn strings.

Roman numbers were used in accounting, with some additions, so that an Indian account sheet looked like this:

Rosario Leyva, en cuenta corriente con el Señor Don
Luis Robertson

"*Debe*" (Debit)	"*Haber*" (Credit)
X X X X X V	X X X V
O O O ∩	O O O O O O ∩
1 1 :	1 1 1 1 1 1 1 :

X for ten pesos, V for five pesos, a circle for one peso, a half circle for a half peso, a straight line for one bit (twelve centavos), a half line for a *medio* (six centavos), a dot for one *centavo*. Debits were entered on the one hand, credits on the other. Complicated accounting for an illiterate Indian, one would think, but each knew exactly what he owed.

Their system of figuring was unique but accurate. Now and then I chanced on them during their rest hour figuring their accounts. To represent the X they would select a large pebble, for the V a smaller, for the pesos little clods or *guamuchil* seeds or grains of corn or beans or *garbanzo*, and so down to the *centavos*. In one pile they placed pebbles or whatever used, to the number of debits. In another pile they placed similarly the number of credits. They then proceeded to throw away like kinds of pebbles or other units, one from debit pile, one from credit, until credits were exhausted. Then they carefully tallied the remaining debits. Certified public accountants take note!

There was much more to the matter of debt than would appear. The amount of debt was the measure of esteem of the employer. If an Indian thought he had cause to question his standing he would ask for an additional loan. Here was created a delicate situation. By leisurely visiting and questioning we tried to determine the real need of the Indian, in the light of acting as a business adviser, which in fact we tried to be. Sometimes the need was real, then almost always we made the loan aware that we would have to go through a long process of collection of a smaller part of the Indian's wages, but with the comfort that until he made repayment we could exercise some small influence on him in regard to his getting drunk on week-ends and so benefit him and his long-suffering family.

If it were determined to be a matter of his learning his

[181]

standing we would assure him that his credit was very good, indeed; in fact up to perhaps some certain amount if he were really in bad circumstances of sickness or other emergency; so he was satisfied and told him family and his fellow workers how esteemed he was by his *patron*.

There was a surprising jealousy among the Indians, in fact even among the Mexicans, as to their comparative ratings in the eyes of the *patron*, a situation that required continued consideration, and despite our efforts at diplomacy occasionally resulted in our losing a good man, *"porque el patron parece que ya no me quiere"*—("because the *patron* appears no longer to have affection for me").

The colonists lived in Sinaloa during the last years of that era when the peonage system was in general usage. Something like the indentured servant system practiced in the early period of the American colonies, it worked in this way: Employers made advances of funds to workers, to be paid by labor, and until such advances were paid the laborer was obligated to remain with the employer under penalty of jail sentence, or of penalties imposed by the employer, in extreme cases even to flogging, such penalties not being legal but condoned by the authorities who were of the employer class. Debts of the fathers were transferred to the children. Laborers compelled by law to work for a certain employer while in debt to him naturally could have little to say about wages.

I can say with some satisfaction that the American colonists disliked the system; that the competition for labor created by their enterprise in the Fuerte River valley contributed much to raising wages and moderating the treatment of laborers. The Indians soon learned to appreciate the fair treatment from the colonists. They persistently ran away from certain native employers to work for some colonist, usually under an assumed name. We did not question them. Sometimes their employers would come with an armed authority, perhaps a private policeman kept by the employer, to search our fields for their men. Often in a few weeks the arrested man would be back to work for us. Occasionally we would pay the account of a worker and so release him from an inconsiderate employer.

The Indians complained that some employers added more debits to their *vales* than had been incurred. A rather pathetic if amusing story is told of the Indian who was standing over his employer watching carefully to see that no extra debit marks were entered.

"Pick me up a little sand to sprinkle on your *vale* so the ink will dry," said the employer.

"I can't reach the sand, *mi patron*, I can't reach the sand," exclaimed the poor Indian, stooping part way down and grasping towards the earth, yet keeping his head on a level to be able to watch his employer's hand on the paper.

Dad, while working long days in various capacities for the expanding sugar company of Johnston had put in long hours at night working on his own farm. When he was able to leave the Company to farm for himself he took contracts to furnish the Company, as well as others, with native hardwood timber for houses, corrals, fence posts, sugar-cane wagon racks, and for many other uses, and to furnish lime made from oyster shells, and mesquite cordwood for firewood for the sugar mill. Later as the sugar business expanded and a private railroad was built we took grading contracts. We freighted for hire; we took brush-clearing contracts—in fact, anything to make a better living.

Timber camps at first were only a few miles out into the woods. As the need for timber increased the lands nearby were stripped, until we extended our roads and made camps in the foothills fifty and sixty miles away.

There are many kinds of hardwood in Sinaloa; none but the cypress (*sabino*), the native cedar (*cedro*), *the* ebony (*ebano*), and mesquite growing to proportions for sawing or hewing into boards.

For fence posts, upright forks for houses, in fact, every use where they were buried into the ground, there was nothing equal to *palo colorado*, a form of rosewood.

For rafters where there was no contact with earth the *amapa* was everlasting.

For wagon reaches and tongues and for eveners, double-trees, and singletrees, the native ash (*asta*) was preferred.

For saddletrees *guasima* was used, with the saddlehorn and fork of mesquite or lignum vitae (*guayacan*).

Oxcart frames were made of cottonwood (*alamo*), *cedro*, or *sabino*. From huge cottonwood logs were sawed solid circular wheels about four feet in diameter by six inches wide. Early oxcart axles were of hardwood. The centers of the solid wheels were boxed with hardwood. Before the advent of axle grease either pitch from the *pitahaya* cactus or beef tallow was used to grease the wheels, when they were greased.

Many a wheel went ungreased. There is no describing the yowling sound of an ungreased wooden-axled, wooden-wheeled *carreta*—agony in slow tempo, as the oxen plodded patiently on—none but an Indian and an oxteam could stand to hear it for hours on end.

Timber cutting was in the fall toward the end of the rainy season while there was still water to be had for man and beast in the woods. Base camp was at the nearest water hole to good timber, usually some deep place in an *arroyo* where a temporary brush corral was built for stock, a shelter with brush sides and roof thrown up for cooking and for storing supplies.

The Mayo Indians were superb axmen, cutting for a day's task 100 hardwood fence posts five to eight inches in diameter, making road for the teams and wagons and carrying the heavy posts to this road. Camp food was good for those days, corn, hominy, and beans boiled with chunks of beef (*posole* to a Mexican), *tortillas*, and coffee. Cooking was done first in *ollas*, later in five-gallon kerosene cans hung from a tripod, *pie de gallo* (literally, "rooster's foot") set over the fire. The *posole* stewed all evening until the cook went to sleep, then stewed again from about two in the morning when the cook began patting out the dozens of *tortillas* for the hungry Indians. By four in the morning the *posole* and *tortillas* were being devoured, coffee was drunk with lots of sugar, and by five, before daybreak, the chop, chop of twenty or thirty or more axes rang through the forest. As the sun bore down, the tough lean brown-backed Mayos would strip to the waist, wearing only long unbleached muslin underdrawers rolled halfway to their hips.

By early afternoon they were back in camp with their *tarea* done and a peso earned—one *centavo* (one-half cent) per hardwood post cut and piled. After another big meal, a long rest under the shade of a tree, before dusk their axes to be ground; perhaps an *iguana* to be roasted, a delicacy for an Indian at least equal to the 'possum for the darkies of the South.

The *iguanas*, woods lizards about eighteen inches in length,

[184]

live in hollow hardwood tree trunks. An Indian can spot a tree with an *iguana* almost as far as he can see it and he never passes up a chance for one. The large wood rats, which built big brush nests in the trees, are very clean animals. The Indians used them for cooking in stews more commonly than rabbits and insisted they were better.

Sometimes they ran across *panales* (wild bee hives) and brought them back to camp.

An American used to being with a group of his own people might think these Indians strange, sitting about on their haunches, eating or resting and visiting. No chatter here. Prolonged periods of quiet. One Indian produces from his *ixtle morral* a bottle full of ground-up *macucho* tobacco leaves and some cornhusks and shares it with his neighbors. One of the group brings from the campfire a hardwood stick with a live ember. A few remarks, short, usually answered by grunts— "*ehe*" for "yes," "*eh—eh*" for "no," "*hei-tu*" for "I don't know." Now and them some clever remark by one of them that sets them all off for a very brief but pleasant laugh, then quiet for another indefinite time.

I wonder now at the courtesy and obedience of those Indians to direction in their work from a mere youngster. There is no doubt that obedience to the *hacendado* and his family were almost as accepted as among the Negro slaves of the old South. In fact, life on an *hacienda* in Mexico had much in common with life on the plantations of the South.

CHAPTER IV

Good Indians

IT SHOULD BE interesting to us who are so surrounded with the comforts and luxuries of life to the point of saturation, to consider just how self-sufficient a group of people can be with only what they produce and create for themselves.

Although the Mayos of the Fuerte River by 1900 had been robbed of most of the fertile river lands and the vast brush wilderness that was once theirs, they still clung tenaciously to little pieces of river lands, owners by moral right, but outlanders in the eyes of the average Mexican. They had learned to be as unobtrusive as possible, but were broodingly quiet and resentful, and well remembered their grievances.

Their little parcels of high land bordering the river were left in mesquite and undergrowth. Their brush houses were to be found by following little trails through the mesquite. Other little trails led down to their river bottom soil where they grew little patches of beans and corn, with pumpkins planted among the corn rows. Farther out in the river bottom where sand banks had deposited they scraped away the sand, in some instances digging holes five feet deep to reach permanent moisture and there planted watermelons, which they really cherished.

Their razorback hogs roamed the woods until corn and pumpkins were harvested. Then those large enough were tethered by the neck or by a leg to a mesquite tree and fed these crops until fat enough to make pork, lard, and cracklings.

The owner of a *yunta de bueyes* (yoke of oxen) was prosperous. They seldom had more than a few cattle. Many had little herds of sheep and goats. They owned a burro or two to ride to the village, to pack wood, to pull a little steel plow if they owned one. Oxen usually pulled wooden plows, some of these with a small steel jacket set on the very front end of the wooden point.

From the milk of cows and goats they made cheese. From the sheep they sheared the wool, carded and spun it for their blankets, jackets, *fajas* (sash belts), and *gorras de lana* (wool hats). Their blankets were woven in black, white, or brown wool, in solid colors, stripes, or various designs, the commonest a diamond shape of various combinations and colors. They added to the natural wool colors certain dyes which they knew how to fix into the wool to hold for generations, dyes of *anilina*, the blueing plant, and of *mora*, the wild mulberry.

Wool jackets were usually deep blue with a little white design, neatly patterned. The sashes, to be wrapped twice or thrice about the body to serve as belts, were woven in colored patterns on a blue background, often with designs such as red and yellow fighting cocks, peacocks, or a stag head with horns.

Cowboy's hats were usually shaped from the whitest wool, pounded between stones into a coarse felt. They were well done, artistic, a typical, high-class piece of workmanship, much sought by the *vaqueros* on the cattle ranches.

From their few cattle, sheep, and goats they eventually dried the meat into "jerky" which could be kept hanging under their roofs until needed. Then it was pounded on the stone *metate* for cooking into a *cocido* or a *guisado* with some chile and onions.

To this store of meat they would now and then add a deer or a wild hog, taken with snare, with bow and arrow, or with cap-and-ball rifle. The deer hides they treated with a mixture of pumpkin seeds, oxbrains, and ashes, removed the hair by scraping, then flexed the hide perhaps for two days over a wedge-topped hardwood piece set into the ground, so producing a fine buckskin. From this buckskin they made *chaparreras* (chaps) for the *vaqueros*, and *cueras* (buckskin coats) for riding through the thorny woods. These garments were neatly made, with ornamental designs cut into the double parts of the buckskin, all sewn with the same buckskin. The *cueras* tied across the chest with buckskin thongs. There was nothing about them not made by the Indians.

For sale they made mats of *palma* in the foothills where wild palm was available, and of *carrizo* (bamboo) along the lower reaches of the river; saddle blankets and thin bed mattresses of the *ixtle* fiber from the *mescal* leaves; curry combs of the same fiber, and even ropes. They made palm baskets of many sizes. Tourists have offered to them at at San Blas station a style of palm basket and *ixtle* fiber hammocks not made in any other place in Mexico.

For their household they require little of civilization. Their houses, brush and dirt roofed, brush or adobe walled, they build for themselves. Their stoves are clay ovens plastered over a support of sticks or adobe. Their utensils are pottery, unless they indulge in the luxury of tin pails for lard and coffee, or of steel pans for frying. Their beds are either the earth floor or a bundle of bamboo sticks about seven feet in length which are tied together with fiber string, to be unrolled into a "bedspring" and laid on two hand-hewn benches set at head and foot for supports. On these with a palm mat spread over they sleep in summer, with little more bedding in winter.

When a Mayo boy and girl marry it is for life; seldom indeed were there any separations. Parents planned the marriages. No doubt the youngsters also contributed their ideas, but parents on both sides conferred, set the date for the wedding, and made all the preparations. .

Granting all the spiritual and moral benefit derived from the ministrations of the Catholic church in Mexico, its priests too often developed a mercenary attitude toward their poor, uneducated, handicapped followers in the faith. Not to be married in the church was a grievous sin, only to be atoned for after civil marriage by repeating with a church ceremony. Charges for church ceremonies were completely out of line with the ability of the Indians to pay. Many a boy and girl incurred for their marriage debts that burdened them for years afterwards. Yet the fathers and mothers as well as the youngsters were made to feel the stigma of being married without the church. Our Indians on the ranch discussed this problem many times with us. We resented the situation, but we soon found that the hold of the church, their awe of its ritual and fear of its displeasure together with the fact of their social life's being so completely interwoven with the church, kept them fast. The frequent result was that the boy and girl took matters into their own hands by running away together to set up a household somewhere away from their people, generally returning in due time to live together for the rest of their lives.

There always remained among both Indians and poorer

Mexican families, who were subject to the same problem, a distinction, a sense of superiority on the part of the women who could boast being married, and a certain fear of those unmarried ones that their men might discard them to marry another woman.

The Indians did not merge their properties at marriage; the woman's sheep and goats and burros ran with those of her master, but only she could dispose of them. If an Indian couple were seen going along a road, the woman riding the burro, one could count it her property; if the man rode, the reverse was true.

Some of our Mayos were incredibly old. Gaunt, shriveled, toothless, they still ate their ground *pinole* with water and *panocha*, chewed on bits of dried meat, ate *pozole*, and along with younger men cut long rows of sugar cane. They brought the bright, broad cane knife down the stock to clear the long leaves, ending with a neat cut at the ground. Then, deftly catching up the cane with the hook on top of the knife, they topped it and scooted it along the flat of the blade to land in a row perhaps twenty feet away. The green cane tops were piled in centers of rows.

One of these old men was Domingo Leyva. I often shared his *pinole* and *panocha* which he broke to small bits for lack of teeth. As we sat under a big cottonwood tree together I learned to help him count his debits and credits with rocks and grains before I could have added them by arithmetic. Domingo was the chief of the La Bajada Mayos, pertaining to the San Miguel Mission. So far as I could see then, his authority seemed to be used chiefly on religious feast days, when he assumed the responsibility for getting his people out to the religious exercises at the mission which were then followed by a fiesta of their own.

After years of association with the Mayos I concluded that they had no really clear-cut conception of what part of their feast days were purely Roman Catholic and what part remained from their own tribal pre-Spanish days. The old missions along the Fuerte River were open to them, sometimes with priests in attendance, sometimes not. In either case they were forever congregating at the missions for Saints' days that they remembered well, taking offerings of bright tissue-paper flowers and small coins for the collection box.

They believed strongly in making offers to God to secure

His favor in restoring the health of themselves or their families, or for certain other much-desired ends. These offerings took curious turns. One of our Mayo Indians with his wife went on a seventy-five mile pilgrimage to a certain church. The man was sick and feeble and rode a small burro. Here they deposited an offering of a sum, considerable for them, all in pennies.

Our Indian cook and washerwoman, Juana, to repay God for saving the life of a sister, wore a hair rope for six months wound about her waist next to her skin. On another *manda* the old lady took the train as far as Sonora, and with an Indian woman companion walked from there a hundred miles to an isolated mission reputed to offer marvelous cures.

Juana was a smart woman in many ways. She was a good listener and liked to argue on many interesting subjects. One day she stopped me with a question.

"Don Tomas, some people say the earth is not flat, that it is round. Is that true?"

"*Si*, Juana, it is round."

"Ugh, and some people say that the earth turns over every night."

"*Si*, Juana, the earth is like a ball. The Chinese live on the other side of the ball from us. It is dark there when it is day here."

"And when it turns over we don't fall off?"

"No, Juana, gravity holds us to the earth."

"Ugh, we shall see if this is true."

The next day she triumphantly led me out to a tree in the yard from a branch of which hung a bucket of water.

"*Mire*" (look you), said she, "I hung this in the tree yesterday, and the water did not spill from the bucket when the earth turned over in the night!"

Rosario, son of old Domingo, was about the age of Dad. He was honest, hard working and faithful, a good friend.

Bernardo Esquer, a Tarahumara Indian from the high Sierras, drifted down as a boy to live among the Mayos, and married one of them.

Rosario and Bernardo ran our two alfalfa hay baler crews for years. They were the best of friends; even on their week-end sprees they never quarreled.

Week after week we would ride to Mochis on Mondays to

The author at 19 years of age. Picture taken when President of High School Student Body at Santa Ana, California in 1917.

LOUIS ROBERTSON *at 22 years of age.*

Cottonwood dugout canoe rigged with wire fire basket for night spearing, Ohuira Bay. The author at the paddle, 1920. Our summer camp and launch in background.

bail out of jail one or several of our Indians, usually Rosario and Bernardo among them. The authorities, besides making a show of keeping the peace, thus collected a tidy sum weekly from fines imposed on Indians and Mexicans who worked for the *colonos*.

They got to know which laborers we rated most useful and tried to levy accordingly. It all got to be a sort of game. Every so often, to discipline the authorities and the men too, we would refuse to pay and just left them in jail. For a few days their poor *mujeres* would carry food to them, until finally the authorities wearied of them and turned them loose. The laborers understood that we were acting for their good in helping to reduce their fines, so took the whole proceeding in good part. We were the ones most annoyed, I am sure.

Indian fiestas might be held anywhere that there were a few families congregated, but more commonly at the old mission pueblos, Tehueco, Sivirijoa, Charay, San Miguel, and Ahome. We did everything possible on the ranch by task. On Saturdays the Mayos would be at work by earliest light to be finished with their tasks and at the *Comisaria* for their week's pay by noon, after which they would set off at a half run for the Fuerte River.

On the central compounds of the old pueblos opposite the missions they had built wide brush-covered sheds without walls, as protection from the tropical sun. By mid-afternoon Saturday there would be gathered there a colorful group, Mayo women dressed in three-piece ensembles, wide skirt of one bright-colored calico, a loose blouse of another bright color, *rebozo* (shawl), always of a sober black calico or of a blue with a small white pattern. Little girls were dressed in the same bright colors, little boys in sober knee-length pants topped probably with a pink shirt, a very favorite color of the Mayos. Men wore freshly washed trousers of overalling or thinner striped material, and a bright solid-colored shirt of pink, green, blue, yellow, or red, topped by a bright handkerchief, sometimes of silk, about the neck, and a new straw hat which was kept tucked away under the roof of their little brush shacks for fiesta days.

The men wore *guarachis* (sandals), the women either shoes with cloth tops and leather soles or more often were barefooted.

The center of interest was the musicians, harpist and violinist. There was not often a guitar player. The gourd in water, or a *tambor* (tom-tom drum), was used for some of their dances. Commonest music was a monotonous jig-time, played over and over for hours on end, while the dancer did his jig-step in one little spot endlessly.

Dancers had wrapped about their legs, calves, and sometimes thighs, a long string of pods called *cascabeles*, after the rattles of the rattlesnake. These pods were cocoons found fastened to bushes. They were tough and firm. With some seeds or little rocks inside, their long chains when shaken produced a fine rhythm with the music.

There were special dances, done in costume, representing the antics of the animals of the forests. For *El Baile del Venado* (Dance of the Deer) the dancer wore a set of stag horns, sometimes with mask down to the shoulders, and a deer hide thrown over the body; for the *Coyote* and for the *Tecolote* (Owl) dances the same type of imitations.

There was a lot of competition among the dancers to produce the best imitations; their mimicry of the dainty walking of the deer, the courting of a stag, the howl of a coyote, the hooting and flying of an owl was most realistic and evoked plenty of laughter, taking the place for the Indian of our perhaps more crude practice of clapping of hands.

The women brought tamales for sale. There was always coffee available, and too much stronger drink, especially *mescal*, which intoxicated quickly and less expensively than beer.

The feasts continued through the night. Before daybreak women offered for sale their really most savory dish, *menudo*, which was tripe cooked with hominy, green onions, and coriander seasoning. With this favorite dish the *fiesteros* took on renewed energy to carry their festivities into the second day. The musicians and dancers carried on a competition to see which could outlast the others. They were known to play and dance for three days and nights, until one or the other lay exhausted.

By Sunday afternoons most of the braves at the fiesta were gathered in groups with arms about each other, weaving on their feet while they carried on their *cantos*, or were stretched on the ground sleeping off the *mescal*. Their *mujeres* chatted with the other women or sat by waiting for the stupor to wear off in a few hours or by another day so that they could take their warriors home. On Mondays following the feast days we had few Indians on the ranch; by Tuesday half our Indian crew, but by Wednesday they were recovered and apparently as tough as ever.

The *Fiestas de Semana Santa* (Feasts of the Holy Week) were the high point of the Indian year. For weeks before, certain of the braves prepared masks, fierce-looking head pieces that fitted down to their shoulders, of peccary, deer, or coyote hide, with wild expressions on their painted faces, long noses or ears attached. The deer skins were surmounted by stag horns. Some head dresses were made with feathers in imitation of owls, eagles, or other birds, and some were hideous caricatures of people. They made long wooden spears, swords, and clubs, and carved and painted them in weird design. In these costumes, often stripped to the waist and sometimes with streaks of paint on their bodies, they were well disguised.

The group representing each mission was led by a *Capitan*, also well disguised and carrying a braided rawhide whip. These were to represent the *Judios*, the Jews who persecuted Christ. For several weeks, I presume during the period of Lent, these bands made excursions about the countryside, singly or in little groups, menacing people with their crude implements, taking liberties with other persons' food, such as corn fields or watermelon patches. They would approach us as we rode on horseback, threatening our horses while holding out their hands for some small coin to be given them for desisting. The occasion called for patience, even though the temptation otherwise might be great.

Once each week the masked *Judios* from one mission area advanced up or down the river *camino real* to meet a group advancing by previous arrangement from the next mission. Upon meeting the groups engaged in a fierce battle, thumping each other without mercy until they were exhausted or fled. There were some serious injuries and even a few deaths as a result of these encounters.

On *Viernes Santo* (Good Friday) there were religious services in the missions, a day of mourning for the death of the Saviour. Saturday and Sunday the *Pascola* dancers performed the religious dance of the Mayos. By daybreak on Sunday

[193]

morning the *Judios* were gathered with a great throng of Indians about the compound near the mission. There were great shootings of rockets and miniature bombs made from gunpowder by the Indians. The effigy of Judas Iscariot was mounted on an ox, effigy and ox being whipped by the *Judios* with long switches until the plunging animal had dumped the effigy. A final ceremony was the running of the gauntlet by the *Capitan* of the *Judios*. The *Judios* formed two lines, armed with brush switches. The *Capitan*, who had wielded his rawhide whip as he chose on his followers must now run the gauntlet between the two rows of braves who whipped him as he ran. This ended the career of the *Judios* for that season. Their masks and weapons were thrown on a pile, together with the effigy of Judas, and all were burned.

There was a strict prohibition against giving up masks, so that it was difficult to secure them as souvenirs. For the onerous duty of serving as *Judios*, I was told by some of our Mayos who so served, they were assured entry into Heaven.

It would be most interesting to know the story of the development of these customs; the tribal customs and beliefs which the priests found among the Yaquis and Mayos over 400 years ago; their attempts at conversion which we know sometimes ended in the death of priests and massacre of their followers; the compromise between Catholic Christianity and the old customs that developed into practices in part described in this story and still existing in Sinaloa.

CHAPTER V

Our Mexican Neighbors

WHETHER OUR WEALTHIER Mexican neighbors comprehended the social and economic aims of the cooperative colony with its program for the leveling of classes I cannot say. However that may have been, they were uniformly friendly and accepted as equals all those Americans who chose to maintain any dignity of living. Many of their children attended colonists' schools, with that beginning often were sent to the United States for higher education.

Many colonists' families were hospitably and pleasantly entertained in the homes of the Padillas, Castros, Lugos, Borboas, Vegas, Renterias, and others. As the original colonists' dream faded, to be replaced by ambitions of personal enterprise, these friendships between colonists and the higher-class Mexicans became easier, of course. I recall many pleasant stays with the Padillas at Higuera de Zaragosa, with the Renterias at Teroque, with Don Patricio Quinones at Choacahui.

With the young Padillas and the young Renterias there was much visiting among the neighbors, many parties, much music and dancing. The visits with Dad to Don Patricio were much more dignified affairs. Don Patricio was a great, dark, robust Indian who had grown to the size and dignity of an *hacendado* through sheer energy. He and Dad for reasons often unaccountable in human relationships became the very best of friends. Don Patricio's visits to us were most austere occasions. His carriage pulled up to our front yard drawn always by four perfectly matched little mules, either a set of roans, or of blacks, or of buckskin yellow. Mounted on the front seat were an Indian coachman and a guard with a Winchester carbine. In the rear seat of the high carriage sat Don Patricio, an impressive figure, gray haired and gray mustached, dressed immaculately in white linen, black bow tie, and a fine broad Panama hat. Sometimes he was accompanied by Doña Rafaela, his buxom, handsome wife, twenty years younger than her lord and master.

There were three other wives, or at least there were children from three other women. They were sent to the best schools. The oldest son, Victor, presumably from wife number one, spoke perfect English, had lived several years in San Francisco. He was as white as any American, a big, florid, handsome fellow. His father set him up in business on an *hacienda* with cattle and horses and mules. Victor took to the life of an *hacendado* with enthusiasm. He became a top poker player, hired the local orchestra to embellish his drinking parties, and generally made lavish use of his patrimony. He was greatly addicted to horse racing, than which there was no more genteel form of amusement in the country.

This behavior was a source of great distress to Don Patricio, he confided to Dad, particularly so his son's extravagance at horse racing, because, Don Patricio said, the boy had no judgment and always lost. Came a day when Don Patricio arrived on a visit, and confided to Dad that he had resolved to cure his son once and for always of his reckless betting on horse races. It seems Victor had *amarrado* (tied up) a particularly bad race, where his horse was pathetically outclassed. The old gentleman had through intermediaries placed bets against the son, enough to break him and so place him in a position to be reasoned with as to the error of his ways.

A few weeks later Don Patricio arrived on another visit. Dad asked him how the disciplining of the son was progressing. With much embarrassment Don Patricio said in effect, not so well. Unaccountably his son's horse had won, so the old gentleman had been busy paying up the bets made in cash, land, cattle, horses, and mules.

The Padilla family through all the years from La Logia days was the most closely associated with the colonists. Don Victor Padilla was for years a member of the colony. The Padilla youngsters, Genoveva, Victor, Anita, Rosario, Placida, Lupe, and Carlos studied in colony schools. Lupe married a graduate of Massachusetts Agricultural College, Harold Spaulding.

Anita was a great favorite of Grandmother Whitzel and a close friend of the daughters of both Grandmother and Grandfather, who had now been united into one family. She stayed with Whitzels to attend school and later taught school. She was a precocious and independent spirit, with talents varying from tight-rope walking to piano playing and teaching. Romantic orchestra leaders composed music in her honor. She was very much the "life of the party," highly esteemed by both Americans and her own people.

From Grandmother's she drove to school, to Don Celedonio Aragon's General Store, where her father had arranged an account for her, and to the post office, in a high-wheeled cart drawn by a little red mule. Presently the activities of Anita began to increase; there were social calls, parties, and dances to be attended. The little red mule went on strike, just to the school, the store, and the post office, his regular routine, but not a foot in any other direction. Much exasperated, Anita took the first opportunity to send the mule thirty miles down river to her father, explaining the problem and asking for another mule. The old gentleman promptly returned the same mule, with the message that those three places were the only ones where she had any business. Furious, Anita forthwith sent the red mule home with the edict that she was walking until she got another mule. "Men have their will, but women have their way." The father recognized when he was beaten in the argument and Anita drove another mule.

On one of many trips with Uncle Bill we stopped along the Fuerte River road at the small pueblo of Zapotillo to call on his friend, Don Salomé Puente. (Curiously, in Spanish countries Salomé is used as a man's name.) Under a great banyan tree by the highway we sat watching his blacksmith forging a pair of spurs for one of the old gentleman's *vaqueros*. Partly shaded by the banyan were the ranch headquarters, a series of adobe rooms built on a U shape, with a hardwood stockade fence surrounding a front yard. Reminiscent of Kipling's description in the immortal "Kim" of the Great Road of India, from the shade of the big banyan we watched the life of the Fuerte River, reflected in the travelers of the *Camino Real*. Indian families padded barefoot in the deep silt dust, women, children, men, cur dogs, now and then a burro; presently a patient yoke of oxen hauling a cart of corn fodder or pumpkins or watermelons; at intervals a string of freight wagons belonging to some *comerciante* or *hacendado*, loaded with dry goods, coffee, sugar, or products of the ranches, such as corn, beans, lard, tallow, hides. There were riders of burros, of mules, of horses, these riders in all degrees of standing in the economic and social scale from ragged old

[197]

men on hard-worn remnants of saddles, astride patient-look-
ing burros, to *vaqueros* in typical Indian-made buckskin coats
and chaps, native-made cowboy saddles and horseman's ac-
cessories; so on to neatly dressed *rancheros* riding their well-
kept favorite horses, often with silver-mounted saddles. The
brisk gait of these spirited horses usually left all other traffic
well behind. Now and again a *carruaje* rolled by, drawn by
four mules at a trot or gallop, giving their passengers a jolt-
ing ride and a thorough dusting.

Where neighbors were known to each other for many
leagues there was much stopping, under shade trees when
possible, for an exchange of news for the duration of a *cigarro*
smoke or two, so keeping up with current events as we do
through radio and newspaper today. Most of the travelers
were known to Don Salomé, and he kept up a revealing com-
mentary as they moved along, one or another pausing for a
courteous handshake and a brief visit.

Don Salomé was one of those incredible characters that
belie all the rules for business laid down since the time of
King Solomon. He had begun life as a poor little Indian. Personally very industrious and thrifty, neither drinking nor
smoking, nor possessing any family to support, he had pyra-
mided his property from a tiny bit of land to a dozen sizeable
farms and two substantial cattle ranches well stocked with
cattle, mules, and horses. During the long years of thrift,
however, he had manifested a weakness (or should we judge
it so?)—he could not resist lending money.

After a preliminary exchange of comments on livestock
and crops, Uncle Bill led Don Salomé to discuss the subject
of his loans. Soon the old man had asked us inside the fence
to a more private place on his big porch, had gone back with
his set of huge door keys, unlocked a room to show us a good-
sized box, which he opened with a smaller key. In this box
were thousands of pesos in gold coins, a little silver, and some
few bills. Also there were piles of papers which proved to be
promissory notes.

Don Salomé could not read or write. The gold and silver
he valued, the bills he slapped contemptuously, no real value,
said he, to be disposed of as soon as possible.

Some of the *pagarés* (notes) were dated so far back that
the makers were only names, people dead many years since.

JUANA, *our Mayo cook and*
washerwoman.

Easter festival at San Miguel Mission on the Fuerte River—1920. In foreground, Mayo Indians disguised as "Judios" (Jews) who persecuted Christ. Face masks were usually of wild peccary hides, with fierce appearing caricatures of faces. They carried whips and clubs and fought similar groups from neighboring Missions, sometimes until badly injured.

The old man had a story for each, the tale told by the borrower to secure the loan. Many of them had never intended to repay. Several of the papers were not promissory notes at all, merely words written on paper to satisfy the old money lender, perhaps stating that the person had received a certain sum, "payment in full," from Don Salomé Puente. These we explained to him.

"Hmm—*cabrones*—*cabrones*, how they deceived me!" he would say, slapping the paper. So he set his papers in two piles in the box, *"Los Buenos"* (the good) and *"Los Malos"* (the bad), for another day. He was the friend and protector of the Indians in his area, always scolding and advising them, and lending them money. He probably did better collecting from them than from various prominent persons whose names we recognized on the *pagarés*.

Another interesting old Indian was Don Ramon Guicochea. With Uncle Bill I made a trip, first in our sailboat across Ohuira Bay, then several miles through the woods on a *jabali* hunt, ending up at the ranch quarters of Guicochea. These consisted of a couple of well-built brush houses hidden in a group of mesquite trees along an arroyo. It was a picturesque little hideout surrounded on three sides by mountains a mile or so distant. Here the big old Indian kept a goodly number of cattle.

After resting a while in the shade of his porch where we exchanged bits of news, I walked out to draw some water from the well by means of the big leather bucket with rope run over a handmade hardwood pulley.

"Don't drink that water, son," called our host. "It is too salty; it is fit only for strangers and for cattle."

He took us away back through the mesquite trees to another well, of good water. He explained to us that although he and his ancestors had lived there for generations there had been several Mexicans come, apparently to crowd in on the old man. After drinking the brackish water a few times they were discouraged and left. The Indians also drank the salt water while the unwelcome visitors were there.

Guicochea was the chief of the Mayos living on the various little cattle ranches along the shores of Ohuira and San Ignacio Bays. Ohuira Bay has been described, twenty miles long, seven miles wide at highest tide, mangrove-lined salt-water swamps on the northwesterly shore, extending to the hills where the port of Topolobampo was built, then low green swamps again for many miles northwestward.

Between Ohuira and San Ignacio Bay to the southeastward are several miles of hills with valleys between. The Guicochea ranch lies far back in those hills, so surrounded by rough cliffs that even the deer, *jabali*, coyotes, and mountain lions chose to move in and out of the valley along the *playa* (mud flat) left at low tide, rather than over the rugged hills. Each day Guicochea would walk down to the entrance to check the tracks. If no cattle had walked along there he was through herding for the day. The flat was too wide at low tide to run a fence across, and besides, the big fellow had little else to do.

Guicochea remembered back to the time of the invasion of the French, when Napoleon planted Maxmilian on the throne of Mexico for a short and tragic reign, 1864-65. His father had been chief then. The Indians from the coast had withdrawn into the little valley with its one low-tide entrance, had piled boulders in strategic places to roll on an enemy, had taken food and water and moved into caves high upon the mountain sides. Their lookouts saw armed bands crossing the playa from one ranch to another, but none ventured into the hidden valley.

With the old man we had a *jabali* hunt not to be forgotten. He called his scrawny dogs and we set out for the hills, he armed only with a sharp *machete*, a sort of broadsword with a curving heavy end, a weapon about two feet in length that serves an Indian for everything from carving his toe nails to building his home.

Don Ramon was a great, gaunt old fellow. In the dozens of times I saw him he always wore one leg of his unbleached muslin *pantalones* rolled above the knee halfway to the hip, and carried one of his *guarachis* hooked over one thumb instead of wearing it on his foot—not that he needed sandals as his feet were tough as shoe soles.

Before long his mongrels were yelping after a group of *jabalies*. Up the mountainside they went. The old boy stood patiently listening, until the barking became fixed at one spot.

"Now the *jabalies* are in a cave," he said, and we moved up the slope to where the grub-hounds were barking fiercely into a dark hole in the mountain. Our guide looked about for some half-dry *pitahaya* cactus, which he placed at the entrance to the cave and set on fire. The dense black smoke soon penetrated the cave.

"Now you will see how to kill *jabalies* without an *arma*," said the big, dignified old Mayo, standing with his *machete* ready.

The band of wild hogs finally was smoked out. As they rushed through the smoke with eyes blinded the old chief dropped two of them with quick strokes aimed at their skulls with his *machete*.

I never tried to get wild hogs that way. They stand only about two feet high, weigh scarcely sixty pounds, but they possess a most uncertain temper, have sharp-edged tusks nearly three inches long; they could tear up a tree root or an adversary *muy pronto*. When alarmed their black and white bristles rise over their backs to make them look twice as big, their beady little eyes look mean as anything, and they pop-pop their jaws together so it sounds like clapping of hands. One never knew whether they planned to retreat or to charge.

This *jabali* hunt was the first of many occasions when we visited with old Don Ramon Guicochea. There was something legendary in the appearance of the old man whether in action against wild hogs or in repose, visiting under his brush *ramada*. Instinctively one knew that here was a descendant of a superior people, of the family of great chiefs of the centuries before.

On the Sinaloa River, at Rancho Salsipuedes, lived one of Uncle Bill's closest friends, Don Onofre Camacho. His brush lands extended for several hours of riding; his cattle were many thousands; his river lowlands produced thousands of *fanegas* of corn and beans; he had a well-kept *hacienda*.

On my first trip with Uncle Bill to meet him, he was away at one of his several cattle ranches, so that we rode far into the night to find him. We were accompanied by his nephew, Esteban.

It was dry season. Don Onofre and two of his *vaqueros* had built a temporary brush corral around a waterhole, leaving only a narrow gap. They were watching for wild cattle which would water only at night.

It was bright moonlight. The *vaqueros* had concealed themselves under some low trees to wait. When cattle came inside the enclosure the *vaqueros* ran a long *riata* across, throwing over it various saddle blankets and trappings to frighten the cattle from the entrance. So they would be held until daybreak, then to be lassoed and tied to a gentle steer for transporting to a fenced-in pasture. Numbers of them were so wild that they would kill themselves by plunging at the end of their ropes, or starve while tied to a hitching post, rather than eat grass or mesquite browse offered them.

Even dressed in his *vaquero* outfit Don Onofre was a man of distinctive appearance. He was of fair complexion and wore a full white beard. One eye had been lost in a run through the thorny woods after cattle. He was most courteous with much dignity of speech and bearing. Uncle Bill had known him for many years, was without doubt in his confidence more than any other person, so knew his life story.

When a boy of fourteen Don Onofre made a trip with his mother, both on horseback, to visit some relatives, a journey of several days into the foothills. On the way they were held up by four bandits who robbed them of their horses, saddles, and all they were taking on their journey. Young Onofre left his mother at the nearest ranch, and, instead of reporting to the authorities, borrowed a rifle and got on the trail of the bandits. From ambush he killed one; they fled, he followed, and another day killed a second. Now thoroughly frightened, the two remaining rode for the high mountains. Onofre stayed with the man hunt until he had killed them all.

The fourteen-year-old boy then had serious questions to consider; whether the authorities would condone his taking the law into his own hands; whether the bandits might have relatives with more influence than one young boy might have. He concluded it was best to evade the law. He was next heard from as a member of a bandit gang that held up pack trains with gold or silver coming down the mountains from Calabacillas, San José de Gracia, and others of the old mines. For about fifteen years he rode with those gangs; became their leader. He was not at heart a thief, he hated thieving, he wished to be an honest man. Getting his band together, he served notice on them that he was through, was making a deal to pay the authorities a substantial sum for his liberty, and theirs if they chose; that henceforth those who remained bandits must count him their enemy who would run them down as when a boy he had those robbers who had waylaid him and his mother.

So the band divided and parted company, also dividing their spoils. Don Onofre soon was made head of the *Acordada*, the Vigilance Committee for the Sinaloa River area, a post for which he was eminently qualified and which he fulfilled so well that it is traditional—a post which he held probably for forty years.

His share of the loot, no doubt a large one, was sufficient to buy his liberty and to secure him lands and cattle, with a goodly portion over. His ranch quarters at Salsipuedes were well planned for protection, the adobe rooms were thick walled, with portholes, and there was a heavy hardwood stockade. There was always a man or two on guard about the place. After we knew each other very well he once unlocked a room to show Uncle Bill and me where he had leaning against the wall a half dozen loaded Winchester carbines, and in a corner various leather sacks, perhaps two feet high, with little silver bars—perhaps some of gold—such was the dignity of the old gentleman that I did not wish to offend it by a show of more than casual interest. I understood by the act of his showing me this treasure that I had his complete confidence, and did not think best to question him further as to its value or how it had been acquired.

He was a rare judge of human nature. Certain offenders against the law whom he concluded were not natural outlaws, only led astray, he would sponsor, taking them from the court on probation and placing them on his ranches where by good treatment and sober counsel he usually made good men of them. If they failed to respond he had authority to make "short shift with a long rope."

Once when I commented on the artistic fences he had built, hardwood brush woven neatly around *palo colorado* posts set about three feet apart, such fences as I have never seen elsewhere, he commented that they had cost him only the feeding of his paroled outlaws, and their clothing. After a certain period, perhaps two or three years, Don Onofre usually would return the paroled man to court and recommend his pardon, which meant that he would be pardoned.

Not so many years ago Uncle Bill brought the fine old man

[203]

up to California to see us. He could not read or write, so Uncle Bill had been able to secure only seventy-two hours' leave for him despite his showing a checking account of $20,000, which he drew on only through Uncle Bill's writing checks if Don Onofre needed them.

Coming over Cahuenga Pass out of Hollywood, marveling at the traffic, he exclaimed, *"Madre de Dios!* There are as many automobiles here as cattle on my ranches!"

Dignified as ever, he sat on our porch giving me an account of his world, and commenting gravely on ours, which he could not well comprehend. He slept outdoors; he had lived outside all the days of his life—inside air, even in the country, stifled him. He was a rare product of an interesting time, a fine gentleman and a good man to have for a friend.

During Dad's employment at Aguila by Johnston he was one day called by Mr. and Mrs. Johnston and asked to take under his care a little Mestizo boy, an orphan about nine years old, Salomé Galaviz. Salomé had drifted into Aguila somehow from Lo de Gabriel on the Mocorito River, over a hundred miles distant. The Johnstons had employed him to carry water with a wooden *palanca* across his shoulders, from the river to their house, paying him a sum liberal for the time. Mrs. Johnston was—is—a charming, gracious, kindly person, and together with her husband took a real interest in the little fellow.

As often happens, prosperity all but ruined the little water carrier. His needs were so small; food wherever he could pick it up, probably largely from the Johnston kitchen; a ragged bit of blanket to curl up in; a minimum of clothes, that was all. So the very young man took to drink. Every day with his pennies he patronized the *cantinas* until he became really just a very young drunkard. Matters came to a climax one day when, fired by *mescal,* he returned to the Johnston home and demanded to see his employers. They received him, listened to a drunken harangue mostly on the proposition of an increase in pay.

The employers decided something positive must be done, so Mr. Johnston asked Dad to take Salomé with him to where he was opening up the first farm project at Los Mochis for his employer. Dad looked up the boy, told him to be ready at a certain time. Salomé had no intention of losing his soft snap.

He hid out, but not well enough. Dad laid firm hold of him by an ear, led him to his wagon, and threw him in, telling him to behave or else.

Salomé was philosophical; he concluded it would be easier to go along quietly and run away later. When they arrived Dad took him in hand, showed him carefully how work should be done, kept him moving, got him interested in learning to do things.

He stayed with us for about fifteen years, became a keen ranch foreman, so able that Dad moved him into a larger field of opportunity with the sugar company. He never learned to read, only to sign his name, but he became superintendent over ten thousand acres of sugar cane plantations. Failing to read, he developed a memory, a storehouse for figures that is incredible to us who leave our memories on a sheet of paper.

Out of his background he has developed a fine and quite humorous philosophy. Plain-spoken, critical when necessary, he has the happy faculty of never quarreling, always making friends. His wife, Maria, daughter of another of our ranch foremen, has interpreted writing to him when necessary. Their two daughters have been sent to the state university, have a good business training. One is married to Tom Jordan, son of one of the old colonist families.

There is a lesson to be found in the lives of such different people as Don Patricio, Anita, Don Salomé Puente, Guicochea, Don Onofre, Salomé Galaviz—that in the main, no matter how classes may be leveled, or how leveling the circumstances of the lives of people, talent will assert itself, and personalities will rise to something like their merited position in life.

CHAPTER VI
Life with a Fisherman

ABOUT TEN MILES from our community, on the northerly shore of Ohuira Bay, the colonists built a summer camp,
Mapaui, named for a nearby estuary and little rocky peninsula. It was here that Owen had first looked on the inland sea
he described in "A Dream." Some few colonists built adobe
houses there, others went on short excursions.

We built a house and spent summers at this camp. We
kept a sailboat and usually a dugout canoe. From this shore
we sailed, sometimes on trips of several days, out past the islands and through the Bays of Ohuira, Topolobampo, Las
Copas, and Santa Maria, camping where we chose, fishing
mornings, sailing afternoons, sometimes spearing fish by
torchlight at night.

My Danish Dad was untiring as a fisherman. Not only
summers when we stayed on the beach, all the year when we
drove Pinto and Rocillo, our little native ponies, the ten miles
to Mapaui usually leaving Saturday afternoon to return Sunday night. Most trips our party consisted of Dad, one of our
Indians (Rosario or Bernardo) and myself.

In the little wagon we carried a grub box, a bale of hay, a
barrel of water, and our fishing tackle. Nearing the camp we
would stop to cut perhaps fifty two-foot lengths of dried *pitahaya*, dead wood but still full of pitch, for our torchlight for
spearing. Thorns were rasped off the fluted cactus trunks, but
many remained to find their way, especially handled in the
dark, into our fingers.

At camp we unharnessed the horses, fed them hay, gave
them water when they had cooled and rested. After making
camp we loaded the *pitahaya* sticks amidships of our dugout
canoe. Into the bow of the canoe we set a pipe, curving up-
ward and forward, from which to suspend our wire fire-
basket, the *candil*. Spears, one or two or three pronged, were
fixed by their sockets onto the hardwood handles, a stout fish-
line tied on the spear socket, then two thirds of the way up

the six-foot handle, leaving about twenty-five feet of line to be held in the left hand. By dusk we had the fire blazing in the basket, ready to depart.

The bay shore was gently sloping; tides dropping six feet left a half mile of *playa* flat exposed. Spearing was usually in water about a foot in depth, to see whatever fish lay on the bottom. Fish moved inshore and out with the tides—mullet, singly, by dozens, or in schools of thousands, leaping into the air as the schools moved along, sounding sometimes like the movement of a herd of cattle. These mullet varied in size from the tiniest ones to two feet in length. They were a lively target, flashing into view under the light, turning, whirling, or leaping into the air in a flash, sometimes landing in the canoe—that one being counted for the canoe man.

There were *roncadores* (croakers), *palometas, curbina* (sea trout), red snappers, and, on the rocky shores, members of the grouper family, *cabrilla* and *mero. Coconacos* were a chunky, short red-snapper type of fish. *Tutoavas,* the big white sea bass, occasionally came into the bays. Some we speared were over five feet in length. In the Gulf outside they grow to seven feet.

To those who do not know spearing it is hard to describe —the king of sports in the realm of fishing. There is a fascination in watching for the fish, seeing them appear in the light, trying to guess their move—towards the canoe, across the bow, straight away or down the side, estimating their depth in the water to allow for refraction, and their speed, then when the spear is heaved they might stop short, side-twist, leap out of the water—anything but what the spearsman figured on.

We took turns, two at the spears, one at the pole or paddle After a dozen fish, a turn at the paddle.

What a contrast in spearsmen, the Indians standing motionless, letting many possible shots go, then a quick stab and usually a fish—the little *gringo* shooting away, missing too many, but having so much fun, ignoring the contemptuous grunt of his Indian friend! Sharks came rushing through, sometimes great big fellows that gave us many a merry tussle, if they didn't take away a spear. Porpoises followed the canoe for minutes at a time, attracted by the light and the commotion of the fish. Once only we erred in spearing one.

It promptly whirled violently, sending up a splash of water that doused our light and soaked us to the skin.

Sometimes by midnight we had returned with a first boat-load of fish, then out again for a second. Next, a few hours sleep—so few—then Dad calling, "Tide must be coming in, Tommie, I hear the red snappers after the mullet. Let's get to fishing." Out through the gray dawn, feet into cold water, pushing from shore a few hundred yards to deep water, where Dad had carefully marked the best patches of red-snapper grass. We were no fancy fishermen—Dad never was converted—we used hand-casting lines with a nice little mullet for bait; and how *Don Luisito* could coil and cast a line, to land the bait a hundred feet away right in a little clear space where a big hungry snapper cruising by could not fail to see it!

Red snappers are gamy, great sport; a beautifully shaped fish, of bright red hue, turning darker out of the water. Large ones were fifteen to twenty pounds, many were ten pounds.

Corbina, coconaco, cabrilla, mero, all were taken by bait fishing. There were several varieties of the mackerel family, including the *sierra,* silver with gold polka dots; *curiel,* similar to yellowtail; *gallo* and *toro*—the rooster fish and bull fish.

At Farallon Island, in the Gulf, we caught huge sea bass, weighing several hundred pounds; for this fishing we came to use quarter-inch rope, for hooks three-eighths-inch spring steel fashioned in our own blacksmith shops. Dad, master fisherman, studied the habits of each fish, knew the best places at certain tides for miles away from camp, kept his fishing tackle just thus and so. The arts of fishing, of spearing, and of casting the *tarralla,* the funnel-shaped net used throughout the tropics and the western islands, all were his for the fullest enjoyment.

His zest for fishing and his seamanship made him a favorite with the Mayo Indians and the Mexicans who made their living from the sea. As we took our sailboat out beyond the Straits of Joshua to the great mangrove-bordered bays, or through glossy green mangrove-bordered salt-water rivers—estuaries—we met now and again our native friends in their dugout canoes, seeking their living from the inland ocean waters—spearing fish, still fishing, casting the *tarralla* for fish or shrimp, or searching for the big sea turtles or ocean tortoise, the *carey*, of which tortoise-shell combs and other 'ornaments are made.

In the shallow inner bays were thousands of these turtles. The colonists never became adept at capturing them, rather they were purchased from the Mayo Indians for a peso or two each. Turtles are speared, the head of the long-handled spear being a single, stubby, four-sided steel barb that, driven full force, penetrates the turtle shell. As the turtle after being speared puts up a desperate struggle, the spear is made with a socket, this socket separating from the handle at the first violent movement, but remaining attached by a cord.

Early mornings, when the waters of Ohuira Bay were glassy still, one could often see a dozen canoes, some in the far distance, usually with two Indians, one wielding a paddle or pole, the other standing motionless, seemingly for hours, in the bow of the canoe. The turtle comes up every few moments for air—just the stubby dark nose being seen and a quiet sigh being heard, then it slips gently under water, to appear presently many yards away, with no certainty as to where the next appearance may be.

The canoemen patiently shift position at a guess—finally, sometimes after an hour or two—flash goes the spear in a mighty heave, and the turtle usually is taken, after an exciting struggle, over the side of the canoe, ever so carefully by his flippers, as a 200-pound turtle may easily upset a canoe.

Turtles live on the sea grass common in southern waters. Their eggs are laid on sand bars, in one of many holes dug ostensibly for eggs, so forcing a long search by man or beast —notably coyotes—for these delicacies.

Cormorants' eggs had provided a substantial addition to the menu of the colonists both at the port and at Los Mochis. They came in unbelievably great numbers. Quoting from the *Credit Foncier of Sinaloa,* "On April 21st our ducks (cormorants) marshalled their forces for their northern flight. Their parade through the Straits of Joshua was a sight not to be soon forgotten. They defiled around the point of Mumicahui on the wing, settled on the water and drifted with the tide— a mass of birds a mile in length by several hundred feet across, looking like a black river flowing through the sea. When all were in order they again took flight, and we shall not see them again until they come home next October to nest and rear their young in this genial clime."

These cormorants nested on Egg Island in the center of Ohuira Bay, covering with their nests an area three quarters of a mile across. For many years Mayo Indians, natives, and colonists took off eggs in canoe loads for use and sale.

By agreement arrived at in a way beyond human understanding, the cormorants one year failed to appear in the bay. They were later found to have changed to Farallon Island, sixteen miles out in the Gulf, and there they still nest each year.

Towards some favorite island in each bay, at close of day may be seen winging their way thousands of sea birds, long lines of blue-gray or white pelicans, formations of cormorants, groups of sea gulls, pairs of osprey (the fish eagles), and of man-of-war birds, scissor tails (*tijeretas*), as they are variously known. Curlews, oyster catchers, sandpipers, and snipe line the little sand bars. Once the gorgeous pink cranes were common, flying along in the early mornings over the glassy still waters, their reflection in the water showing as clearly as their plumage in the air. Now they are rare, but there are many of their white-plumed cousins.

The night resting places of these many sea birds were also literally bird hospitals. At the Bird Rocks in San Ignacio Bay usually can be found dozens of cripples, pelicans or cormorants or other birds with broken wings or damaged legs; from the scenes of their unfortunate adventures they unfailingly endeavored to reach their bird havens to recuperate or tragically to die.

Out in the shallow bay from the village of Ohuira the Mayos had pooled their energies to construct a primitive fish trap, a tightly packed brush wall extending fully two miles in an incomplete semicircle from the shore, so that the fish at incoming tide were diverted by this great wing into the space between wall and shore; later with the falling tide to follow the inside line of the brush fence, seeking their way to the open bay, but finding instead cleverly constructed little diversion fences which led them into brush pockets, traps where they lingered too long until the tide left them stranded, to be taken by the Indians. The fish were opened down the back, spread to appear like a pancake, the flesh cut into long

[210]

ribbon-like strips, heavily sprinkled with salt, then sun dried. When cured they were packed on burros to be sold in the up-country villages along the Fuerte River.

Another method of taking fish by the Indians should be described. Choosing an *estero* small enough that all the water emptied from it at lowest tide, they constructed across its entrance from the sea a solidly packed brush wall. The center, where the channel was deepest, they left open for several days, until fish no longer turned away from the wall. Meanwhile, they built the center section of the wall, leaving it lying near the entrance. One day—or night—at full high tide, before fish began moving down the estuary, with the outgoing current, they would complete the barricade.

Canoes were placed end to end outside the wall with sails or blankets raised along their length. When the schools of mullet arrived to find the obstruction they would swim violently about; eventually, as the tide continued to lower they would leap through the air, high as a man's head, many of them striking the sails or blankets to land in the canoes. Other fish milled about until left stranded by the lowered tide.

Some estuaries had large, deep pools to which part of the fish retreated. Into these the Mayos cast handfuls of mashed San Juanico berries. In a few moments fish would rise to the surface, gasping for air, to be easily picked up by the fishermen. Some chemist might give the explanation for this swift contamination of a large volume of salt water by a few tree berries.

CHAPTER VII
Game Trails

AMERICAN SCHOOL TEACHERS being hard to come by in Sinaloa, we youngsters had so much more time for the fishing and hunting abundant there. Small game came to the door, practically speaking. An hour's ride on horseback took us far enough into the woods for deer and *jabali*, which we usually stalked Indian fashion, moving slowly along the game trails, set for a quick shot, as game is found close and moves swiftly in such dense woods, disappearing before the careless hunter could raise a rifle.

In those early days the Mayo Indians, besides snaring deer in various curious ways, would run them down—not by speed, but by perseverance. Two or three Mayos, starting a deer at early morning, would take turns at keeping on its trail, at a fast walk or Indian trot, permitting the deer no rest. Now and again the runner would call to the others, and, the deer customarily running in a wide circle, another runner would presently take up the chase, until by midafternoon the poor animal must rest, and so let an Indian get within bow shot for the kill.

Jabali usually move out of view as swiftly as a deer. If wounded, however, they are apt to make a stand. I recall an anxious afternoon because after wounding a *jabali* its squealing brought a rush of fifteen or more grunting, jaw-snapping *jabalies* towards him—and me—from several directions. After shooting a second I decided for the relative safety of a small *palo colorado* tree.

Despite my killing three more of the brutes, they hung around for over two hours, not moving over thirty yards away. With three cartridges left for my rifle I sat, most uncomfortably, in the small tree. When the sun had set I finally made my getaway without disturbing them.

Another time I shot a sow from a band, leaving it to trail the others. They moved into such dense woods that I left them, returning to recover the kill. Coming upon the pig from around a bush at a distance of perhaps six feet, I was putting down my rifle when I was startled to see a boar, standing partly concealed under a low bush not a yard from the sow. He never moved, just looked balefully at me while I dropped him at less than two paces. I have wondered what would have happened in another second of waiting.

The meat of the young *jabali*, particularly of the sows, is delectable, superior in flavor to venison or any other large

game I have tasted. Boars have a strong taste, derived from a scent bag lodged oddly along the top of their backs, between front shoulders and hind quarters. Another oddity of the *jabali* is that it has no tail.

In a country so rich in small game there are many coyotes, bob-cats, and a goodly number of mountain lions. Howling of coyotes in the evening and the early dawn was as expected as the crowing of roosters or lowing of cattle. I learned to imitate them well enough that they would answer, coming closer and closer to the call, until they caught the human scent or otherwise decided they were being deceived. While hunting we were often followed by them, their occasional yipping being likely to warn away our game. Once I hid well

enough to drop one in its tracks two steps from me, as it trotted along on my trail.

Coyotes may play dead like a possum when in a tight spot.
While riding with a group of *vaqueros* I chased one that had
been wounded some days before, lassoed it, and dragged it by
the neck for fifty yards—not that I had any feeling of cruelty
towards animals, simply that coyotes were our most serious
menace to poultry, livestock, and game, to be killed when
possible. We removed the lasso to continue on our way. After
traveling a hundred yards or so we looked back to see the
coyote making off, apparently none the worse for his dragging at the end of a rope.

The mountain lion, cougar, puma, panther, as it is variously termed, is the most disputed animal as to its habits of any
wild animal known. I am inclined to believe that, so scattered as it is over North America, its characteristics vary
with its environment to cause this sharp conflict in state-
ments by various naturalists and hunters. By some it is
termed cowardly—yet I shall tell a personal experience that
proves otherwise.

One summer upon moving to our seashore home at Mapaui
we found the signs of a lioness' having during the preceding
months bedded its cubs on some hay left in storage in our
kitchen. A few days later Mother took a walk some hundreds
of yards up the road leading through the brush. Presently I
faintly heard her call, as from a long distance, "Help, Tommie, help!" Snatching up a rifle I hastened as fast as a ten
year old may up the road, to find her, walking slowly backward while the lioness stalked her, moving in the road towards her. Upon hearing my approach, the animal slipped
into the woods before I could get into position along the road
for a shot.

One evening some weeks later we had turned in for the
night, when we heard the scratch, scratch of an animal on
the closed windows of our house. Whispering, all concluded
it must be the lioness wanting to take shelter inside. Failing
at one window or door, she moved to the next. Suddenly
Mother shrieked, "I left the kitchen window open," and out
we piled to close it.

When we broke camp at the end of summer, the rest of the
family drove back to the farm in a buckboard, an Indian,

Julian Bacame, and I remaining another day to finish load-
ing our household goods into a larger wagon. It was still
warm—a bright moonlit night. I was sleeping on the typical
canvas cot inside. Julian chose the cooler air outside, covering himself only with a sheet to reduce the annoyance of occasional sand gnats and mosquitoes.

The lioness screamed that night—no need to describe the
heart-chilling sound to those who have heard it—it strikes
fear into any ordinary soul, yet it has such a similarity to the
sound of a distressed person—the woman's voice—that it well
can bring uncertainty as to being a lion. My half-grown
Great Dane, Moreno, rose at the sound, barking furiously.
Eventually we all settled down again, I at least to a restless
sleep, when I was brought upright out of bed by a yell more
human still, as our Indian, Julian, came streaking through
the door with his sheet tailing out behind. When his excitement subsided he told his story.

He had settled down to sleep, the sheet pulled up to leave
his feet exposed. He came to with the nuzzling of an animal
against his toes. Thinking it to be the dog, he raised his head,
to stare by full moonlight into the face of the lioness.

The noise Julian made should have chilled the heart of a
Bengal tiger, but no—we were kept awake by a curious game
of tag between the lioness and the dog, the latter chasing up
the slope towards the woods, barking furiously, then being
chased back yowling when the beast turned on him. On one
of these exciting excursions from a window we glimpsed the
animal, with the dog chasing after, coming along the open
porch of the house. Now well armed, I with Dad's .45-caliber
sixshooter, Julian with a big rosewood club, we rushed
through the house to intercept the brute at the house corner.
As she flashed by I fired wildly while Julian brought his club
down in a fierce swing, missing the lioness completely, landing with a sound thud on the earth floor of the porch. This
excitement was enough even for the lioness. Some while later
she once more screamed into the moonlight, but we never
saw her again.

Native hunters of jaguars have successfully used a cow's
horn to blow a rumbling sound in imitation of the female, so
calling the male jaguar which answers the sound as he ap-
proaches. A hunter I know near Alamos, Sonora, does this

calling at night, lying in ambush, then when the male jaguar is a few steps away a flashlight is focused on him while he is shot with a rifle. Just when to flash the light would seem to be the most delicate point in this way of stalking a tiger.

A Mexican friend told me of stalking a tiger that was feeding on his young livestock. The man took a young goat to a clearing on a hillside, killed it, put some strychnine poison on the meat, then, armed with a rifle, a pistol, and a big knife, climbed a large tree nearby to wait.

It was full moonlight. A coyote came into the clearing, found the goat, ate of it, soon writhed in agony and died near the carcass of the goat. Later that night the man heard the tiger rumbling, rumbling, first far up the hillside, then nearer and nearer and ever more terrifying to my hunter friend. Suddenly the tiger showed head and shoulders in the moonlight, his mouth wide in a fierce rumble. My friend swears that his hair stood straight up and that he shook so much that his hat bounced up and down on his head.

The big cat bounded over to the dead goat, sniffed, then to the coyote, which it took up in its huge jaws, and trotted away into the woods. The valiant hunter had completely forgotten about his weapons. Moreover, he was so profoundly impressed with that jaguar that he stayed perched in the tree until morning.

In contrast, near Fuerte a Mayo woman, while milking a cow, saw a jaguar leap into the corral, take a good-sized calf in its jaws, and make for the fence. This woman seized a mesquite club, and, while the tiger was busily tugging at the calf, laid it dead with a blow over the head.

Jaguars were once quite common, now they are rare, most of those remaining living in the wilder reaches of the west coast sierras. Once, on a sandy island, I tracked one for hours, in something of a circle, its track appearing over mine several times as it moved out ahead, but it was too wary to be stalked. Another time I heard the call of a tiger, similar to the rumbling of a bull, far up the peak of Cabezon Mountain, overlooking San Ignacio Bay. Another I saw slip like a shadow out of view into dense wood; only these in many years of hunting.

Caimanes (alligators) are to be found at the mouths of the Fuerte, Sinaloa, Culiacan, and other southern rivers. The natives developed a most ingenious way of catching them, constructing a hook, as it were, in the form of two sticks crossed, one hinged. This they baited with a jackrabbit or a small pig, attached to it a good-sized rope which at its opposite end was staked securely into the river bank. As the *caiman* swallowed the bait and moved away, the rope tightened to set the hinged cross piece across inside the throat so that it held the *caiman* securely as the fishermen dragged it ashore to finish it off with clubs.

Lying on the sand banks they appear sluggish, but can move swiftly, raising their bodies on all fours as a smaller lizard does when running.

Camped at the mouth of Culiacan River, Thanksgiving Day 1917, being low on provisions, we skinned out the tail of a young alligator, boiling the white fish-like flesh for three hours or so to tenderize it, then fried it to make some very palatable steaks.

Alligator steak—slightly tough—squash from a nearby Indian garden, flour tortillas, and tea—not a usual Thanksgiving menu, yet the memory of it still pleasantly lingers.

This chapter closes with the most curious hunting story I have heard. Among various enterprises together, Uncle Bill and I raised cattle and horses. Some of these we ran in the woods near the Fuerte—at Vialacahui Ranch—in the care of Longino Valdez, a *vaquero* well past seventy years of age. After a day of hard riding in the woods we would sit about the campfire exchanging stories.

On one of these nights I was rolled into my blankets, just about gone in slumber, when old Longino asked, "Don Tomas, did you ever kill a camel?" Somewhat startled, and provoked, too, I answered, "No, Longino, nor have you!" "Ah, but I have!" said he. I came to and heard his story.

When about fifteen years of age, perhaps between the years 1870 and 1875, Longino was out hunting in the woods a short distance out of the pueblo of Sinaloa, once capital of the state. He was armed with a cap and ball rifle. Emerging from the woods into a good sized trail he came face to face with a hideous monster, so shocking to behold that Longino knew it could be naught but a devil in form of animal. Shaking to his toes, he barely had courage to raise and fire his gun. At his shot the "devil" fell dead.

While Longino was still rejoicing in a shaken way over his escape, a man came hurrying to find the camel. It was one of a caravan being sent down the West Coast to central Mexico, a gift from the President of Mexico. The angry caretaker hustled the young hunter into town to face the local judge, demanding a thousand pesos fine and a letter of explanation to clear the keeper. Young Longino stoutly protested that under the circumstances he was not to blame. To decide the case the Judge went to view the camel caravan, and immediately released Longino, declaring he would have acted as quickly to kill such a beast.

At San Miguel on the Fuerte River the caravan had a bad time. The local Mayos, upon seeing the camels, sent out a call for a council meeting, to debate whether the hideous creatures were animal or devil, and ended by resolving to kill them. Fortunately, the local Mexicans heard of the tribal gathering, and warned the camel drivers, who quickly moved some miles away, so escaping the calamity that was so nearly upon them.

The fact of importation of camels during the last century into the deserts of Texas and Arizona is well known. Western publications have carried stories of them from time to time. This was one they missed.

CHAPTER VIII

Local Lore

ONE COULD NOT LIVE in Mexico without becoming interested in buried treasure. For more than 300 years there had been constant production of gold and silver. Pack trains carrying those metals were frequently robbed and the loot buried. Pirate ships had plundered other ships and had raided seaports, later landing at secluded shores to bury their ill-gotten riches. There was not a bank in which to deposit money, short of the state capital of Culiacan, 200 miles away, or Alamos, Sonora, where so much silver and gold were produced that a Federal Mint was constructed there to handle the vast output.

From the wealthy *hacendado* to the lowly *pelado*, burying gold and silver was the usual way of hoarding.

Churches in out-of-the-way places were considered apt locations for buried treasure.

The greatest protection afforded the owner of a buried treasure was a firmly rooted superstition that to unearth an *entierro* was to bring a curse upon the digger in the way of death to himself, probably to others of his family as well. This was smart propaganda, whoever first conceived its use. However, there were rugged souls who braved the curse. Along the *caminos reales*—the highways—even along the by-ways, in all sorts of unexpected places, one can find excavations of many ages, where there has been search for treasure. Now and then some poor man suddenly has riches with which to buy land, cattle, to build a home—the discoverer of a buried treasure.

The accepted phenomena by which treasures are located is that at night a light shines over the spot of burial. Once two of our laborers climbed the roof of a house to better watch for the light. One of them, coming out of a deep sleep, fancied he saw a flare. His companion aroused, they hastened toward it, running off the roof, one breaking a leg. This was patent evidence of the ill fate awaiting treasure hunters.

Uncle Bill was keen for finding treasure. During one of his various searches, near the village of Bamoa, where he had several men digging, he unearthed a village of the ancients, where bodies were buried in a sitting posture inside huge pottery *ollas*.

Another search was made by him with an old Indian who had herded goats over the hideout of a bandit gang, their headquarters being a huge cave on the slope of a lonely mountain. Although the old man had not returned to the spot since a boy, he found his way from point to point as he had remembered, until facing the place where the cave had been. Within the past twenty or thirty years there had been a slide moving thousands of tons of earth over the spot. Who may tell what treasure therein lies!

My fine Indian friend, Lino Jocobi, constant hunting companion in trips about San Ignacio Bay, told two interesting treasure tales.

San Ignacio Bay is a miniature inland sea, sprinkled with rocky islands. Across its western shore to shelter it from the Gulf extends an island of the same name, twelve miles of drift sand. Pointing toward this island from the north is Ajoro Peninsula, protecting an inner bay. Along the western shore of this bay lies Cerro Barcino, a cactus-covered mountain sheltering a fine anchorage concealed from the sea, likewise from land, that is, for all but a few Indians living in two small villages on the peninsula.

According to the father-in-law of Lino, as a small boy he had hidden with other Indians and watched a pirate ship sail into this sheltered place, anchoring off shore at a certain protruding rocky point, where they spent several days. The pirate crew dug on the saddle of the mountain a great hole, where they dumped bars of metal and placed various heavy boxes. Several times during two or three years the same ship put in to shelter, sometimes adding to their store of treasure on the hilltop. The Indians were fearful; they did not let themselves be seen. As fearful of any other ruling force, they never divulged the story to the Mexicans, and fearful too of the consequences of unearthing treasure, it is probable that no one of them went too near the place.

There was a story among local natives of a pirate "Crom" —perhaps Cromwell—putting into San Ignacio and Topolobampo Bays at various times, probably in the early 1800's. He is reported to have perished with his crew in the upper reaches of the Gulf of California.

This same Cromwell frequently raided the picturesque seaport of La Paz, on the southeastern shore of the peninsula of Lower California, and for many decades the most important center of the pearl-diving industry of all the world. So often was his pirate ship, with sails full set, seen borne down the Bahia de La Paz by the northwesterly winds, that the term *"El Coromuel"* is still applied by the natives there to those cooling ocean breezes so welcome during summers in that tropic land.

Thought of the treasure of Cerro Barcino was intriguing to Uncle Bill, Lino, and me, but the hill is rugged, the exact spot uncertain, and the years have left it undisturbed.

Cabezon Mountain stands, impressively solitary, on the eastern shore of San Ignacio Bay. Out from Cabezon a few hundred feet lies a rocky little islet, dry at low tide. On its summit, perhaps forty feet above tideline, was a very old, much weathered hardwood cross, its base wedged firmly into a fissure in the rock. The Indians of the nearby village of Carrizo, where Lino lived, had inherited a story; that the Spaniards had worked a silver mine on Cabezon, using Mayo Indian labor captured by lassoing them from on horseback, herding them at night into a high hardwood stockade well guarded by Spanish soldiers. During some upheaval, perhaps the war for Mexican independence dating from 1810, being compelled to abandon the mine, the Spaniards had erected the large hardwood cross on the islet, carefully pointing its horizontal arm to indicate the entrance to the mine, which they concealed before leaving. The cross, grooved from age, was too unfirm for us to have any assurance of its original position. Perhaps geologists may some day discover what legend has handed down.

Of all the persons of my acquaintance I am the only one who has actually discovered a buried treasure! In 1935 a group of us, adventurous residents of Southern California, drove in two pick-up cars down the peninsula of Baja California to the beautiful Bahia de Los Angeles, lying in the Gulf, protected by the forty-mile length of Angel de la Guardia Island. The stories of fishing we can tell from that trip are something hardly to be believed, but again they are not a part of our story. We had camped near an abandoned stamp mill of the Las Flores Mine, which had operated in 1892 when Dad had come into the bay on his way to the colony.

One day, walking on the beach after swimming, my toes rested on a round object in the sand. Taking it to be a sea shell I toed it over to discover it a silver peso, covered with green corrosion that had cemented to it a layer of ocean sand. I soon found several others; marking the spot, I returned to toss my pesos onto our camp table, with most gratifying results. Our whole crew went to digging and soon we were finding little stacks of pesos, welded together by corrosion. However, our illusions somewhat dampened when we reached a top loot of two hundred and eighty-four pesos. The latest date on any peso was 1894, forty-one years before.

For all our jubilation we soon concluded that we had brought upon ourselves a problem of the first magnitude. The law required us to deliver half the treasure to the Mexican government. Half of two hundred and eighty-four pesos! I had a picture of us trying to persuade some skeptical Government official that we were reporting it all, and finally all being thrown into jail until further notice. For days we fished and pondered our problem. Divided among five of us there were little over fifty pesos each which would scarce last us as souvenirs for the years to come. We concluded we must either divide it for souvenirs, or throw it back on the sand. We threw it back, you may be sure!

Treasure hunting sometimes led to the playing of practical jokes among the natives. Near Zapotillo on the Fuerte River lived two men, Modesto Galaviz and a close friend and *compadre*, the latter reputed to have a substantial treasure underground. As often occurred, the man died without telling his heirs or his friend of its hiding place. Don Modesto's brooding over the matter suggested an idea to Uncle Bill, then a young fellow, and to Don Modesto's mischievous nephews. They told Don Modesto that as they passed a certain bridge along the highway at night the deceased had appeared, appealing to them to summon his friend for the following night. Don Modesto must not fail his deceased *amigo*, so appeared as requested, and was startled to hear a sepulchral voice greet him.

"Compadre," said the voice, "since my death I have not rested. I cannot rest, for I have died leaving a debt to be paid. I now ask that you should pay it for me"—mentioning the sum and to whom due—"You will find my money buried at the foot of the mesquite tree in my corral. Whatever remains after payment I wish to be yours."

"It shall be done," said Don Modesto, "exactly as you have asked."

"Ah, now I may rest in peace," said the spirit, "yet first I wish to embrace you before departing," and one of the boys advanced from the darkness shrouded in white, spreading wide his arms, over which a white sheet was draped.

"Ay, eso no mas no!" ("Ay, anything but that!") gasped the startled Don Modesto, and fell in a faint.

A great person for perpetrating jokes was Don Napoleon Sanchez of Higuera de Zaragoza. On his ranch was a mountain with a deep cave, where the devil was reputed to be in hiding. My uncle Clyde scoffed at the idea, offering to traverse the length of the cave after dark to disprove the belief. Don Napoleon and his sons begged Clyde not to do so, but no persuasion sufficing, he was requested to sign a statement that he had been duly warned and therewith relieved his hosts of all responsibility for what might befall him.

Meanwhile they hired an Indian to go into the cave to play the part of *El Diablo.* According to agreement Clyde proceeded ten steps into the cave before calling *"Diablo,"* then another ten to repeat the call. Upon the third call the *Diablo* answered *"Ay voy"*—(there I go). Terrified, Clyde sank to his knees in the narrow cave; the Indian, nervous also, dashed for the entrance. As he brushed past Clyde the latter, in a gesture of protection, flung himself upon the man, whose screaming caused Clyde to guess what had been planned, and he came out of the cave with the Indian held tight to be delivered as the *Diablo.*

Don Napoleon kept a store in town. The boys, as willing to trick the old gentleman, came to town with news that the ranch *vaquero* had been bitten by a mad dog. Some days later the boys took Don Napoleon out to the ranch, saying they were going rabbit hunting. As the old joker was waiting about for the boys he beheld his *vaquero,* his clothes in disorder, foam covering his face and beard, coming across the yard toward him, growling like a dog and doing a most horrible snapping of his jaws.

Across the fields fled old Don Napoleon with his supposedly rabied *vaquero* in pursuit, finally catching up to leap on his back and bite at him with all the realism that might be imagined. Rescued by the boys, Don Napoleon was returned to town, where he went to bed sick with fear, so sick that the boys concluded they must tell him the truth. However, the truth the old sinner would not believe, and he lay for days in an agony of fear before being convinced that he was not becoming a case of rabies. The cure was most effective; he desisted from his "practical joking" thereafter.

Rabies was all too common in a country so replete with dogs. Epidemics extended to livestock bitten, to coyotes in the woods, and people. During one bad three months' period I killed seven dogs with rabies. Believe it or not, there is a rabies treatment known to certain Mayo Indians through the generations for no one knows how many centuries past. I have talked with several persons bitten who have taken the cure, and heard of a multitude of others. Such is the faith of the people that they come from all over the State for treatment, and of many, many dozens treated during the years a case has never been known to die of rabies.

The treatment seems simple enough. Near the Indian doctor's house he has another little house where the patients are placed, after a complete change of clothing and a bath in a liquid prepared by the Indian doctor. Once a day for three successive days the patient is given a drink which immediately induces terrific perspiration, after which the patient has another bath. At the end of the three-day treatment the patient is released, assured of being cured.

It is stoutly maintained by many who should know, as our old foreman, Salomé Galaviz, that these Indian doctors cure cases already with the seizure upon them, cases brought to them lashed to beds. In such cases the cure is more drastic, a drink which induces extreme vomiting, followed by a series of steam baths in an earthen pit, meanwhile taking the liquid that induces perspiration.

Wise men may scoff. I urge them to investigate for themselves. Science can make use of such startling cures by people to whom science is an unknown world.

Many of the cases may not have been inoculated with rabies, but over the years many others must have been. Mexicans and Indians know many cures that we might make use of. Once upon a time when a veterinarian gave up my saddle horse for gone from a great inflamed wound that could not be drained, our Mexican *vaquero* healed the animal in a remarkably short time by the simple remedy of cooking some common lily-looking swamp plants called *Yerba del Manzo* and bathing the wound with the liquid.

Long before the technique of healing infection by use of worms was developed in World War I, we had learned from an Indian cowboy in Sinaloa to rid a mule of fistula, a cancerous growth, by infesting it with worms which ate the cancerous flesh to leave a clean wound which soon healed.

A few weeks ago I saw at Los Mochis Charles Hays, one of the few remaining colonists, nearing 80 years, but ruddy and vigorous as a man 20 years younger. A year before he had given up hope of living, was suffering from uremic poisoning, and in a general run-down condition that no physician's treatments would alleviate. In despair he turned to an old Indian woman for advice. For the uremic poisoning she prescribed a clove of garlic with each meal for two weeks—and the poisoning was eliminated. For the run-down condition the prescription was a tablespoon of turtle oil daily until one and a half gallons were taken, by which time our friend's vigor was restored to that of twenty years before. Powder of the ovaries of the turtle is well known along the coasts of Mexico as a gland restorative of the nature of the well-advertised Dr. Brinkley of some years past. Instead of diving into the swampy pools of Florida, Ponce de Leon might have restored his youth by fishing the waters of Topolobampo Bay!

CHAPTER IX

Viva la Revolucion!

DIESISEIS DE SEPTIEMBRE (16th of September) is the Mexican National Holiday, commemorating the famous *Grito de Dolores*, when in 1810 the Patriot Priest, Miguel Hidalgo, gave his historic call to arms, somewhat as our own Patrick Henry gave during the stirring days preceding our War of the Revolution. The Centennial of the Mexican National Holiday, on September 16th, 1910, was, of course, cause for great celebration.

A boy of thirteen years, I chanced to be visiting Mexican friends at the pueblo of Muchicahui. The central plaza was adorned with colored paper streamers extended between lamp posts, the central *kiosko* (bandstand) was hidden in flowers. Many hundreds of people were congregated. There was music from two competing bands. A speaker's stand held the town and country notables, the local *oficiales*, the more prominent *comerciantes* and *hacendados*.

From the rostrum after the *Grito de Dolores* given by the top local official had been enthusiastically applauded, distinguished, handsome young Donato Borboa, son of the town's leading merchant and local *Jefe Politico*, pronounced a stirring discourse dealing with the glories of Mexico, the greatness of its government, the happiness of a free people. It was most inspiring, and drew a fine round of applause after which the celebration continued, the aristocracy with the best orchestra holding a dance in one location, the poorer class in another. The Mayo Indians, few of whom were interested enough to attend the speaking, celebrated in their customary manner with their own music and dances, no doubt chiefly glad because it was a day free from labor. They had little cause to rejoice over the type of government that robbed them of their lands.

The poorer Mexicans, too, had little reason to rejoice over their condition, as contrasted to that of the ruling classes. However, there was an everlasting patience on the part of the Indians and the poorer Mexicans that would have been reassuring to the most questioning mind.

President Porfirio Diaz was old, past eighty years; his generals and closest advisers too were old. Their control had extended through two generations, a hereditary aristocracy of power. The contemptuous bitterness of a few Indians, the cautious if caustic attitude of some of our laborers towards our aristocratic friends such as Don Patricio Quinonez, Don Manuel Borboa, Don Francisco Orrantia, these evidences of feeling seemed of little consequence to me as I considered their lowly position and their impotence to do anything for themselves.

There were state elections, the first I recalled when anyone seemed to even know who were the candidates. *Licenciado* (lawyer) José Ferrel, termed a radical, was running against a fine gentleman, Don Diego Redo, a wealthy sugar plantation owner, the Government's selection. We were surprised to learn how very many of our Mexican friends, not only small merchants, shopkeepers, and poorer people, but the upper classes too, were for Ferrel. Don Diego Redo was elected, by Government control of the ballot, it was said. He was admittedly a fine, able man, but his source of support was not the common people. There were murmurings. Such things were happening all over the country.

One day there was startling news. A revolution was beginning in northern Mexico. Its leaders were not just outlaws, but men of wealth and influence like the Madero family. We heard that a force from the Sinaloa River under the command of Macario Gaxiola, a well-esteemed young rancher, was on its way to assault the Federal garrison at Mochis. Next I was astonished to learn that when they arrived they had established headquarters at the ranch of Uncle Bill, who was a close friend of Gaxiola.

After an exciting three days of gunfire, in which a very few combatants, three innocent bystanders, and several burros were killed, the garrison surrendered. Living three miles out of town, we were fairly secure. However, we counted seven holes from stray bullets in our house walls when the fracas was over.

Most American families within the perimeter of attack were removed. Some of the men stayed to protect their homes.

[227]

The Americans had quickly organized a sort of Militia for mutual protection, with Ross Page as its Captain and Factory Superintendent Tom Boyd as Lieutenant. Telephone communications were cut before the attack. Boyd managed to get Dad by phone, asking him to send someone to warn Scally, Burr, Newton, and Weeks, who were in a house in the line of fire, to leave immediately. Not daring to leave the family, Dad sent me. Catching a dark saddle mare, Queen, as I walked through our pasture, I took cross cuts through fields, passed a Federal outpost a hundred yards away without being challenged, and emerged from a cornfield near the Scally home. As I peered through the pitch-dark night my heart must have missed a beat when I saw standing on the canal bank opposite a whole line of persons—soldiers, no doubt. They kept motionless, except for an occasional flutter of clothes in the gentle night breeze. I froze against the side of the mare, expecting to be shot. There was no challenge, no shot, so I cautiously looked over the neck of the animal again. I studied the figures more carefully; they were clothes hung along a barbed wire fence!

By then the shooting had begun. I rode on to the house, but had the startling and unhappy experience of being knocked off the horse by a clothes line stretched in the yard. Imagine my let-down when "Uncle Joe" Scally, who was deaf and could not hear the shooting, refused to leave, causing his two brothers-in-law to stay also. With one recruit, old Mr. Weeks, I returned the same course to arrive safe at home in the early morning.

Our laborers and their families, uncertain as to their treatment by either *Federales* or *Revolucionarios*, were ready to flee to the sugar cane fields on short notice. They kept someone on lookout in the branches of a large cottonwood tree overhanging the canal that passed through the ranch. The last day of fighting a squad of eight *Federales*, deserters from the defending garrison, came tramping out our road. Dad and I saw them in time to fall in close behind as they moved towards our ranch quarters. As they neared the tall cottonwood tree we were all surprised to see a body come tumbling out of it, falling with a loud splash into the canal below. An Indian boy placed as lookout had dozed off, coming to just in time to see the soldiers, which frightened him into tumbling off his perch.

Viva la Revolucion!

Our laborer families began scurrying for shelter. However, the *soldados* were not looking for trouble. When they saw Dad and me they insisted on surrendering to us, pleading that we intercede for them.

We stacked their arms in our foreman's house and sent them to hide in a nearby cane field. Presently there came galloping down the road a company of the victorious *Revolucionarios*. Reining up, they asked if we had seen any of their *enemigos*. They were quite startled when we told them there were some near by. After some discussion they agreed to spare the lives of their former adversaries. We delivered the arms and brought the poor trembling *Federales* out of hiding. One of the defeated soldiers lived in the town for years after. He never failed to lift his hat high and bow low when Dad or I met him on the street, in gratitude for our intercession for him that day.

A gesture of courtesy much appreciated came during this siege, when the attacking rebels, being advised that American women and children were in a house in line of fire, gallantly moved across open fields to a new position. One colonist young lady, Lilla Newton, was barely missed by a bullet landing in the wall above her.

The closing incident of this siege is burned in my memory. The last defending Federal officer was Artillery Lieutenant Saracho, a graduate of the fine military college of Chapultepec. He had made a gallant stand, exciting the admiration of the attackers. He was well known and well liked by the townspeople. After the surrender he was offered the alternative of execution or a commission in the rebel army. Tauntingly he replied that he would rather die a patiot than live a traitor. He was marched through the main street of the town. His wife ran crying from a house to plead with him. Adamant, Saracho marched on, arms folded on his breast, out of town, to be stood against a high canal bank. Refusing to be bandaged, he protested that the firing squad was not properly formed, and placed them to his satisfaction, seemingly more calm than his executioners. The volley rang out, he was lifted off his feet, the depressing yet inspiring occasion was over. Hundreds of us who had gone in curiosity returned in admiration of that brave soul.

Just a few years ago I met in Lower California a Colonel Saracho, graduate of Chapultepec. Learning I was from Sinaloa he told me of a cousin who had been lost in the early fighting in Sinaloa. I was grateful then to be able to give to this cousin the story of the bravery of Teniente Saracho.

In an incredibly short time the first wave of revolution was over, with President Diaz deposed into exile in France. What appeared to be the end of revolution, however, was in reality only the beginning. From the first the chief objectives were free elections, more representative government, more education, more even distribution of lands and other wealth among the people. Attainment of these idealistic ends was impeded by all the difficulties to be expected from the upsurge of a new leadership largely uneducated and inexperienced in government.

It seemed to us colonists, caught as interested third parties in the struggle, that each succeeding wave of revolution brought more disrespect for personal and property rights, more waste, more poverty. In the beginning we were little molested. The wealthier Mexicans were the first to suffer— first their properties, then themselves. Many of these were our friends, as too were many of the poorer people. In desperation they turned to us foreigners for sanctuary and we had no heart to refuse them. Don Patricio Quinonez and wife and the Renterias lived with us for many months; their farms had been wasted, their livestock taken, only a small part of their wealth, what could be moved to store with us, had been saved.

During the wave after wave of revolution and counter revolution the wealth of the country, material improvements such as railroads, steamships, harbor facilities, factories, mines, and *haciendas*, was greatly wasted. Construction projects such as the Kansas City, Mexico, and Orient Railway and the Southern Pacific of Mexico were abandoned for many years.

The financial economy of the country collapsed, paper currency became worthless, and only silver pesos and gold pieces maintained their value. Generals of the opposing armies carried hand printing presses, putting out their own currency, which they forced on the country by the effective method of shooting those who refused to accept it in exchange for what they might have to sell. After a few months the General in charge of a certain area usually moved. The next General taking his place soon issued a decree substituting a new issue currency. Trying to guess the date of departure of a General, in order to get rid of his currency in exchange for anything that could be purchased became an important part of the local economy.

When the shift in command came because of a revolutionary upheaval we faced another problem—local officials were replaced, including tax collectors; then these new tax collectors would demand from us a show of receipts from their Government for one, two, or three years back, and these being impossible to produce, they demanded back payment of taxes, sometimes with fines for non-payment. To show tax receipts from the party in power just previous was an insult, even possibly to be used as evidence that we had been conniving with the enemy.

Americans in Mexico during those years were a real headache to United States government officialdom. Through their consulates they appealed for protection for life and property. It was tough to lose the earnings of a lifetime of pioneering for causes so completely disassociated with us—yet, there could be no adequate protection for us during those years of revolution, short of intervention, which would have been a most unhappy and unfortunate situation for the government and people of both countries.

Through the United States Department of State permission was secured from one of the revolutionary governments for Americans to carry arms for protection from bandits. An American gunboat was stationed almost continuously at Topolobampo to serve as a place of refuge in case of extreme necessity. Americans were urged to leave the country, but generally they stayed on, hoping to save their farms, factories, mines, railroads, or other properties.

There were several raids by bandit gangs of a hundred or more, such as Chico Mesa's or Fortunato Heredia's. Usually we learned of the approach of these in time to run our livestock, particularly saddle horses and mules, into the cane fields for hiding, and to send our families by back roads through the woods down to the seashore on Ohuira Bay, which, being away from any center, offered no incentive for plunder.

During one of these raids I hurried home from school to find a whole group of bandits' horses tied up in our yard, while the bandits themselves were sitting at our big dining table taking a meal with Dad. He was just sitting down to eat as they arrived, guns held on him, demanding money, commissary supplies, and horses. Dad said in effect, "All right, boys, we will see what we can do for you, but I'm going to eat first. You might as well sit down and eat with me," which they did, feeling in such good humor after a meal and good visit that they were content to leave with some provisions from our commissary.

Rumors coming of another raid, I hurried home from school, about a mile, harnessed a team to our buckboard, threw in hay, blankets, food and water, drove back to school, picked up the dozen or so pupils and the teacher, driving them through the woods to arrive at our beach camp at Mapaui after night. Dad had sent some of our Indians to tell the various parents where we had gone. Most of them arrived at Mapaui the next day, some after driving about all the dark night, lost on the winding roads used for wood hauling. In the excitement of leaving at night Charlie Hays had put his pants on backward and George Drake had tried to pull on the pants of his small nephew, Vin Mulkey, getting them on so tight he was almost permanently hobbled.

Most of us were cheerful enough through those years, laughing at our little misfortunes, always figuring on a brighter day ahead.

A friend of Dad, Mr. Dean, roundhouse foreman of the Southern Pacific at San Blas, brought his Mexican wife, his mother-in-law, and his sister-in-law to us for refuge. The K.C.M. and O. railway passed within a mile of our seashore camp at Mapaui, so we moved the Dean family down there on a track car, one of the hand-pumped variety, on which Dean had built a longer platform to accommodate their many items of luggage. It fell to my unfortunate lot to stay with them in camp. The wife was pleasant enough, the sister-in-law fat and fussy, but mama-in-law was impossible to please. After a few days she insisted on returning to Mochis. Nothing would have pleased me more, but there we were, without transportation except one heavy track car, a mountain of baggage and three big women, for one fourteen-year-old boy to transport, slightly up-grade, for ten miles.

A brainstorm suddenly came to me as I puzzled over this

problem. I lugged the baggage a mile to the track car, loaded
it on with the ladies on top, unfastened the track car handles
to prevent their pumping, and rigged the sail from our large
skiff onto the center section. As the daily westerly breeze
stiffened we set sail. Away we went at a fast click-a-click
over the rails. Never was an ocean skipper more proud of
himself than I as we rounded the curve and sailed into the
town of Mochis to astonish the crowd of onlookers. And what
a relief to leave mama-in-law with their friends, the family
of the station agent in town.

As the years of revolution continued, it became increasingly difficult to make a living. B. F. Johnston somehow managed to keep his field and factory organization together for
producing and processing sugar cane. Alfalfa hay was always salable when we could secure rail transportation to the
larger centers, as Culiacan and Mazatlan, or across the Gulf
to the big French copper mine at El Boleo at Santa Rosalia,
Lower California. The Yaqui Indians of Sonora were constantly on the warpath, their aggressiveness making them a
desirable asset to any revolutionary element, but whatever
side they turned to there was soon disagreement. Yaquis were
not to be turned off easily with careless promises. They
avenged their grievances by raiding towns and burning
bridges of the Southern Pacific of Mexico railway, so causing us heavy losses of winter vegetables either in the fields or
en route to the markets of the United States.

Uncle Bill, always a trader, during these troubled times
moved about the country, buying and selling. I made many
trips with him. Buying at Mochis, with the paper currency—
bilimbiques—such manufactured products as clothing, bolts
of dry goods, thread, buttons, shoes; and food, such as sugar,
coffee, and cigarettes, we freighted them with a half dozen
wagons driven by Indian or Mexican teamsters, to villages
and ranches farther removed from routes of rail or sea transportation, like the villages down the Sinaloa River. On these
trips of ten days or two weeks we traded our goods for silver
or gold hoarded by the ranchers or storekeepers, or for a back
haul of local products such as hides, dried beef, or lard—
sometimes for livestock, particularly cattle, to be sold on our
local market.

In out-of-the-way villages, during those troubled days,

there was usually no civil or police authority. Small bandit groups, often disbanded soldiers, made raids for their food, clothing, and some money where it could be found. We rode on horseback, carrying pistol and rifle. Our teamsters did not go armed.

One night we rented a corral for our stock from an acquaintance at the village of Tamazula, pulling our wagons up between the corral and the back of the house, which was given over to a little store kept by a Chinese. There was a mescal distillery in the village, always a source of drunkenness and disorder. Bedded down under one of our wagons, we heard a drunken group moving along the street, presently coming to a halt at the porch of our host who had a little mesquite fire burning, sitting by it, in the custom of the country, before retiring. During the drunken harangue we heard them demand to know the whereabouts of us *gringos*. Evidently the man of the house diverted their attention, because they next considered the Chinese storekeeper and soon were gathered at his door. His place being only a shack of sugar-box material, they pushed in the door, rolled the frightened Oriental out of bed, demanding money. Upon his insistence that he had none a rope was placed about his neck and over a rafter in the little store. Still protesting his poverty, the unfortunate man was choked by the tightening rope until he pointed to a place under a counter, where the raiders found enough to satisfy them.

Uncle Bill and I had crawled from under the wagon to watch through the cracks in the boarding what was happening.

"We can't let them hang that poor Chinaman, Tio," said I.

"Oh, yes we can," said my wiser uncle, "We will do well to save our own necks tonight."

In the group Uncle Bill soon recognized an old acquaintance, and when they had released the frightened victim and returned to the fire at the front of the house Uncle Bill stepped out with a hearty greeting. The friend, half drunk as he was, embraced Uncle Bill with fervent enthusiasm and introduced him to his pals. From that point on the occasion was in our hands.

Another time when I stayed over at the village of Amole to trade, Uncle Bill going on with another part of our outfit

Revolutionarios of Sinaloa. JOSE M. OCHOA, the figure on the white horse, was released from prison at Fuerte to lead in the defense of the city—later became a General in the forces of the famous Pancho Villa, later still held the same rank in the forces of the Federal Government.

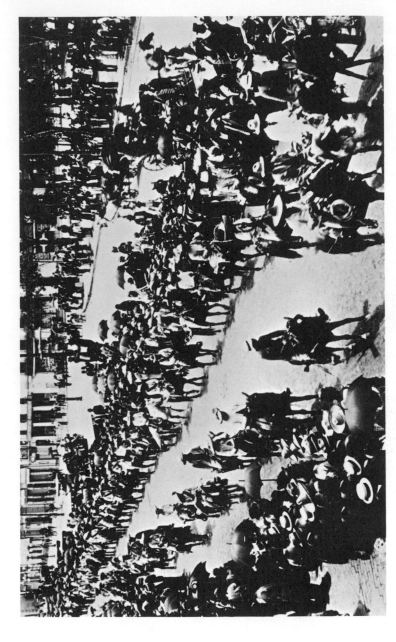

GENERAL ALVARO OBREGON, *Revolutionary President of Mexico, entering Mexico City on horseback from Tacubaya, May 9, 1920.*

for a few days, I observed a little group, apparently ex-revolutionaries, talking on two occasions with the Mexican at whose house we had stopped. Telling Uncle Bill of this on his return he assured me our host was to be trusted and suggested we wait to see if he might bring up the matter. This the friend did, in a devious way, by suggesting that for our return trip we could take a certain short cut that he would show us through some fields, that would save us some time. This we were pleased to do, thus by-passing whatever danger was in waiting.

Another trip when Uncle Bill was alone he was approached by four armed men at a village, offering to accompany him to the next town. Thanking them, he said that he traveled faster alone, and quite securely, pointing to his gun. The men left down the main highway through the woods. Uncle Bill sent his wagons, now empty of goods, down the highway also, himself taking detours along trails as long as possible, now and then dropping into the *camino real*. Emerging from one of these side trails, he saw in a bend of the road about twenty-five yards away, rifles across their saddles, the four men that had left before him. Yanking his revolver from its holster to cover the bandits, Uncle Bill set spurs to his horse and rode directly at them.

"*Que buscan?*" (what are you looking for?), he demanded.

Caught flat, they protested, "*Somos amigos*" (we are friends).

"*Bueno*," said Uncle Bill, from one side of the road, keeping them covered, "ride back the road as fast as you can."

Away they went, and as they rounded the first bend Uncle Bill turned to ride as fast in the opposite direction.

Uncle Bill was not only daring, he was as well versed as the natives themselves in every last detail of their existence, of their manner of thinking and acting.

Departing from a stay at Guasave on the Sinaloa River with our wagon outfit, a comely young *señorita*, a visitor at the house where we had stayed, made him a present of a carton of *coricochis*, very choice corn doughnuts, baked by her own hand. As we rode along through the *monte* my mouth watered in anticipation of a tasty snack. In due course I suggested as much. Uncle Bill pulled the package from his saddle bags and gave it a mighty heave into the woods. "I don't know the girl well enough to be given *coricochis*," said he; "maybe someone has paid her to poison us!"

There is a story to be written of the years of revolution in Mexico from 1910 through to recent years—I have not seen it, nor is it for me to write, but the source material is incomparably colorful—the contrast in living, before 1910, between the needy many and the aristocratic few—the tragedies in the downfall of the great families of the country—the upsurge of the masses—the forging, in the flame of revolution, of a new leadership—the development of another, a plebeian, aristocracy—the infiltration of Communism into the leadership of the masses—its failure to achieve its presumed goal of a better way of life—the return to the body politic of the remnants of the old aristocracy in the second and third generation—the present search for the middle way of life as best for most people.

During this period there has been a kaleidoscope of colorful, rare, outstanding personalities—Francisco I. Madero, the idealist and martyr—Victoriano Huerta, the hard-boiled reactionary—Pancho Villa, the Robin Hood of many moods —Venustiano Carranza, hard-headed opportunist—Alvaro Obregon, outstanding in practical sense and military intuition, but considered by many the archplotter of his period—Plutarco Elias Calles, hard, taciturn idealist dictator—Abelardo Rodriguez, middle-of-the-road man of business—all these being Generals—then Adolfo de la Huerta, a man of deep sentiment for his people, astute, but too idealistic to withstand the political pressures of his day—General Lazaro Cardenas, champion of the Indian and the poorer classes, perhaps to the point of diminishing returns—General Manuel Avila Camacho, elected by radicals and turned conservative—and now Miguel Aleman, the first nonmilitary President of his generation, and the most nearly representing the composite aspirations of the public of any President of Mexico within my recollection of forty years.

Of these I have been privileged to know casually Generals Obregon, Calles, and Rodriguez, better Don Adolfo de la Huerta, who during World War II, as Inspector General of Mexican Consulates in the United States, handled Mexican labor relations, it being my function to serve as consultant in charge of farm labor for our government in the western states. Sr. De la Huerta is a fine, fair, courteous gentleman, still the idealistic champion of the common people, with a very special knowledge of and sympathy for the Yaqui Indians of Sonora, of whom he has without doubt been the most ardent champion.

I have very recently visited with President Aleman. He impresses me as a man of destiny—keenly intelligent, idealistically practical, courteous, attentive, having the common touch so necessary to great men.

It has been my good fortune to be assigned by the President to a part in the agricultural development of Mexico. The call to that country—of that country—strikes a responsive note, and is accepted with interest, and with gratitude for being considered in some measure a useful element in their movement towards a better life. The Party of the Revolution, dominant in the political life of the country for many years, may well shape itself soon into the party of peace— and of a more abundant life for a long-suffering people.

CHAPTER X

The Mayo Indian Uprising

IT IS MY PRIVILEGE to possess, carefully rebound, one of the few copies of a book containing the grammar and vocabulary of the Yaqui and Mayo language. This book was prepared in manuscript form about 1600 A.D., 347 years ago, by a Jesuit priest, Juan B. de Velasco, with a Catechism prepared about twenty years later by another Jesuit father, Tomas Basilio, and was used by the priesthood following these men in missionary work among the Indians. Having been raised among the Mayo Indians and learning something of their language, and from talking with Yaquis, I have found that the languages are quite identical except for certain changes of accent and in the endings of some words.

This hand-written manuscript was used for 137 years, then printed in book form in 1737. In 1890 the Federal Government prepared a reprint with a revision and an introduction by Licenciado (Lawyer) Eustacio Buelna, prominent historian, once Governor of Sinaloa. Licenciado Buelna writes that to his knowledge there were in 1890 only three, possibly four, copies of this old book in existence. From three incomplete copies he was able to reproduce the work in its entirety.

The title is expressive, *"Arte de la lengua cahita, por un padre de la Compañia de Jesus"* (Art of the Cahita tongue, by a father of the Company of Jesus).

The word *"cahita"* in Indian means "there is none," which perhaps signifies that Padre Velasco intended to convey the thought of its being an unwritten language. Among the Indians today their language is termed merely *"la Lengua"* (the Tongue). These Indians today have no knowledge of their language's being written; few of them could attempt reading it.

The historical introduction of Buelna is most interesting, and probably as authentic as any information available on the early history of the Indians. He divides the language into three dialects, Yaqui, Mayo, and Tehueco. Two of these,

Mayo and Tehueco, now are merged in one. He states that the tribes of the province of Sinaloa, which embraced all the west coastal plain and lower mountains, bear definite resemblance in speech and habits to the Toltecs and Aztecs. Following his opinions further we learn that the migration of the Aztecs or Nahoas is traced westward from the region of Georgia and the Carolinas to the Gila River in Arizona, where they remained from about 300 B.C. to 544 A.D., their influence spreading southward almost altogether because of the savagery of the tribes to their north. In that year, wearied from incessant warfare with those northern tribes, they determined to migrate southward in search of more tranquil surroundings. They traveled in large groups and by different routes, because of the need to subsist on the country as they moved.

The Toltecs, which formed one of these groups, made their way down the west coastal plain, being forced to fight many battles with the Indians indigenous to their route of travel, and after eight years occupied in moving perhaps one thousand miles, founded the pueblo of Culiacan, now capital of Sinaloa. The major portion of this group, after three years, in 555 A.D. continued southward to found the city of Jalisco, then to Tula, State of Hidalgo, east of Mexico City, arriving there in 661, after a peregrination of seventeen years. The evidences of this Toltec race show it to be outstanding in its development, over that of the savage tribes through which it passed. Señor Buelna traces some influence in language and habits of the Sinaloa Province Indians, Yaquis and Mayos, to the Toltecs.

A significant fact given is that from the Fuerte River south the indigenous tribes proved more friendly to the Toltecs. Probably for this reason, today, from this point south there are no Indian tribes along the lowlands of the northwest coast. They have been absorbed into the Spanish-speaking people. In contrast, the Mayos and Yaquis retain their tribal unity 400 years after the Spanish conquest.

Buelna gives another interesting bit of history, that another group, the Aztecs or Mexicans, proceeded at the same time, 544 A.D., from the Gila River towards the southeast, remained a century in the region now Chihuahua. crossed westward over the Sierra Madre now inhabited by the Tarahumara Indians, descending to Culiacan in 648 A.D., three years later recrossing the Sierras to continue southward down the central plateau, arriving at the hill of Chapultepec, now in Mexico City, in 683 A.D., 215 years after leaving the Gila River. Their founding of the ancient city of Mexico is an epic, most intriguing, but not a part of our story.

Buelna gives a graphic, if not pleasant, account of the Spanish invasions of the northwest coast, the province of Sinaloa. The first was by Nuño Beltran de Guzman, leaving Mexico City December 22, 1529, with 300 Spaniards, equal numbers of foot soldiers and horsemen, with 12 cannons, and with over 8,000 Indian auxiliaries. This expedition passed northwestward through what are the present states of Michoacan and Jalisco and down toward the west coastal plain along a large stream, probably the Santiago River in Nayarit, south of Sinaloa. The Spaniards everywhere treated the native Indians most cruelly, murdered some, made many slaves, and severely lacerated or disfigured others.

On the coast lowland they were deluged by one of Mexico's terrific *"chubascos"*—tropical storms. Drowning, starvation, and tropical diseases reduced their Indian allies by seven thousand men and the Spaniards in large numbers. Despite many difficulties this expedition pushed on through hostile Indian tribes to arrive at Culiacan, site of the present capital of Sinaloa, in March 1531, about sixteen months after leaving Mexico City. Two years later, in 1533, expeditions were made into the Mayo and Yaqui Indian territories, beginning many years of savage fighting. After being defeated many times in combat, the Spaniards gradually made peace with these Indians through the offices of the priests who accompanied the expeditions, and so began the slow process of readjustment, not yet complete, of these Indians to Catholic Christianity and to civilized customs of living.

By 1886 when the first American colonists arrived at Topolobampo Bay, Spanish and later Mexican civilization had absorbed many of these Indians. As has been described, the Mayo tribes had been forced to adjust themselves to living in a situation to outward appearances bordering on servitude. They were deprived of their lands through every imaginable chicanery; false arrest, imposition of fines, falsification of land titles, securing their signatures to documents which later proved to be deeds to land—every devilish method that dishonest local overlords could conceive was used.

Pathetically they fought back, pooling their poor resources to pay, often in poultry, hogs, sheep, or cattle, some local half-lawyer to plead their cases, perhaps only to be betrayed by that person also. There came a time when a wave of counter-revolution found revolutionary leaders on the west coast at a standstill, Federal soldiers holding such key points as the ports of Mazatlan and Guaymas, with garrisons extending down to the town of Navajoa in southern Sonora, these forces being supported by ocean water transportation from the south.

Squarely up against it, the *revolucionarios* made a deal with the Mayo Indians, that these should fight for them through the revolution, in exchange for a promise by the revolutionary leaders that the Indians' lands should be restored when the fight was won.

The first objective to be taken was the pueblo of Navajoa. I shall always remember the thrill of seeing the Mayo warriors, hundreds of them, standing, in several lines, in the street before the little railway station at Mochis, my friend of the adventure with the lioness, Julian Bacame, a major, his cousin, our faithful Rosario, a *Capitan*, my boyhood playmate, Miguel Vainoro, a warrior in the ranks, dozens of others of our former laborers scattered among the rows of men. The old Chief Domingo, father of Rosario, was by then close to a hundred years old, so he remained on the ranch to work in our sugar-cane fields.

Their only organization insignia was a red parrot feather in their straw sombreros. Few carried guns. Their weapons were long bows and the heavy hooked machetes for hand-to-hand combat. Across their backs hung two quivers full of steel-barbed arrows, more than a few of which carried rattlesnake poison on their barbs.

A red blanket each, folded at the middle over a *morral*, which carried some provision—*pinole, panocha, carne seca,* with a cow's-horn cup to mix the *pinole* in—the *morral* hung over a shoulder—this completed their equipment. Four adventurous Americans went with them, Bill Cartilage, who constructed hand grenades from Indian-made black powder packed into tin cans; Fred Drewien, a boy raised in the colony; a chap named Ellis, and Roy McComas, the latter two young men down on visits and yearning for adventure. The three last named operated the only machine guns possessed by the attackers. A local mechanic and amateur bull-fighter, *"El Cacahuate"* (The Peanut), had drilled out a solid steel shaft to construct a small cannon for which he had ammunition salvaged from some previous battle. José Maria Ochoa, son of Don Zacarias, former partner of Johnston, led the expedition. He was destined to become a General in the years following.

Our American friends returned a few days later with a thrilling story of how the Mayos, tom-toms beating, with fearful war-cries, advanced at earliest dawn through grain fields, and, supported by Cartilage hurling bombs over the adobe walls, by the fire of three machine guns and questionable assistance from the homemade cannon, these Indians scaled the garrison walls over the shoulders of each other to face trained soldiers with modern rifles, and with bows and arrows and machetes cleaned out the entire garrison in a matter of an hour.

Our friends Julian Bacame and the boy Miguel were killed in that fight.

From there the Mayos continued, many of them being joined with their blood cousins the Yaquis. By 1915 the fighting appeared to be over. Many Indians had been slain. Our friend Rosario was separated from his regiment, together with about fifty of his men, was taken south to fight for Carranza against the Zapatistas, lost all but four of his Mayos, and spent eleven years, patiently holding his little group together, securing any transfer northward, until they finally secured a release to return home—our ranch being home for Rosario.

Perhaps a thousand Mayos were garrisoned at San Blas, on the Fuerte River, then provisional state capital for the forces of the revolution. It was now time to present their demand for discharge and for delivery of their lands by their Mexican leaders.

I cannot say with what sincerity the promise of their lands was made, but it was not kept. There were negotiations that resulted in nothing, then threats of reprisal by the Indians. Finally the Mayos were discharged to go home, carrying with them their arms. Word of this spread terror among the residents of the Fuerte River valley. The day the Mayos marched down river from San Blas I had ridden to Teroque, on the river, for a visit with my friend José Renteria, son of a landowner and merchant. Not finding José at their Teroque ranch, I continued up river towards their home in the pueblo of Mochicahui. The road was filled with people, on foot, on horseback, in oxcarts and wagons, fleeing from the wrath of the Indians.

When I arrived at the pueblo after night there was not a light to be seen. Not a dog barked. The Renteria family had stayed, and I was with my horse Captain let through their heavily barred front door. By now we heard Indian drums beating at intervals across the river at Jaguara, an Indian settlement. The family barricaded themselves in a remote storeroom of their huge home. The house, including their store on a corner, and a high wall in the rear, covered a half block wide and ran front to rear from one street to another. José and I chose to keep our horses saddled in the corral at the rear of the courtyard, next the street, ourselves staying by them.

By midnight the drums across the river were being answered from up the *Camino Real*, and soon we heard the tramp of the Mayo soldiers, the yells of some who were drunk, the talking of their women and children. They slowly moved through the town, most of them along the street just across the wall from us. They did no plundering that night, but continued down river for a parley at San Miguel, after which they established headquarters at Jaguara.

Soon they began living from the countryside, then making raids on the river towns for the double purpose of finding loot and of killing those certain persons they well remembered to have been their persecutors in former years. They became increasingly uncontrolled. At Fuerte they beheaded Dionisio Torres, a lawyer who had aided in taking their lands, carrying the head about for days impaled on a pole.

They made three major raids on our community at Mochis. A few Indians continued to stay with us. Bernardo Esquer, the Tarahumara married to a Mayo wife, was completely faithful. We always knew of the raids in time to move out of physical danger, down to the seacoast, if we chose to do so. Many Mexicans were killed, and three Americans. The name

[243]

of the Mayo chief, *Bachomo* (Bamboo, translated from the Mayo), became one of terror.

My precocious younger brother, Bill, eight years of age, without telling us, together with Bernardo's small son Vidal, rode on burro back across the Fuerte River to the Indian stronghold, staying overnight. During one of the raids on Mochis Bill was gone from home. Dad's search for the boy finally led him into the town, facing stray bullets of the raiders. He found Bill sitting in the midst of a group of Indians eating watermelons from an oxcart load they had raided. "They are all my friends," insisted Bill—and it appeared they were!

When conditions became so tough that the American families moved to the seaport of Topolobampo to be near a United States warship, Bill organized two groups of the local Mexican boys, himself as "Bachomo" leading the "Indians" in fights that finally ended in heads being thumped, so that angry mothers complained to the authorities. (That disposition has served Bill well as an officer in Uncle Sam's Navy, with a record of seventeen Jap ships sunk by various ships on which he has served.) The young Captain of the U.S.S. *Yorktown* stationed to protect the Americans at Topolobampo was William H. Standley, now Admiral Standley, retired, and recently our Ambassador to Russia.

Another incident of an Indian raid during which Dad was in town was of a Chinese storekeeper, possessor of a fine gold bridgework on his front uppers, being sat on, a big Mayo Indian digging at the gold uppers with the end of a wickedly pointed dagger, the Chinese groaning in terror. A slip from the lip would have been disaster!

Before the worst raids, José Renteria and I had risked crossing the river on some urgent business. As we rode up the opposite shore we were covered by two armed Indians, one with Winchester rifle, another with a big single-action .45 Colt's revolver which the holder, being slightly intoxicated, held somewhat uncertainly pointed at me, cocked and ready to fire.

We had puposely ridden mules, not so much desired by soldiers, and had used old saddles. However, José had a revolver of which he was relieved. Our chief concern was that José might be recognized and held for ransom or shot. This fact we hurriedly discussed in English, until we were cut short by our captors, after which I conversed with them, explaining that we were Americans, not unfriendly toward them, but insisting on not being molested. The U.S.S. *South Dakota*, stationed in the Gulf twenty miles away, each night played its huge searchlight over the up-country, the powerful beam lighting the woods almost like day even across the Fuerte River. I pointed out to our captors how they were being watched by the American forces to see that we Americans were not molested. We were moved down river a mile or so as this persuasion was in progress, before being released to swim our mules back across the Fuerte River to neutral territory, very much relieved to have escaped so easily.

This reign of terror continued for most of a year. American families moved out on United States transports. A few men remained, Dad and Uncle Bill among them. The only markets paying good cash for farm products during those months were the United States gunboat in the harbor and the warship in the Gulf. Keeping Bernardo and two other men to help, Dad worked strenuously. Between raids of the Indians on the one hand and the loosely organized opposition on the other, he drove back to the ranch at night to harvest green corn and vegetables grown by a Chinese renter, butchered beef and hogs; everything salable he hauled to our camp at Mapaui, transferred to two sailboats, and delivered to the ships. He admits he even gathered up stray chickens now and then from the deserted town of Mochis to add to his cargo. In this way he supported his family in the United States until the uprising was over.

Most of our farm laborers and families had loaded their small belongings and some farm implements into our wagons, and, with our foreman in charge, had fled to the Sinaloa River, where they remained for a year, renting land and raising corn and beans to feed themselves until they could come home to us. Every American family had its exciting experiences during those months.

There were several ineffectual attempts to drive out the Indians. Finally the revolutionary government sent against them General Don Herculano de la Rocha with his "men of the mountains." Don Herculano was one of several brothers who together owned a vast portion of the mountainous areas of the States of Sinaloa, Chihuahua, and Durango. For a generation he had served as *Jefe de Acordada*, striking fear into the hearts of dishonest men by filling a mountain cemetery —the *Camposanto de Don Herculano*—with men who disobeyed the law. Wherever captured he took them to this private cemetery for thieves, on a main pack trail high up on the summit of the mountains, for execution.

Preferring the government of the state of Durango to that of Sinaloa, the de la Rocha family had declared their western property line the state boundary, although this reduced the width of the state of Sinaloa by thirty miles. There they kept the boundary, until cartographers drew the map that way, and so it remains today.

In a series of well-planned raids Don Herculano drove the Indians out of their village strongholds, capturing their leader Bachomo, who was returned for execution at Mochis. Thirty years after the Mayos still are burning candles on his grave. For several years there were scarce any Mayos to be found on the Fuerte River. They dispersed to the mountains, to the Mayo and Yaqui Rivers, for a cooling off period. They are back now living again in their little houses among the mesquite trees, in much the same situation as before the revolution.

I did not meet Don Herculano until some years later when I went to the state capital at Culiacan. To pass the time between appointments I went to a cockfight, at a ring that belonged to the old General. I was completely astonished to see him—a very short, stooped, slight old fellow, complexion light as a Scandinavian, wearing a unique *piocha* (Van Dyke) beard, his one eye a flashing bright blue, sporting a huge Stetson campaign hat, and a long old-fashioned Colt's .45 pistol that hung halfway to his knee. Retired, he was kept on government pay just to insure his being on the right side of the fence politically. Knowing the old warrior's background, I was doubly entertained, hearing him exchange taunts and insults over the respective merits of his game roosters and those of his adversaries, especially because some of the latter were just boys in their teens who showed little respect for the old man's legendary past.

Don Herculano now lies buried, at his request, on the summit of the range overlooking the thieves' cemetery, that even in death he may still watch over them, and serve as a warning to all who pass by of the fate that may await them if they should drift from the ways of honest men. Among his pallbearer escort were my fine friend B. H. (Hal) Shepley and General Angel Flores, Governor of Sinaloa, then Military Commander of the Western Area of Mexico, both these men of the type appreciated by Don Herculano—pioneers, developers of that southwest, straightforward and rugged of mind and deed. Both have since followed their gallant old friend down that mysterious trail from which none of us may turn too long aside.

CHAPTER XI
Gabriel Gamez

SOUTH OF THE Fuerte River valley fifty miles, along the Ocoroni Arroyo, from the plain up into the lower Sierras for twenty-five miles, lived the Gamez clan, perhaps a hundred families. They were a turbulent lot, and so controlled their part of the country that in those days of law enforcement by *Acordadas* the Governor of the state had to choose between naming a Gamez chief of the *Acordada*, so putting to flight their enemies, or, if of the opposite faction, the top men of the Gamez took to the woods.

During the revolutions the Gamez fought as a unit under a Gamez colonel and lower officers, sometimes for one revolutionary movement, sometimes for another.

A few years before the revolution we became acquainted with Gabriel Gamez. He was anything but a roughneck type —a man of medium stature, slender, light skin, shining black eyes, finely shaped sharp features, very honest, serious in his associations. From working with us as a sub-contractor in brush-clearing contracts we made with United Sugar Companies he continued, to become our ranch foreman, later Administrator of the irrigation system of the Mochis area, and by 1914 the *Sindico* of Mochis, a position combining approximately the duties of mayor and sheriff.

The landing of American marines at Vera Cruz by President Woodrow Wilson in 1914 naturally stirred a terrific resentment by Mexicans, placing Americans in Mexico in an extremely dangerous situation. Mexicans hearing of their country's being invaded quite naturally saw us all as enemies. There were many hair-raising experiences by·Americans in making their way to the safety of the international border or the seacoasts, where they might be picked up by American ships. There were many, many instances where American families were saved through the protection of their Mexican friends.

At Mochis we were advised by the consular agent to move immediately to Topolobampo Harbor to the protection of an

American warship. A railway train was hurried to the station and soon loaded with the Americans from the colony and from the sugar plantation and factory.

An angry mob gathered about, led by a well-known *gringo* hater, threatening to kill the Americans. Uncle Bill, rather than join the crowd on board the train, chose to sit quietly on horseback, moving from one to another group of Mexicans, chatting with those he knew, sobering them by his cheerful calmness.

Gabriel Gamez met the most exacting test of wisdom and friendship. Daring to face his angry fellow countrymen, his own friends and constituents, he placed policemen at the locked doors of the coaches, and addressing the crowd, pleaded that regardless of the action of the United States these Americans were friends and neighbors of many years, that to murder them would be a crime they would forever regret, that any violence would be fought by his policemen and himself. The mob subsided and the train departed.

After the Vera Cruz incident, although many Americans returned, relationships were more difficult than ever. We deeply appreciated the friendship of Gabriel Gamez and of many other Mexicans during those trying years.

About six years later Gabriel became *Presidente Municipal* of the Sinaloa District. He was highly respected, a just man in his administration. Wish it or not, through blood ties and natural ability, he had become the acknowledged leader of the Gamez clan. They were a daring, quarrelsome lot, for whom he was constantly intervening, trying to keep them at peace with their neighbors and the authorities.

Through one of frequent political turnovers in state government the Gamez enemies came into power. Claiming that some Gamez men had been in a train derailment and robbery, they made a dash to take Gabriel, probably planning to assassinate him. He escaped on horseback into the mountains, gathering Gamez followers as he rode. There was a bloody battle, in which Gabriel was said to have been killed.

A year later his wife paid us a visit to tell us that he was alive, in hiding in the mountains, that he had resolved to make his way to the United States, far away from his former ties, to establish himself anew with his wife and little daughter, that he appealed to us to assist in his escape.

What would anyone so indebted have done? We knew

Gabriel for an honest man, a patriotic citizen who should be spared to live a useful life. We did not interfere in Mexican politics, we had good friends even among the enemies of Gabriel. We had no illusions as to what might happen if we were discovered. However, his hope was to leave the country, no longer to be a factor in any quarrel. Primarily he was a fine friend to whom we were deeply indebted.

Traveling all one day in our Model-T Ford, with a Gamez guide, at sundown I picked up Gabriel and a cousin at a ranch far up in the hills, returning through the night.

Some incidents of that return trip I have cause to remember. At dusk we drove through the one main street of a tiny village, almost deserted an hour before, but now lined with natives. Suddenly from out of the crowd there sprang a bearded giant of a man, to stand before us waving his blanket. Quickly I turned to Gabriel, who sat, wrapped to his eyes in a blanket, beside me.

"Dele" (practically translated, "Give it the gun"), said he, and I bore down on gas and horn, missing the great fellow by scant inches as he made a last second leap to the safety of the roadside. I was quivering with excitement when we had left the village and entered the woods beyond. Gabriel and his cousin laughed heartily as they explained that the chap was the village *loco* (moron), apt to pull just such unusual surprises. Nevertheless, we were most fortunate not to have been stopped.

As we crossed the sand bed of the Ocoroni Arroyo just south of the village of Naranjo, on the Southern Pacific of Mexico Railway, we were helplessly stalled, churning away in bottomless loose sand. This was the heart of enemy territory. However, there was no course but to find help. On the suggestion of Gabriel I roused the nearest enemy *ranchero*, who obligingly saddled his horse, came down to fasten his rawhide riata to our car, took some turns about his saddle horn, and with engine roaring, wheels spinning, and my two blanketed refugees pushing, we were towed out to firm ground.

Our congenial horseman was all for settling down to build a fire to warm us by, which would never do. He was well paid and we rambled on, risking his displeasure rather than discovery of my friends.

[250]

In the early hours of the morning we were so stiff with cold we pulled off the road into the woods, built a fire, and sat down to a basket of food I had taken from home.

"Ah, for some hot coffee!" exclaimed Gabriel.

"Nothing easier," said I, pouring it from a Thermos jug, the first either had seen. Picture their astonishment and delight at such a (to them) marvelous invention.

For many weeks the refugees lived in a cave along the seashore, a spot where during the revolution Dad had kept hidden in the mangroves a dugout canoe stocked with water and provisions in event of extreme necessity.

No shipping came bound for Lower California or northern ports. Meanwhile came a letter from an uncle, colonel of the Gamez regiment, by fortunes of war now located in central Mexico, offering Gabriel a commission in this regiment under an assumed name. Back we drove into the mountains to where there were horses waiting, one a fine roan that had been given to me by Gabriel, which I now gladly returned for his long journey over the Sierras.

I never saw him again. His wife and daughter went to him. For some years I received letters from *Capitan* ———, then the letters ceased. If still living I know he is an asset to his country. Time has erased the risk in this story's being told; it is related here in grateful acknowledgment of the services of a fine friend.

CHAPTER XII

The Cattle Ranches

THE NEXT RIVER south of the Fuerte is the Sinaloa, known as the Petatlan when Spaniards first watered their horses on its banks before the middle of the sixteenth century. The headwater of this river is the top of Cerro de Mohinora, 11,-408 feet elevation, located in the State of Chihuahua.

In 1924 with two other Americans, using a mule pack outfit, I had the pleasure of exploring this stream from the lowlands through the foothills and mountains to its source. That trip would be another story. The first day of it brought to mind the days of the old west coast cattle ranches.

We drove by Model-T Ford to the town of Sinaloa, one of those historic old pueblos once a center of wealth, its cobblestone streets lined with substantial and ornate store buildings and dwellings. This was the gateway to the mountains, a major point of call for the stagecoaches before the coming of the railroad, shopping center for the mining of the hills and for the farming of the valleys. The revolution had emptied the fine homes of their *hacendados*; some had escaped to the United States or to Europe; some had been killed or impoverished. A few were living in modest ways as local merchants, or as small farmers. The pueblo of Sinaloa still showed through the ravages of time and human carelessness evidence of a once beautiful small Mexican city.

We called on an old friend, Gabriel Peña, with whom we discussed the fate of his family properties. Between the Fuerte and Sinaloa Rivers, fifty miles apart, were cattle ranches of his uncles, Francisco, Octaviano, Manuel, and Genaro Alcalde, and of their sisters, one the mother of Gabriel Peña. Their ranch headquarters were many miles apart, connected with roads through the woods. Washes crossing the flat lowland brush country had been dammed to form great lagoons for watering cattle and for irrigating parcels of land planted to pasture or to food crops, principally corn and beans.

The ranch quarters were lordly—great brick houses with

patios encircled by brick walls—workmen's and cowboys' quarters of adobe nearby, solidly constructed corrals of mesquite or rosewood set upright in the ground, with gate head posts of solid hardwood blocks, holes being cut into these blocks for drawing through the hardwood gate bars. There were horse pastures full of tough little Mexican ponies, and pastures for the calves during milking season.

Each ranch was a little community. The owner kept a small store for his ranch people. Cattle roamed the wooded ranges by the tens of thousands. Several families were hired for handling these cattle, milking the cows, and making cheese for sale to the pueblos. Sometimes there was butchering and drying of meat. Often a rancher operated a tannery, curing the hides with native barks. Bark of the *mauto* tree was used for shoe and sandal sole leather, of *chino* and *guamuchil* trees for saddle and harness leather.

The cowboys were most picturesque in their leather trappings, chaps and coats of buckskin, and woolen hats made by the Mayo Indian women. Their saddle trees were made of their own hardwoods, covered with scraped pigskin, this covering being done by their leatherworkers, with much hand tooling of the leather. Riatas were of rawhide. Hackamores (*jaquimas*) were made with rawhide nose pieces. Variegated colors of horsehair ropes were made for reins and tie rope. Bridles and spurs were often silver inlaid, by local smiths; the bridle headstalls of plaited rawhide or leather or of horsehair. Spur straps were hand tooled, sometimes with wildcat or jaguar fur on the piece that shows outside the boot.

Cowboys, although responsible to the "patron," led a life more free than any working men I can recall. Days when they rode the brushy ranges they saddled leisurely and took the trails, checking cattle tracks, little groups of cattle, keeping a sort of continuous inventory of the cattle and their locations on the range, cutting out those needing special attention such as doctoring for worms, or cows soon to calve.

Calving was heaviest in summer when the rains brought on green feed. Cows were milked after the new grass was growing well, calves were gentled by handling at milking time. Cows were handled by the cowboys; milking and cheese-making was the chore of the women. The care of the calves fell to the lot of the small boys or of some old Indian

[253]

in cases where there were not enough small boys on the ranch.

Milking Mexican range cows was something apart from all other dairying. In the early mornings, calves were brought from pastures to a calf corral opening into the larger ranch corral. The ranch corral encircled a well or water hole so that all animals were forced to enter in order to drink, and could be handled without having to be chased in the open range.

Cows would feed in the woods all day, coming back to their calves at night or early morning, to stand outside the calf pen bawling lustily at intervals until milking time. A cowboy would rope a cow, tie her short, head high, through the fork of a mesquite tree, then throw a doubled lasso about her hind legs above the hock joints, draw them together, tie in the tail to avoid switching, and call for the *becerrero* (calf boy). The boy would have the calf picked from a bevy of others in the pen, roped by the neck, and dragged to the little gate, from that point on being towed in a grand rush towards mama cow. Getting the cow to give down her milk was a tricky task. His fingers in one side of the calf's mouth, the boy patiently kept the calf from getting too much milk, just enough to interest the cow in letting down; then the calf was yanked away and held struggling while the *"ordeñadora"* lady milked away, another boy, girl, or cowboy holding the big milking gourd from the opposite side of the cow. Sometimes the cow "raised" her milk and the performance must be repeated. Some little milk was left for the calf to enjoy; the cow's legs were untied and another secured. Calves were presently put back in the corral or pasture and cows drifted off into the woods for feeding.

Cattle, meat, hides, and cheese were cheap and plentiful. During the revolution the livestock of these large ranches was appropriated by whoever came first and in greatest strength. Cattle were shot by thousands for the hides, faster than they could be eaten either fresh or as dried meat. Hides of uncertain ownership were moved out by shiploads and carloads, some to Mexican tanneries, others to tanneries in the United States and other countries.

In all the years since, this great cattle business has not been restored. Just the memory of those days remains for some of us who lived them in full enjoyment: the memory of the riding through the woods to the "cling-clinging" of spurs, chasing cattle, roping, resting ourselves and horses in the shade of some mesquite, returning in midafternoon to a feed of broiled beefsteak, cheese, juicy beans, tortillas, and coffee. That was indeed the happy life. Would that it could be lived again!

CHAPTER XIII

Time Marches On

WITH THE PASSING YEARS the colonists, Kickers and Saints, had come to be good friends. The vicissitudes of the revolution brought them into a more than usually close relationship with each other, and with their Mexican neighbors.

There were those who persisted in their socialistic beliefs. Hobart Brink, married to a hard-working Mexican wife, never farmed more than a few acres, read his socialist papers, and planned for the return of Owen.

Tom Whitzel, married to my grandmother, read the "Appeal to Reason" and followed the tribulations of Eugene V. Debs, perennial socialist candidate for President of the United States, from week to week, in complete detail. Many an hour I spent with the fine old gentleman, out in his grape vineyard or following along with him behind the plow pulled by Polly and Molly, his team of bay mares, listening to his splendid booming bass voice as he told of his arguments over politics and religion while he had been teaching school or running for the Nebraska legislature.

George Page, still a socialist, farmed and ran surveys. His sons Chester, Ray, and Cecil farmed with him. A fourth son, Ross, after attending Salina Normal University in Kansas, returned to Mochis, married Miss Julia Drake. Through his energy and ability some years later he became General Manager for Johnston's United Sugar Companies, then Field Manager for one of the largest sugar concerns in Porto Rico.

Festus "Fess" Ward, one of the staunch Saints, married Code Whitzel and early became Manager for Johnston. He died in the prime of his young manhood, leaving to his widow and two children a substantial inheritance in farm land.

The Kneeland family lived for many years at Sivirijoa, on the Fuerte River, next to the foothills of the Sierras. From her rich store of local lore Clarissa Kneeland wrote "Smugglers' Island," a story for young people which has been popular for many years.

"The Scallys" was the term used for fifty years to designate not only the Dr. J. W. Scally family, but the families of his sons-in-law, John Newton, Grant Burr, and James Jordan. They were all enterprising people, and each struggled through those early years to develop substantial farms. For many years they ran a *panocha* mill which gave outlet for some of the sugar cane, best "pay" crop of the colonists in those early years.

The Drake family, Mayville, his wife Julia, and their eight children, were truly of "the salt of the earth."

Mr. Drake, staunch socialist, had been a Union soldier, then a farmer in Rooks County, Kansas.

Mrs. Drake was one of those rare personalities of a time perhaps gone forever. While "raising" a fine, sturdy family, she still made time for running a boarding house, and for serving as community nurse. In the style of those pioneer women, she rode on horseback, only Mrs. Drake used no side-saddle, she sat sideways on a blanket, holding to a strap bound around the back of the horse.

When there was sickness in the community, Mrs. Drake would soon be seen arriving on horseback at full gallop, a true angel of mercy who not only attended the sick, but likewise fed them well with many a fine jam or jelly or other delicacy from her own store. Her girls rode horses as expertly while sitting sideways on a blanket as most men riders of the day.

"Young George Drake" is past seventy now. From driving the long string of oxen at the building of the Los Tastes Canal he rose to become Superintendent of the vast farming operations of Johnston at Los Mochis. Greatly liked and respected by both Mexicans and Americans, he and his wife, Flora Korfhage Drake, are living near the Korfhage family relatives in Denver, Colorado.

The Korfhage family, splendid people, threw all their resources and effort into the colony in its later days. They, with many, many others of the old colonists, have made a substantial contribution to the building of a better world in both countries.

The Drewien family, colonists for many years, moved each to separate fields of endeavor. "Young" Bill Drewien has remained on the Mochis farm of his father for fifty years.

Charles Jones, son of the colony shoemaker, and Fred Mulkey, colonist since La Logia days, are the two remaining farmers on *El Publico*, the Public Farm, the Saints' community for many years.

Charles Hays remained to become a wealthy property owner at Los Mochis.

There were many marriages of American colonist men to Mexican *señoritas* in the Fuerte River valley: W. W. Green, Charles Jones, William Bunker, Charles Hays, "Don Eugenio" Tays. There are many children from these marriages, and of other Americans arrived separately before and since those days, children who have generally contributed creditably to society in the places they have lived.

The sugar enterprises of Johnston have passed through many vicissitudes of low prices, revolutions, expropriation of their farming lands, and strife with labor. In the 1900-1927 period these enterprises grew to an industry controlling 400,-000 acres of land, producing 250 tons of sugar a day, giving work to many thousands of employees. Now restricted to its factory operations, it still operates successfully, a monument to the energy and ability of B. F. Johnston, recently passed on to leave the business to his wife, Agnes Sherwood Johnston, a lady greatly esteemed by those of us who have been privileged to know her well.

Expropriation and redistribution of lands is a policy that is close to the heart of millions of Mexican Indians and Mestizos. A certain percentage of them are not yet dependable enough to make a success of running their own farms. There is sometimes corruption in administration of parts of the land program. Production of food under the new program is not always sufficient for the people. Yet the movement has taken hold, has become a great part of national life, and because of the love of the people, especially the Indians, for their land, it will in some fashion be carried forward.

Another change has been in greater education of the poorer classes. Their indoctrination to Communism as a part of their education I cannot agree with, but having lived for twenty-three years in Mexico, most of it before the advent of Communism, and knowing the nature of the people, I am convinced that even what of Communism now remains with them is a passing phase in their national life. Mexicans love their homes, their families, and their personal possessions. They are generally individualistic, not interested in being made over to conform to any plan or pattern. These characteristics will eventually lead them down the road of Democracy, with its liberty for individuals, not of Communism, with its regimentation of personal life.

It is a great tragedy that in the era before the Revolution their leadership was not wise enough, strong enough, or unselfish enough to bring about gradually, systematically, a better distribution of lands through the development of millions of additional acres of land still lying idle, and to provide general free education.

Recognizing the failure of revolution and of Communism to provide that abundant life and that freedom which have been their aspiration, the people of Mexico today are gradually but surely turning to production through private enterprise, supported by Government through the creation of credits, by the encouragement of sound business enterprises, the building of highways, the impounding of water for irrigation, the sale, in direct ownership, of substantial acreages for agricultural production.

The socialistic dream of Owen and his followers has faded into history. The colonists are almost all gone from the Fuerte River valley. Los Mochis has grown to a city of twenty thousand. A paved highway is being completed thirty miles from Mochis to San Blas on the Southern Pacific of Mexico Railway.

It is better so. The development of Mexico by its own people will bring a better relationship between our two countries in the years ahead. We should form a progressive part of that development, but not a dominant one.

There is much to enjoy in Mexico, in Sinaloa in particular, for us who do not demand the luxuries of modern life, but who love the natural beauty of a shore line, a mangrove-bordered estuary, an inland bay, islands, the wild woods, the scenery of the higher hills.

These are little changed. For some of us there also are pleasant memories of friends, some living, many now gone, as Uncle Bill, Lino, Bernardo, Don Onofre Camacho, Don Salomé Puente, Guicochea, José Renteria, and some others as close who have not formed a part of this story.

The early colonists were well received and kindly treated by their Mexican neighbors of the Fuerte Valley. In contrast, the later periods of revolution and of experiments in Communism have brought many difficulties for Americans in Mexico. We sold our properties there in 1925, before the advent of Communism. I am confident that the joining of our two countries as allies in the World War just won marks the beginning of a new and happier era of relationship between the United States and Mexico. It has given each country an opportunity to discover the good characteristics of the other, to learn to what degree each is striving for the same objectives for its people.

To some of us who feel that we are traveling towards home when we have passed our southern border, this gives a very special feeling of pleasure. If this narrative in any small degree helps more Americans to become better acquainted with our friends of Mexico, it will have been worth relating.

If there is something of interest to readers in the story of the colonists of Sinaloa I shall be glad to have recorded it here—a small bit of the history of a great world.

EPILOGUE

The Fuerte River Valley of 1963

WE HAVE TRAVELED today up the Fuerte River Valley from Los Mochis, which is now a city of 50,000 inhabitants, surrounded by over 300,000 hectares of luxurious fields of sugar cane, alfalfa, wheat, cotton, rice and winter vegetables. Our first stop was San Blas, which we found converted into an important railway junction. Here the line of the Pacifico Railway (formerly the Southern Pacific of Mexico) has been crossed by the recently completed "Chihuahua al Pacifico" whose first lines, traced by Owen, were for many years called the "Kansas City, Mexico y Oriente."

The "Chihuahua al Pacifico" railway begins at Ojinaga, on the northern border of Chihuahua, facing Presidio, Texas, crosses the plains and Sierras of Chihuahua and, after conquering the most abrupt and intricate precipices, descends towards the plains westward to Sinaloa, touching at the enchanting old pueblo of El Fuerte, and terminating at the Port of Topolobampo.

The pueblo of El Fuerte takes its name from the last third of the sixteenth century, when the Count of Montesclaros, then Viceroy of New Spain (Mexico) ordered the construction here of a fort that should resist the attacks of the barbarous Indian tribes indigenous to that region. It fell to the lot of the valiant don Diego Martinez de Hurdaide, in the first part of the seventeenth century, to complete its construction, naming it in honor of that dignitary, the "Fuerte de Montesclaros."

Seven miles eastward of El Fuerte the new Presa Miguel Hidalgo captures the waters of the Fuerte River, originally the Rio Grande de Zuaque. These waters come pouring down from many streams, great and small, from out of the Sierras of the four states of Sinaloa, Sonora, Chihuahua and Durango, in volume sufficient for the irrigation of more than a half million hectares (one and one quarter million acres) of magnificent plains.

Thus finally we see realized this magnificent dream of Engineer Albert Kimsey Owen. The Chihuahua and Pacifico Railway

[261]

is the shortest route from middle western United States to the west coast of Mexico; the great Valle del Rio Fuerte can now be irrigated; and the Port of Topolobampo begins its development which, in the dream of Owen, and in reality, should make it one of the great ports of the world.

For almost a century that vision of Owen was maintained in the minds of farmers, engineers, capitalists, legislators and even of various Presidents of the Republic of Mexico. We must stand in admiration of the valor and tenacity of those who have brought this great dream to fruition.

The ultimate accomplishment is to be measured in terms of human welfare; the details of the struggle are simply a part of a great cooperative effort that has been dedicated through various generations to the realization of this dream that has so permeated the minds of all these people.

A hundred thousand persons from every part of Mexico, and from every profession, every philosophy, every occupation, are busily transforming these woods of Sinaloa. These "arcabucos y espeluncas" are most aptly described by the Jesuit Padre Andres Perez de Ribas, the same who, in the early part of the seventeenth century, faced all the perils of man and nature, as the first missionary to thousands of those primitive peoples. In the words of Perez de Ribas, "The greatest part of the Province of Sinaloa is a great plain, but covered with woods, brambles and forest trees . . . sometimes so dense for many leagues that even birds cannot fly through them, and they are only the shelter for wild beasts."

Perez de Ribas gives a beautiful description of the area; the vegetation, the bird and animal life, the various Indian tribes; their manner of living, and especially of the effect upon their lives of the Great River, and of the Sea of Californias.

By his count there were then 30,000 Indians; Ahomes, Zuaques, Teguecos and Sinaloas inhabiting small villages from the entrance of the river to the sea and upwards into the Sierras.

This careful record of Padre Perez de Ribas relating to the region is the work of a gifted writer, an ardent missionary and a patient philosopher. I am at present enjoying briefing and translating it into English. It is indeed a precious record for those interested in the background history of the west coast of Mexico.

An intriguing history, that of the Fuerte River Valley. It is told in many parts; first, in the wealth of its Indian artifacts, petroglyphs, paintings on stone, arrowheads, stone hammers and other utensils of stone and clay; then in the known histories of Baltazar de Obregon (1585), Perez de Ribas (1645). Licenciado Eustaquio Buelna (1890), and in the written folklore of our good friend Licenciado Raul Cervantes Ahumada, followed by other recent written records, and finally, in personal narrative that comes down from one generation to another of people of the frontier.

For those who live with a background of its past, there is still much to enjoy here. At El Fuerte we wandered into the great courtyard of the once elegant Hotel Diligencias owned by the same Ibarra family that contracted the lands of Los Mochis for the Colony. For a hundred years or more this was a charming haven of rest for travelers by stage coming from such far away places as Hermosillo, Sonora and Mazatlan, Sinaloa.

The Señora Doña Luisa Ibarra de Ibarra, 92 years of age, graciously received us in a living room furnished with the finest of a century ago. Her son, Doctor Roberto Ibarra, entertained us with a piano concert of the same period. These people lost the greater part of their wealth during the revolutionary years. Their culture and graciousness has remained.

At Varobampo, nestled into the northern slope of the Sierra de San Pablo, and forming a natural gateway to Sinaloa from the north, our good friend Professor Conrado Espinosa, Director for many years of the Scholastic Center of the Northwest at Los Mochis, is now busily engaged in planning and organizing a Museum of Sinaloa, to be situated in this interesting background of the flora native to the area.

At Los Mochis, a fine friend of our family for six generations, the Señora Anita Padilla Vda. de Peyro, at 80 years of age, is surrounded by pupils to whom she is teaching English, the latest of many hundreds she has taught since she attended the school of Doctor Edwin Schellhous, colony leader, at Higuera de Zaragoza 70 years ago. Anita is diligently collecting material to assist in conserving the History of the Valle del Fuerte, beginning with the days of the Topolobambo Colony.

At the home of our friends since ever we can remember, the Jordan family, and at the home of Hubert and Clemmie Jordan Mulkey, we have been shown what is no doubt the most complete collection of stone, pottery and bone artifacts in the State

[263]

of Sinaloa; the result of following a pleasant and instructive hobby for the greater part of their lifetime.

Mrs. Irene Mulkey is the only one of the earlier colonists living in the Fuerte River Valley today.

At San Ignacio Bay, where we have spent so many happy vacations in sailing, swimming, fishing and hunting, with the best Indian guide of a lifetime, Lino Jocobi, we have just spent a glorious few days reliving the past, now with Lino's stalwart Indian sons as guides. We have feasted on fish; fried, broiled over the coals of a campfire, or marinated; on shrimp, oysters, clams and crab. We have heard the mountain lion scream within fifty yards of our encampment at night; have hunted the little white-tailed deer, still there, although not so plentiful as in the days gone by.

Most of what there was is still there for us and thousands of others to enjoy; the refreshing ocean, the moonlight on the beaches, the phosphorescence on the dark nights, when the porpoises race after the mullet to create a gorgeous display of light; these beauties will never fade, and to those of us who have thrilled to them, it is pleasing to know they will remain for the coming generations to enjoy.

At the Hotel Santa Anita this evening we again relived the past in the music of the stringed orchestra of the "Cachoanas" a group of musicians who should be woven into the history of the valley, for their fine music during fifty years.

Finally, using the experiences of years past in Mexico and in California through which to look into the mists of the future, it seems to me that there will surely be a time, when the limitations imposed by custom and economy shall bow to the demands of people for a more abundant life, a future time when the Fuerte River Valley will be a very major source of products not grown in the north countries; the United States and Canada. Not only winter vegetables, but endless acres of tropical fruits, which will be planted instead of wheat and corn, as these latter can be grown more economically in the north countries and given in exchange for crops much more valuable that can only be produced in a tropical land.

So those of us who have thought that ours were the golden days must philosophically trade one advantage for another, comprehending that the days ahead are those that will be called the greatest in the history of the Fuerte River Valley and the west coastal area of Mexico.

Measured in terms of social progress, the story of the sincere friendships of those early colonists with their Mexican neighbors may serve as an inspiration for a fuller understanding among the people of the two countries, as they mingle in greater numbers through the years.

A prosperous Mexico, with happy people, is the greatest guarantee to the United States of having a country of democratic philosophy along it's southern border, and is for Mexico itself it's greatest guarantee of complete liberty and independence in which to develop it's final pattern of national life, which is only just in the making, and holds much promise for improvement for the lives of those to come.

"With malice towards none, and charity for all" in the words of Abraham Lincoln, and with the guiding principle that "Respect for the rights of others brings peace," so perfectly expressed by Don Benito Juarez, the great Mexican statesman contemporary to and friendly with Lincoln; with these words of simple philosophy to guide us, the future should multiply in blessings to our peoples.

Acknowledgments

I wish first to express my thanks to Mrs. Ida Hoagland Dawkins, who has without doubt the most complete record of the Topolobampo Cooperative Colony extant. She has given me unlimited access to the files of the *Credit Foncier of Sinaloa*, of which she was long Editor and Publisher, as well as of her time for discussion and comparison of data without which it would not have been possible to have given so fully the facts relating to the experiment, then of worldwide interest, in Integral Cooperation carried on by many hundreds of American colonists in Sinaloa, Mexico, during the latter part of the past century. The quotations used at the beginning of each chapter in Book I are reprinted from the *Credit Foncier of Sinaloa*.

Next I thank our dear friend Anita Padilla de Peiro, that vivacious young *señorita* so friendly to Americans in a land new to them, now a grandmother, who retains the brightness of youth and a keen interest in the welfare of her people and of the people of all the world.

I am grateful to various other colonists and children of colonists for their interest in this story.

In conclusion, I wish to express my gratitude for the assistance given by Thelma McKinney Riess, a daughter of the old southwest, in typing and correction of phrasing and friendly criticism so needed by writers but not of the profession.